Reading Biblical Poetry

READING BIBLICAL POETRY

An Introductory Guide

J. P. Fokkelman

Translated by
Ineke Smit

Westminster John Knox Press
LOUISVILLE
LONDON ·LEIDEN

Cover design by Kathy York
Interior design by Sharon Adams

First edition
Published by Westminster John Knox Press
Louisville, Kentucky

This book is printed on acid-free paper that meets the American National Standards Institute Z39.48 standard. ∞

PRINTED IN THE UNITED STATES OF AMERICA

01 02 03 04 05 06 07 08 09 10 — 10 9 8 7 6 5 4 3 2 1

Library of Congress Cataloging-in-Publication Data

Fokkelman, J. P.
    Reading biblical poetry : an introductory guide / J.P. Fokkelman.—
1st ed.
        p. cm.
    Includes bibliographical references and index.
    ISBN 0-664-22439-3 (pbk. : alk. paper)
    1. Hebrew poetry, Biblical—History and criticism. 2. Bible. O.T.—
Language, style. I. Title.

BS1405.2 .F67 2001
221.6'6—dc21

                                                            2001026227

Contents

Preface

This book is intended for those who do not read Hebrew but have to rely on a translation of the Bible. I have tried to put myself in their position as much as possible, and when I started writing I was fully resolved to refrain entirely from using information from the original texts, or at least to limit references to the original text to the utmost minimum. Now that the book is finished, however, I find that I have not always succeeded in this aim. Occasionally I have been forced to refer to the original language after all, in order to keep my argument transparent, and because the poem under consideration demanded it. Moreover, I have frequently resorted to using my own translations.

This is not surprising. Poetry is the most ingenious form of verbal expression. Furthermore, the poet's virtuosity permeates every level of the text, from sounds and syllables to strophes and even higher textual units; there is a box of tricks for every layer. The result is that anyone who discusses poetry should be able to draw on a similar extensive repertoire of tools; dealing with poetry is a much more technical job than interpreting narrative prose. Then there are the readers, from whom considerably more patience and stamina is required than in the case of prose with its familiar forms of organization such as plot, time, etc.

This book is the complement to *Reading Biblical Narrative*, the American edition of which appeared in 2000. At the same time, however, *Reading Biblical Poetry* is perfectly able to stand on its own. This time I have made more allowances for the fact that the book will be consulted by college students. For their convenience, I have taken two measures: in the first place, every now and then there is a footnote containing a reference to the Hebrew Bible or secondary literature. Secondly, I have also taken great pains over chapter 12, "Guidelines for further reading," which offers, among other information, for the first time ever the strophe divisions for all psalms. These data may serve as an incentive and a guide to the reader to try his or her own hand at tackling these puzzles. Even those "average" readers, who lack knowledge of the original text, will find that the tools offered here will enable them to embark on this challenging enterprise.

February 2001

1

Preliminary exercise

A strophe by Isaiah and a poem by David

In search of the poets of the Bible

Within the Bible, poetry is almost exclusively confined to the Old Testament. Although poetic lines do occur regularly in the Gospels and the letters of the New Testament, these are actually quotations from the Psalms and the Prophets. In the first chapter of his Gospel, Luke includes two poems: the song of praise spoken by Mary when she visits Elizabeth, who is later to become the mother of John (vv. 46–55), and shortly afterwards, when John is born, the prophecy spoken over the child by his father Zechariah (vv. 68–79). Both texts, however, owe everything to Hebrew poetics and its rules; they are mainly a collage of expressions and phrases from the Old Testament. This means that we can safely confine our attention to the Old Testament,[1] which I will henceforth refer to as the Hebrew Bible. This is a term that is better suited to the Scriptures of both Ancient Israel and Jesus of Nazareth, as it is a collection of writings whose origin predates the Greek of the New Testament by centuries, and is totally independent of it from both a literary and a religious point of view.

Where do we find the poems? The Hebrew Bible consists of 1,574 printed pages in the standard edition that is used worldwide for the study of the original text.[2] A fairly accurate estimate would be that more than 37 percent of these, about 585 pages, contain poetry. These figures, however, are fluid, as especially in Jeremiah, Ezekiel, and Ecclesiastes it is hard to determine the proportion of poetry to prose. Some scholars see more prose there than I do. If I humor them and lower my figure to 550 pages, this still means that almost 35 percent of the pages in the standard edition consists of poetic lines. If we take into account that these pages contain more white space than do the pages of the histories and law, we can conclude that roughly one third of the Hebrew Bible consists of poetry. I call that quite a lot.

Where exactly are the poems situated? For most texts, there is a quite definite answer to this question. The books of Psalms,[3] Proverbs, Song of Songs, and Lamentations consist exclusively of poems, the book of Job almost exclusively.[4] The books of Isaiah and the twelve so-called Minor Prophets (bar one)[5] were also largely written in poetry; the fact that the demarcation of the poems is often difficult does not alter this. Finally, there are a number of individual poems, distributed throughout the narrative prose. They occupy carefully chosen positions; varying in length from a few words to many strophes, they articulate the mass of narrative prose, throughout the entire "history" track that runs from Genesis through to Kings. I will mention only the most important ones here: the strophes in which Jacob, and Moses after him, characterizes the tribes (in Gen. 49 and Deut. 33), Moses' Song at the Reed Sea (Exod. 15), his long didactic speech in Deuteronomy 32 (no fewer than sixty-nine full poetic lines in twenty-seven strophes), Deborah's Song of Victory in Judges 5, the Song of Hannah in 1 Samuel 2:1–10, David's lament in 2 Samuel 1:19–27, and his great Song of Thanksgiving as king in 2 Samuel 22.[6]

This is all very well, but can we actually see the difference between prose and poetry in our Bible translations? This is a question we have to ask, as I am writing primarily for the many readers who do not read the Bible in the original languages.

The difference between prose and poetry has generally been carefully observed in recent translations, as for instance the bestselling New International Version (1978, revised 1983), and the Jewish Publication Society's 1985 translation of the Hebrew Bible: prose has been printed continuously, but poetry is immediately conspicuous by its typography: the lines are ragged instead of justified. In the older translations—the many reprints of the King James Bible and the widely available Revised Standard Version of 1946–52—this is unfortunately not the case. In these versions, only the Psalms, Proverbs, Job, Song of Songs, and Lamentations are printed in the desired typography of true poetic lines. The abundant Prophetic texts have regrettably been printed as prose, often in two columns per page. The unfortunate results of this will soon become clear, as I introduce two of the greatest poets by discussing a strophe from Isaiah and a lament of David's.

Wash yourselves, make yourselves clean (Isaiah 1)

The first thing that strikes us when we open our translation is the typography in which the poems are presented: their appearance on the page. Here is a passage from Isaiah in the RSV rendering:

> [16] Wash yourselves; make yourselves clean; remove the evil of your doings from before my eyes; cease to do evil, [17] learn to do good; seek justice, correct oppression; defend the fatherless, plead for the widow.

(Isa. 1:16–17)

Typography like this blocks our view of the true literary situation by printing the text continuously, as if it were prose. Moreover, the text is printed in two columns per page, a procedure which in itself is already detrimental to the poetry. The two biblical verses I just quoted are actually composed of three verses in the literary sense—i.e., full poetic lines—which each consist of three segments. Their 3 x 3 exactly fill one strophe, and thus the unit may also be printed as follows:

	line
Wash yourselves; make yourselves clean;	1a
remove the evil of your doings	1b
from before my eyes;	1c
cease to do evil,	2a
learn to do good,	2b
seek justice;	2c
support the oppressed,	3a
provide justice for the fatherless,	3b
plead for the widow.	3c

This is a working translation that keeps a bit closer to the original text. There is one substantial difference from the RSV rendering, which appears at the beginning of the third verse. The Hebrew word *hamots* usually refers to an oppressor ("oppression" in the first quote), but this time (line 3a) the object of this action is meant. In the following, I will have to resist the temptation to go back to the Hebrew, as this introduces information the reader cannot check, which is something I want to avoid. For once, however, I will depart from this rule, and for a good reason: the very articulation of the third trio guides us in the choice of the right object.

The correct arrangement or division of the strophe is the ideal starting point for a compact and simple analysis of the structure. The presentation of Isaiah 1:16–17 as three trios offers a perfect view of what happens. Each verse contains three forms of the imperative (in the plural). Although the first verse is about physical cleansing, the focus is on the symbolic and moral meanings. With these three verses we are in the middle of a long poem in which the deity itself is fulminating against the corrupt compatriots of the Judaean Isaiah; this is the long oracle*† of doom of Isaiah 1:2–20, some forty poetic lines. The addressed have to cleanse themselves because they have blood on their hands (thus the end of verse 15, which immediately precedes our strophe), and because their cult is only a lot of pomp and show (vv. 11–14).

The second verse is a new series of three, where the imperative (another three times, all of them in the plural) always has an abstract noun as its object: do evil, good, justice. In line 2a I used the word "evil" for the first object to show in my translation that this makes the phrase an echo of the evil in line 1b. This instance of repetition is linked to another in the second verse: the root for "just" appears in 2c and is also used in 3b, in favor of the oppressed. The central command imparting meaning to the nine injunctions is 2b, "learn to do good," and starting from this pivot there are only positive commands in the text.

The poet does not get bogged down in a noncommittal exhortation to such abstract virtues as "the good." In his last trio he presents the practical application. The commands (another three, still in the plural) of the third verse all have concrete direct objects: people of flesh and blood who are under great duress and deserve to be protected. So much for our brief analysis of the structure of the strophe; it has now become obvious that line 3a indeed refers to the object of oppression rather than the subject, and the more recent translations have fortunately seen this.

A sentence such as "I have seen you" or "You will praise him" needs only one word in Hebrew. Moreover, the classical poets aim

---

† The first occurrence of each glossary term is marked by an asterisk (*) following the word.

for succinctness even by Hebrew standards. This is why in English we almost always need far more words to render a verse than there are in the original. And this in turn creates the situation that biblical poetry works when each segment (half-verse, colon) is given a line of its own in the typography. The complete verse in translation simply becomes too long to be printed on a single line. Let us see how this works for Isaiah 1:16–17:

> Wash yourselves; make yourselves clean; / remove the evil of
> your doings / from before my eyes!
> Cease to do evil, / learn to do good, / seek justice!
> Correct oppression; / provide justice for the fatherless, / plead
> for the widow.

Even now it hardly works, although I have used a smaller font. As a staccato of commands, phrase after phrase, the passage is so dense that even by Hebrew standards it is exceptional; in terms of meter, we here have three times 2 + 2 + 2 beats. In the following, I will call the first segment of a verse the A-colon, the second the B-colon, and the third the C-colon. From a visual point of view it is good practice to indent the B-cola in translation, and then indent the C-cola one extra level, so as to show staggered articulation, which is the true hallmark of the poetic line.

For a good understanding of a poem it is essential to discover the contours of the units or textual layers above the level of the verse. This form of structuration and other matters will be discussed together with David's poem; I will first print it in its entirety, in a working translation of my own.

David's lament for Saul (2 Samuel 1)

The situation at the end of the first book of Samuel is as follows: under the command of king Saul and three of his sons, the Israelite army tries to fend off an attack by the Philistines, but is utterly defeated. Three days later the bad news reaches David in Ziklag, in the southwest of Palestine, where he is formally still the vassal of one of the Philistine kings.[7] He composes a dirge for the fallen king and his firstborn Jonathan, who is David's closest friend. The text is in 2 Samuel 1:19–27; the author of the book first provides some information (vv. 17–18) that in three prose lines tells us a surprising amount about subject, genre, aim, target group, and source of the painful message, and as such helps to guide our reading:

David composed this dirge over Saul and his son Jonathan   [prose]
and he said
[in order to instruct the Judaeans through the hard message;
see, it is recorded in the Book of the Upright]:   [vv. 17–18]

strophe   stanza

Your glory/gazelle, O Israel,
　　[lies] slain on your heights;   1
　　　　how have the mighty fallen!

Tell it not in Gath,   2   I
　　do not proclaim it in the streets of Ashkelon,
lest the daughters of the Philistines rejoice,
　　lest the daughters of the uncircumcised exult.

Hills of Gilboa, [let there be] no dew   3
　　and no rain on you, fields up high,
for there the shield of the mighty was desecrated,
　　the shield of Saul is anointed with oil no more.

Without the blood of the slain,
　　without the fat of the mighty   4   II
the bow of Jonathan did not come back,
　　and the sword of Saul never returned empty.

Saul and Jonathan, the beloved and most dear,   5
　　in life and death they never parted.
　　　　They were swifter than eagles, mightier than lions.

Daughters of Israel, weep over Saul,   6   III
　　who clothed you in crimson and finery,
　　　　who decked your robes with jewels of gold.
How are the mighty fallen in the midst of battle!

[It is] Jonathan [who is] slain on your heights!   7
I am devastated because of you, my brother,
　　Jonathan, you were most dear to me,
your love is a miracle to me,
　　more than the love of women.
How have the mighty fallen,
　　the instruments of war perished!

The seven strophes have been arranged into three stanzas, as a short analysis must show. The first strophe consists of only one tripartite verse (a so-called tricolon), and has to serve as an introduction in more than one respect. The very first word of strophe and poem is *ts^{e}vi* in the original language (also spelled *Zvi*) and wrong-foots us on purpose: we just cannot understand it at this stage. The word is a homonym* that means both "jewel, glory" and "gazelle," and we are forced to defer our decision as to which meaning to choose. Moreover, we do not know who or what the metaphor* refers to. The information that Zvi lies slain on the heights of Gilboa—the low table-mountain where the battle took place—suggests that we have to do with one or more persons, but who? Is it the king, with the princes at his side, or the army? Here, too, we have to defer our decision—and, as we shall see, as far as the final strophe. In other words, the poet immediately presents us with a riddle.

The second sentence of the poem is the C-colon of the opening verse. While the first sentence contained an unevenness because of the awkward position of the vocative* and remained incomprehensible, the rhetorical exclamation is smooth and simple. More than that, it is a cliché, a general statement that also might have been exclaimed after the battles of Waterloo or Hastings. At the same time, however, its "normal" and cliché character is undermined by a strategic decision. The poet makes this exclamation a seed that will grow. At the end of strophes 6 and 7 the sentence returns, first accompanied by an adjunct of place, and then (at the end of the poem as a whole) with a new clause in the B-colon as its counterpart. For this reason, "how have the mighty fallen!" merits the label of "refrain phrase." The worst cliché effect has been removed anyway, as it has been placed *after* the sentence about Zvi: fortunately, the poem does not start with a platitude. The riddle of Zvi I will call the theme phrase.

Stanza I consists of two strophes, which are both determined by two commands placed in front, followed by two negative sentences. In strophe 2 David forbids certain persons to carry the "joyful message" to the Philistine home front. But who exactly are these people? In reality, the cities on the coast have heard of the outcome of the war at least two days before David does, and exuberant festivities must long since have started in the Pentapolis, the

league of the five major cities of the Philistines! I conclude that
here David is addressing imaginary messengers in a desperate
attempt to reverse reality. As yet, he absolutely cannot bear the
thought that the other camp is now joyously celebrating its tri-
umph on the battlefield, and tries to prevent this party by magical-
poetical means. This is indicated by the double "lest."

In strophe 3 David again opens with two prohibitions, in sentences which have been so shortened by anger that they do not
even contain a verb. Their content is remarkable: he curses the
slopes of Mount Gilboa. David tries to condemn them to permanent infertility by blocking the supply of life-giving water. But
which person is capable of stopping rain? There is only one: the
deity. In the Song of the Vineyard (Isa. 5:1–7), God does indeed
command the clouds not to grant their rain to the vineyard he has
decided to curse. All this demonstrates how David here tries the
impossible, exactly as in strophe 2. Against his own better judgment he places himself in the position of God. He feels so power-
less in the face of this catastrophe that he deploys all the power
tools in the language he must work with as a poet, in order to turn
back the clock. In this way, great poetic expressivity becomes the
mask and the sign of complete impotence.

All these prohibitions of David's, so characteristic of stanza I, are
apotropaic*: they aim at fending off disaster by denying and aveng-
ing the inexorable course of history. The poet makes a titanic effort
to eliminate the *fait accompli*. This in itself is also a message: the
warding-off gesture is a form of avoidance. David will not and
cannot relate to the catastrophe directly and personally at this
point, which may in turn be explained by his distress and pain.

After two strophes, David still has not reached that point. Stanza
II stands out sharply from its surroundings—i.e., the first and last
stanzas—by referring to the times before the battle, and surprisingly exchanging the minor key of the complaint for the major
key of a song of praise. This central part praises the courage and
victories of Saul and Jonathan as the heroes of earlier battles. Stanza
II is a eulogy* that forms the center of an elegy*. The maximum
contrast between center and flanks creates a formidable dynamic
in the perception of the poet and the empathetic reader.

I have rendered the usual "heroes" of the refrain phrase by

"mighty" here, as the root "strong, mighty" is an important key word in the song. It occurs in v. 25a and parallel to this in v. 27a, indicating a closure or finish at strophe level, and it is the counterpart of the name "Saul" in the strophe about the shields (v. 21). The most telling aspect, however, is its placement in vv. 22a and 23b. Its position on the edges of the central stanza gives the root a structural function, that of demarcating and framing that unit. Moreover, here it appears with a reversed key signature. In the verses of the flanking stanzas I and III, "mighty" is in a minor key and refers to the fallen heroes of David's own party; at the top and bottom of the middle stanza its effect is exactly the reverse: in v. 22 it refers to Saul's and Jonathan's former enemies, and at the end of v. 23 it aims to honor father and son themselves: "they were stronger than lions."

At the beginning of stanza II, Jonathan receives a much longer sentence than his father. This is mainly because the word "empty," which further specifies the return of Saul's sword, is the exact counterpart of two wordier complements that characterize the return of Jonathan's bow: "not without the blood of the slain . . . not without the fat of the warriors." Formally speaking, our attention is directed toward the weapons rather than their bearers. The same already happened in strophe 3, when the poet's gaze discovered "the shield of the mighty, tainted" on the battlefield, and "the shield of Saul [was] anointed with oil no more." Polishing one's shield with oil was one of the things a soldier had to do in preparation for battle; this was supposed to make blows from the enemy glance off it. But the introduction of "oil" in this strophe is first and foremost a subtle allusion to Saul's status: he was the Lord's Anointed, meaning that he held the sacred office of king, and as such was inviolable. Now, the shield smeared with blood and mud symbolizes the terrible and desecrating end he met with.

The shift to speaking of weapons instead of their bearers is an example of metonymy*. This form of indirectness again betrays the poet's emotional condition: he is still intent upon avoidance. At this point, however, strophe 5 appears as a complement. Suddenly, father and son are juxtaposed, and the order of their names has been reversed. The two names are followed by two appositions ("beloved and most dear"), and two adjuncts of time of maximum contrast, "life and death." Finally, in the last position of the double verse, the actual sentence core follows: "they never parted." This predicate* is the only element in the sentence that is not duplicated.

For the Israelite, life and death cannot be meaningfully linked or united in any way: they form the ultimate polarity of human existence. Here, however, their opposition is put in perspective, I would almost say negated, by the mutual loyalty of father and son, whose force is so strong that it cannot be split up. Verse 23 is an arena in which unity and duality are at war, and all duplications in the [outer] form ultimately prove to serve the Saul-and-Jonathan unity. The entire poem is a chain of twenty-five predicates in all. The middle one—number 13—is this one verb that, thanks to the negation, conquers or surpasses polarity and division, and so tries to exorcise the divisive ravages wrought by death.

The distribution of the two proper names throughout the poem is in itself an important beacon, which points the way to the solution of the Zvi-riddle. Within stanza II, both names occur twice, in a chiastic* order. If we take strophe 1 to be a part of stanza I, a pattern becomes visible:

I	Zvi	II	Jonathan	III	Saul
			Saul		
	Saul		Saul		Jonathan
			Jonathan		

The balance between these occurrences is the first clear suggestion that the name Zvi might be the cover for the person most beloved by David. If this is true, the two names under III mirror the two of the beginning in a crosswise construction. In that case, the poem starts and ends with the one person whose loss David can never get over; first denoted enigmatically as the glory of Israel, he appears under his own name in the final strophe, which clearly forms the climax.

Stanza III consists of two strophes. The first, strophe 6, is devoted to the king; the other one, the seventh and last of the song, speaks about Jonathan. In the one strophe the women lament the king; in the other David himself, in the first person, laments the prince, his bosom friend.

Around the center, which was in a major key, the poet creates a balance between stanzas I and III. This is immediately visible in the exhortation of strophe 6. While in strophe 2 the poet refuses all joy to "the daughters of the Philistines" (as the original text literally reads) and hence tries to stop the message of victory by means of a prohibition, in strophe 6 he issues a command, so that throughout the land "the daughters of Israel" express their grief in mourning rituals. They should weep for a king who gave them prosperity in better days. Saul's care is expressed through attributes and terms of outward pomp, and a chiasm* keeps the core of the strophe together:

[weep over Saul] who clothed you   in crimson and finery,
                 who with jewels of gold decked your robes.

This is followed by the exclamation about the mighty having fallen, which as a repetition of v. 19c becomes the refrain sentence and concludes the strophe.

The final strophe is much more personal, with its intense exchange between "me" and "you." Borrowing a term from love poetry, David calls Jonathan "my brother"—which is what the girl from the Song of Songs calls her lover (and he can address her as "my sister"). In the center, the poet applied the adjectives "beloved" and "most dear" to the king and his son in a rather objective tone. These two terms now turn out to have been used in preparation for the final strophe as well, where the word "love" appears twice exclusively in honor of Jonathan, and follows "dear." The relationship with the middle of stanza II is again chiastic:

Saul and Jonathan:
    the beloved,   the most dear . . .   [middle of strophe 4]

Jehonathan, you were   your love is a miracle to me,
    most dear to me   more than the love of women.

Next to this unique praise for his friend, David places his personal pain—a formidable contrast. He speaks his name twice, in its full form *Jehonathan* (literally: "Yahweh has given"), and now expresses his grief uninhibitedly and directly with "I am distressed for

thee"—for once I will use the English of the almost four-
centuries-old King James Bible. The original text literally says
something like "I am hard-pressed," in the sense of "I am in a terrible plight." The avoidance stage has passed, and David is now
ready for the naked truth. He is crushed and shocked. His grief
makes him aware of the full depth of their love for each other,
while the love lends depth and a voice to the grief.

Meanwhile, David as a speaker has made his most surprising
move on the threshold of the strophe. He started it with a nominal sentence, which is nothing but the theme phrase v. 19a with
which the poem opened: "Jehonathan—[lies] slain on your
heights." He has changed only one element: he has replaced the
word Zvi with his friend's name! Suddenly we have received
the poetic answer to the question of who is hidden behind the
metaphors "jewel" and "gazelle." The substitution of the name
Jonathan for the very first word, together with the hint provided
by the structure, proves that Jonathan = Zvi. While the last strophe
sings of the love *of* Jonathan (for David), and immortalizes this
with a unique comparison—"your love is more wonderful to me
than the love of women"—we may call the love *for* Jonathan (on
David's part) the alpha and omega of the song as a whole.

The refrain phrase "how have the mighty fallen" is repeated, and
is expanded even further than in v. 25a, as it is given a parallel in
the independent clause that flanks it: "the weapons of war have
perished." This last clause combines the shields, the sword, and the
bow under one heading, and so concludes the metonymical
speech. This half-verse about the weapons thus also refers to the
owners of the weapons and their deaths. The indirect character of
the reference now no longer means avoidance, but offers a discreet
way to provide the lament with a not-too-vehement ending, by
means of a certain distance.

These preliminary exercises already demonstrate that the
Hebrew poet is a master of proportions. At every position in the
poem, and at every level—whether we are dealing with sounds
and words, or whether we are looking at half-verses or verses,
strophes or stanzas—he always adapts himself to the proper dimensions of his material. However conscientious, a translation can
never take into account all subtleties of style such as alliteration*,

number of syllables, rhyme, and such, but at the levels above vocabulary even a translation can show much of the poets' measured composing. We have already seen this in the meticulous as well as playful handling of the "three-units" principle in Isaiah.

The poems in the Bible are extremely varied. We notice this when we look at genre: there are proverbs and poems from the Wisdom tradition, songs of victory and defeat, lamentations by individual voices or groups, hymns, songs of thanksgiving, love poetry, oracles of doom or salvation pronounced by the prophets, and much more. But however diverse the poems, they have a number of powerful rules and literary conventions in common; and after we have learned to recognize and apply these, the texts are generally self-explanatory: this is the subject of the rest of this book.

The number of English-speakers who read classical Hebrew is so small that I will here assume the position of readers who have to take recourse to translations. I want to find an answer to the question of what the primary tools are that such readers require for an independent and creative reading of the translated poems. I will start from the reality that there are three commonly used translations: the Authorized (or King James) Version (usually in some sort of modernized spelling), the 1946–52 Revised Standard Version, and the New International Version. I will regularly quote from the Jewish Publication Society's Tanakh translation, 1985.

Legend

I must first point out a pitfall: the term "verse" is ambiguous. When I write "v. 16" or "verses 10–14," I am referring to the traditional verse numbers of the transmitted text. The numbers here indicate *biblical verses*. A biblical verse can be prose or poetry, and its length may vary from a few words in one sentence to as many as ten sentences and thirty words. They have been transmitted or demarcated as textual units by the rabbis, for the purpose of recitation in the synagogue. In a book about poetics, the other term "verse" is much more important: this refers to the complete poetic line, as when we talk about texts by Yeats or Wallace Stevens, lines by Homer, Horace, and Shakespeare—the verse in the literary or poetical sense. In the Hebrew Bible, the traditional verse numbers almost always coincide with the actual poetic lines in the books of Job and Proverbs: a happy coincidence. Outside these, however, in the Prophets and in the books of Psalms, Song of Songs, and Lamentations, or in the strophes that here and there adorn and enrich the prose from Genesis through to Kings, the biblical verse is not at all the same as the (literary) verse = the poetic line.

As I expect this book also to be used or consulted by all sorts of students, I have added endnotes to each chapter at the end of the book which may be of service to Hebraists. Readers without knowledge of the original languages can safely skip them. For these readers I have included a glossary of foreign and technical terms at the end of the book. The first occurrence of such a term (for instance, "metonymy" or "merism") has been marked by an asterisk, indicating that it will be explained in the list. Finally, I should point out an important terminological distinction: I use the word "poetic" as an adjective relating to *poetry* (i.e., primary literature), and the word "poetical" as an adjective referring to the scholarly discipline of *poetics*, which produces secondary literature *about* poetry.

2

The art of poetry: a definition and analysis

Components I and II: language and number

Density; language as a system of differences

Sensitivity to verse has something to do with aptitude, and a lot to do with the proper training. A correct perception of poetry is based on the art of reading. Competent reading, and the right kind of experience, I consider more essential than drawing up a definition of the art of poetry. Yet, it is worth the effort to try and define Hebrew poetry. An adequate set of specifications has many practical advantages and will lead to effective insight and increased pleasure in reading.

What exactly is "poetry"? The German term for it, *Dichtung,* by a lucky coincidence sounds as if it was derived from the German root *dicht,* meaning "dense," a similarity I simply must take advantage of. The sounds create an association that we can put to good use, even if it is no more than my own opportunist popular etymology*.

What a poet undertakes does have a lot to do with creating "density." Poetry is the most compact and concentrated form of speech possible. By making the most of his or her linguistic tools, the poet creates an immense richness of meaning, and this richness becomes available if we as readers know how to handle the density: how we can cautiously tackle complexity, probe the various layers one by one, and unfold them.

The poet creates this abundance of meanings by visiting all the nooks and crannies of the language, and by being an expert at it. I may draw a comparison here with the visual arts: it is a well-known fact that the greatest painters and sculptors spend their entire lives lovingly studying their materials and experimenting with them: paint and canvas, clay and bronze. The same holds true for the poet: his raw material is language, in the first instance, and very few poems are born without the poet's exploring and trying out various forms of language and style, without outlines and deletions.

Our language is a well-ordered and subtle system of signs, which may be described as a network of relations and differences. These forms of cohesion were discovered only at the beginning of the twentieth century, which means that scholarly attention to them is comparatively recent; the poets, however, have been actually working with them for thousands of years. They brilliantly exploit the differences and contrasts inherent in their language as a system.

In the case of Hebrew, an additional factor is involved: the difference between that language and English. We should remain aware of that difference when reading translations of poems from the Bible. Hebrew needs fewer words than our mother tongue. Take, for instance, the sentence: "I have listened to you." In Hebrew this is only one word, of three or four syllables, which moreover contains an extra element of information as compared to English: it shows whether "you" (the direct object) is a man or a woman. A phrase such as "the people who pursue me without reason" in the original language consists of only two words, five syllables in all.

Because English needs more words, it is often impossible to print a complete verse on one line (as we have already seen in the Introduction). As a result, the RSV, NIV, and many other translations have had to decide to print one verset (colon, plural *cola*) per line in their presentation of biblical poetry. And sometimes even that is hardly feasible. I will illustrate this by an extreme case of divergent lengths. In Psalm 69:5a/5b, the Hebrew text contains 5 + 4 words filling cola of regular length. Two popular Dutch translations print the equivalent of these words (taken from the RSV) as follows:

> More in number than the hairs of my head
> > are those who hate me without cause;
> > mighty are those who would destroy me, those who attack me
> > > with lies.

A rather unfortunate typography. The text itself consists of two cola, because we easily recognize two sentences of almost completely parallel structure. The translators needed a lot of words (no fewer than sixteen) to render v. 5a, and have succumbed to the temptation to cut the first sentence in two. Thus they have divided a syntactically and rhythmically close-knit unit into two lines, on the basis of a criterion that has nothing to do with writing Hebrew verse but is determined by the receiving language: the length of the translated English phrase. Which leads to a second mistake: printing the B-colon in the position of an A-colon. The RSV cuts both sentences in two, which leads to the illusion that we have two A-cola and two B-cola here.

The poet traverses the system of relations formed by the language, and is very adroit at exploiting the differences that as it were form the clue to this system. Below I am giving a list of the most important differences determining the usage of the Hebrew language. As in English, many of these contrasts are binary*:

- masculine/feminine
- singular/plural
- past/present/future
- stating, noting, or describing versus wishing, begging, and commanding
- positive/negative
- figurative/non-figurative
- active/passive
- transitive*/intransitive*
- speaking about/speaking to
- abstract/concrete
- regular/irregular word order

This list is mainly about language and text signs (signifiers*), but we could go on with a list of meanings (signifieds*), i.e., concepts and things the language refers to:

- high/low
- God/man
- native/foreign
- good/evil
- joy/distress
- fear/security
- trust/despair

... etc., but I have to admit that this short list is fairly arbitrary. This second list, however, makes us realize something much bigger: the number of meanings or subjects is simply inexhaustible, so I will immediately stop adding on to it.

However many there are, all these differences do not yet have a specifically literary quality; they also may be observed and studied in an ordinary newspaper article or some other piece of everyday language. So, it is time to consult the poet himself and see how he juggles binary and other differences. Here is a short poem from the Psalter, a unit of nine verses:

verse	Psalm 113	strophe
1a	O servants of Yahweh, give praise,	
b	praise the name of Yahweh.	
2a	Let the name of Yahweh be blessed,	1
b	now and forever.	
3a	From the rising of the sun to its setting	
b	the name of Yahweh is praised!	
4a	Yahweh is exalted above all nations,	2
b	His glory is above the heavens.	
5a	Who is like Yahweh our God,	
b	who is enthroned on high,	
6a	who looks far down,	3
b	in heaven and on earth?	
7a	Who raises the poor from the dust,	
b	and lifts the needy from the ash heap,	
8a	to make them sit with princes,	
b	with the princes of his people,	4
9a	who gives the barren woman a home,	
b	as a happy mother of children.	

We only need to look at the kind of sentences, and the use of space on the page, to find the right way into the work and to be able to see its articulation in various parts. The division into verses and the way they have been cut into halves (cola) originates from the Jewish text tradition and is undisputed. The division into four strophes, however, is mine, and therefore need not be accepted without question.

In vv. 1–2 we notice two verbs in the imperative, followed by a wish. This volitive* quality sets off the first strophe from the second, which contains positive sentences. In this indicative* mode they point to attributes of the deity; hence, there are no actions here, but rather three ways of saying "is." Speaking *to* (people) has been replaced by a hymnic speaking *about* (God).

Verses 5–6 are again different in tone, as they form a rhetorical question. The four versets are parts of a single syntactic unit.[1] The point of the question is that God is incomparable. In v. 6b we recognize the very first merism* of the Bible (as we find it in Gen.1:1), pointing to the domains of God and man: heaven and earth, respectively. This pair has been placed in a remarkable position: the two halves do correspond to God's activities—i.e., being enthroned and looking down—but they have been cut loose from these and placed together as the final line of the strophe. In this way, the poet has avoided writing a three-part verse, which would run: "who is like Yahweh, our God, / who sits on high, in heaven, / and looks far down, on earth?" His actual point is slightly different. Furthermore, he wanted to stick with his bicolic* design, and has created a third quartet of cola.

The center of this foursome, vv. 5b–6a, is taken up by a spectacular vertical axis linking the provinces of God and man. The axis is embedded in descriptions of God, and in the two halves of the spatial merism. The words for God and for cosmic space form two pairs, which provide a good balance and a perfect finish to the strophe. The only remaining question now is why the poet has delayed using the terms of space until v. 6d, and there presents them together. The answer is that in so doing he has them work in two ways: not only as an explanation and topographical indication of God's actions (being enthroned/seeing), but also as a gauge of God's uniqueness. Strictly speaking, the point of the strophe is: neither in heaven nor on earth do we find anybody comparable to Him. Thus, we may also reorganize the quartet, and interpret it as:

Who is like Yahweh our God, / in heaven and on earth?
There is nobody who sits so high / and looks down so far!

Reading on, we reach strophe 4 and see six rather than four versets. These are largely adjective clauses, and we are struck by at least three transitive* verbs indicating sovereign action. Although we all know the answer to the rhetorical question in the exact center of the poem ("nobody," of course!), the poet has decided to seize his opportunity and add an answer of his own after all. He again presents a series of actions on God's part, which at last govern the object omitted in v. 6: here we see the people, more specifically the weak and needy, who appear in the position of beneficiaries. The three transitive verbs demonstrate the constitutive power of God's liberating initiative. God proves to be a totally committed person, instead of a neutral physical phenomenon. His proper name occurs, in descending frequency, three, two, one, and zero times in strophes 1–4. His activity shows a reverse development: it started at zero and reaches its maximum in strophe 4.

The strophes not only show variation of tone and mode (in the verbs), but also form a quartet on their own level, in an AB-B'A' pattern: first, they view the earth/heaven, next heaven/the earth. The characters we meet in them are arranged in a similar crosswise structure: the people are exhorted to action in strophe 1 and liberated in strophe 4, while God is praised in the central strophes 2 and 3.

The lyrical world as evoked by this poem is one of sheer space, and the reader is provided with plenty of space thanks to the intersecting horizontal and vertical axes, which have been dynamically positioned by the poet. In the second strophe, v. 3 shows the horizontal axis at its widest by tracing the course of the sun from East to West. Verse 4 duly follows with the vertical axis, for a moment showing us God enthroned high above the human struggle. But not for long: in v. 6b the hymnic question that constitutes the *poetic* axis and points to God's uniqueness reverses the order earth/heaven, so that our attention is bent back toward the earth, following God's gaze. Next, strophe 4 fills up the plane of our history with the images of God's intervention.

In this plane, too, the horizontal and vertical axes are contrasted. The poor are raised from the dust, and we can see how this symbolizes the reversal of their fortunes; they are now able to straighten their backs. The horizontal orientation of vv. 8–9 is not prominent, but certainly recognizable and lends an aspect of harmony to the people gathered there. They are presented in the plural (princes, children), by which the poet takes us back to the beginning. In this way he effectively rounds off his song with a form of *inclusio**, a frame. Only after we have crossed the finish do we realize that there are excellent reasons for the call to "praise God" in v. 1: these are given in the long final strophe.

The prosody* of Psalm 113 cannot be called representative of biblical poetry, for a positive reason: this poem is one of the top five as regards regularity. By way of exception I will demonstrate this by a count of the syllables in the original Hebrew, so that these exact figures may again give the reader an impression of the precision the poet can employ at will. The left-hand column shows the number of syllables per word on either side of the caesura* (indicated by a slash), and the middle column adds up the totals for the versets:

verse			
1	3.2.2 / 3.1.1.2	7 + 7 = 14	
2	1.1.2.3 / 3.2.2	7 + 7 = 14	strophe 1 = 28
3	3.1.1.3 / 3.1.2	8 + 6 = 14	
4	1.1.1.2.2 / 1.3.3	7 + 7 = 14	strophe 2 = 28
5	1.3.4 / 4.2	8 + 6 = 14	
6	4.2 / 3.3	6 + 6 = 12	strophe 3 = 26
7	3.3.1 / 3.2.2	7 + 7 = 14	
8	4.1.3 / 1.3.2	8 + 6 = 14	
9	3.2.2 / 1.3.3	7 + 7 = 14	strophe 4 = 42

The total number of syllables is 28 + 28 + 26 + 42 = 124. We may be allowed to rewrite this as 40 (a very biblical number, the total of vv. 5–7) plus 3 x 28. The greatest regularity is found at verse level: eight out of nine verses contain fourteen syllables, a total that in five cases has been reached, moreover, by doubling the sacred number seven. The minimal variation in colon length, which nowhere exceeds a range of 6–7–8 in the poem, is not representative either: there are quite a number of psalms using a range of five to twelve syllables (as a measure of colon length); there is usually considerable variation within one poem.

The old definition of Hebrew poetry

Until some thirty years ago, Old Testament scholars entertained a rather inadequate view of Hebrew poetics. Exegetes worked with a seriously flawed definition of poetry, and I fear that it is still floating about in a number of heads. Nevertheless, their view of Hebrew verse contains two small grains of truth, which are worth mentioning. I will therefore use the old formula as a starting point for a quest for a comprehensive definition: a formula that will do full justice to the true riches and complexity of the poem, rather than reduce it.

The old definition rests on two pillars, as it holds that the biblical poem is determined by a) meter, and b) the parallel arrangement of versets (for which the technical term is *parallelismus membrorum*). In how far is this correct?

I will discuss the first pillar, that of *meter,* only briefly as the details are relevant only to readers of Hebrew. In the nineteenth century, biblical scholarship reached an important negative conclusion: however strong the impression of rhythm emanating from the verses in the Hebrew Bible, they are obviously subject to rules totally different from those governing the metrics of Graeco-Roman poetry and its various branches and offshoots in the poetry of the European languages. Homer and Virgil, Sophocles and Plautus used quantitative meter, based on an unambiguous distinction between long and short syllables. In Arabic, too, poets have the option to work with verse feet that may be determined quantitatively—Arabic is related to Hebrew within the Semitic family, and it was the world language with which Jews in the Middle East, Northern Africa, and the Iberian peninsula came into contact more than a thousand years after the canon of biblical books had been finalized.

In classical Hebrew, the distinction between long and short syllables does not work. At the end of the nineteenth century, scholars concluded that the Hebrew poetic line was best described as a string of alternating stressed and unstressed syllables: it is an accentual verse. What we need to do is count the number of stresses (beats) per colon, while between the beats there is a varying though not too large number of unstressed syllables. A verse may be schematically represented as separate syllables, or in a short notation. This looks as follows (for once, I will give some Hebrew words in a scholarly transliteration—Ps. 44, v. 7):

I do not trust in my bow / it is not my sword that gives me victory.

ki lo bᵉqashti ebṭaḥ / wᵉḥarbi lo toshiˁeni

to be pronounced roughly as follows:

kee lo bᵉkashtee ebtakh	/	*uᵉkharbee lo toshee-eini*
o ó o o ó o ó	/	o o ó ó o o óo

An "o" represents a syllable; accents indicate a beat or stress. The practical short notation for this would be 3 + 3, which has led the Germans to call this sort of line a *Doppeldreier*. Frequent patterns are 2 + 2, 2 + 3, or conversely 3 + 2, 3 + 3, 4 + 4, and 4 + 3 or the reverse. Half-verses often differ by one accent or beat (one point). A pattern such as 3 + 3 for a two-part verse (a bicolon) may be nicely varied by 2 + 2 + 2 in a tricolon (three-part verse), so that the total of six syllables remains the same.

I realize that all this is not going to help the user of a Bible translation much. And there are two more pieces of bad news. First, scholars are often bitterly divided on the correct scansion*, as of course borderline cases constantly crop up—for instance, about the question whether a specific secondary stress may be viewed as a metric accent, i.e., a beat. Second, there is the question that strikes at the very roots of the problem: can we speak of metrics at all in connection with Hebrew verse? The interpreters whose sensitivity to verse I admire almost all answer in the affirmative, but there are renowned scholars who radically deny the possibility of determining any meter at all. In short, there is a vehement discussion about the point, or lack of it, of scanning Hebrew verse, and it is highly unlikely that the debate will ever reach a consensus.

The consequence of this battle is that this first pillar of the classical definition is tottering, and has probably fallen already. What can we do? Making a virtue out of necessity, I can point to two escape routes. In the first place, this book exclusively deals with Bible translations. A rendering of a Hebrew poem in English cannot hope to approximate the rhythm and meter of the original, due to the enormous gap between source and target languages, and the fact that Hebrew uses far fewer words. Consequently, we had better leave the entire complex of metrics and scansion aside.

Yet, the text that is left in translation still shows two faces. Even though meter has gone, there is still a powerful rhythm, which is even stronger in Hebrew and is not denied even by scholars who have no time for metrics. The rhythm is kept reasonably intact thanks to *parallelismus membrorum*, which will be discussed in the next section; I will return to rhythm in due course.

The second escape route from the yes/no metrics deadlock is a roundabout one. It is possible to circumvent the entire issue, and go back to counting the original syllables to measure and describe the powerful rhythm of Hebrew verse. I return to Psalm 44, v. 7: the $7 + 8 = 15$ syllables that I just presented as an accentual verse were also 15 in the old Hebrew from centuries before Christ.[2] Some 65 percent of the cola in the book of Psalms are seven, eight, or nine syllables long. Recent investigations have shown that the poets themselves counted their syllables, and often used the syllable totals to make patterns in their verses and strophes.[3] Hence, the poems have an explicit and precise numerical aspect—in Hebrew. As this is taking things too far for most readers, I refer the Hebraists among them to note 2 on page 232 for more information. Still, in the previous paragraph I have lifted a corner of the veil: the figures for Psalm 113 are a good example of numerical precision.

Parallel arrangement of versets

The second pillar of the obsolete definition is known among scholars as *parallelismus membrorum*. The Latin plural "membra" has the same meaning as the Greek plural "cola"; the singular "colon" means "a member, a part."

This way of arranging verse parts is not unknown to us. Take for example the most straightforward example from our own literature:

> Here lies Fred:
> He is dead.[4]

Words and syllables coincide; this $3 + 3$ is a miracle of efficiency, certainly if you realize that even a haiku still needs seventeen syllables. The lines start with an alliteration because of the h, and their first words, *here/he*, indicate the spot and the man. The verbs are intransitive* and static: they indicate duration and condition rather than action; the consonant s provides assonance*/phonetic cohesion. By their rhyme, the line endings best demonstrate the importance of sound. The rhyme *Fred/dead* invites us to semanticize*:

we make a semantic link between two words that was not there before, and find that the man becomes fused with his horizontal, still position. It is a kind of identification that leads to the point of the poem: an attitude of complete acceptance of the end, and one of great sobriety and dry humor.

This preliminary exercise shows how each word in one line has its counterpart in the other, in the same position even, and also how essential is the function of the sounds. Only if we pay close attention, and appreciate even the smallest detail, do we fully realize how much sheer technique has gone into this. And then I am not even talking about everything we do not see, i.e., everything that has been left out.

Back to the biblical verse (in the sense of poetic line). The importance of parallelismus membrorum has been clear since the middle of the eighteenth century, when the English bishop Robert Lowth wrote a book about it.[5] His discussion of the phenomenon has long set the tone for the study of biblical poetry. He described parallelism at verse level, distinguishing three types: if the parallel versets say the same thing, Lowth called it *synonymous* parallelism; if one is opposed to the other we have *antithetical* parallelism; and if there is a different relation, it is called *complementary* or *synthetic*. This is demonstrated by examples (a), (b), and (c) below:

(a) Ps. 2:1   Why do nations rage
                and peoples plot vain things?

(b) Ps. 1:6   Yahweh knows the way of the righteous,
                but the way of the wicked is doomed.

(c) Ps. 3:5   When I cry aloud to Yahweh,
                He answers me from his holy mountain.

The first notable aspect of example (c) is that it contains a compound sentence, the parts of which—subclause and main clause—neatly coincide with the cola, and present the actions of the speaker and his God. Hence, in this case the complementary aspect has been realized mainly by sentence structure and consecution (progress of the action). In example (b) we immediately recognize the simple opposition good/bad. While the righteous is "known" by God, something which to an Israelite implies attention and support, the wicked dies a miserable and lonely death, as a result of what seems a quasi–autonomous process: the intransive verb does not mention an agent. Consequently, we have a second contrast, conveyed by the difference between the verbs: the first is transitive, the second is not. In example (a), the synonymy is based on two word pairs. The terms in one colon are illustrated and explained by the terms in the other colon.

Lowth's division of "parallelism of the versets" into three types has been influential, and there are still theologians who consider it adequate enough to work with. Yet, the triad synonymous/ antithetical/complementary cannot withstand critical scrutiny. Already if we take Lowth seriously at the level of his own words, we immediately see that the label "complementary" is a basket term that covers everything that cannot be called synonymous or contrasting. Thus, the term is exposed as a counsel of despair, and this realization immediately strikes at the root of the entire triadic structure.

We now have entered the path that leads toward an adequate definition of Hebrew poetry, and in order to clear it, more radical criticism of Lowth's three-part structure is needed. I see three main areas of objection: an approach that mounts an epistemological attack on his terminology, a strictly literary counter-campaign, and an insight of a structural nature. In the following explanation I will make use of examples (a), (b), and (c) above, all taken from the beginning of the Psalter.

I will play the amateur philosopher for a moment and look at the binary division, synonymous versus antithetical, from the perspective of observation and epistemology. If you call the segments of a verse synonymous, you obscure the fact that actually they are not the same. Because their words are never identical, they do not really have the same meaning, and this opens up a crack between them. It is this crack that invites us to open the door wider. By "wider" I mean the following: in a case of synonymous parallelism we first notice, as Lowth did, the great similarity in meaning. Without losing sight of the resemblance, we nevertheless should not stop there and think we have finished. The similarity between the two cola, as for instance in the case of Psalm 2:1a and 1b in example (a), becomes a jumping-board or take-off point: against the background of the similarities, subtle differences begin to stand out. The nervous bustle of the peoples—they rage, as example (a) says—is further clarified in the B-colon, which disqualifies their activity as vain plotting. We now understand that the verse as a whole with its "why" (which does double duty, i.e., governs both cola) is no informative question, but a rhetorical and caustic one. There are thousands of verses that at first sight seem to consist of synonymous cola, but upon closer scrutiny turn out to cover potholes of difference. This is not to say that we should start expressing the relation between the similar and the different in figures or percentages; poems wilt when subjected to this sort of boorish and wooden treatment.

Lowth's second term deserves similar criticism. If you call two elements X and Y antithetical, you have in fact already seen or assumed a significant relation between the two. Only when X and Y have something in common is it possible and meaningful to speak of an antithesis between them. This dialectic consideration may be illustrated by example (b): "Yahweh knows the way of the righteous, but the way of the wicked is doomed"—a verse that forms the conclusion of the first Psalm. The entire poem has been based on the opposition between good and bad, to such an extent that there are only few cola in which the righteous or the wicked are presented with their own qualities, but many cola where they appear as the opposite of the other, by means of the word "not." I will print the negations in strophes 1 and 3 in italics, and follow the JPS here, with some small adaptations.[6]

verse	Psalm 1	strophe

1a   Happy the man

b   who has *not* followed the counsel of the wicked,

c   who has *not* taken the path of sinners,   1

d   and has *not* joined the company of the insolent;

2a   but finds his delight in the teaching of Yahweh,

b   and studies that teaching day and night.

3a   Yea, he is like a tree planted beside streams of water,

b   which yields its fruit in season,   2

c   whose foliage never fades;

d   whatever he does, prospers.

4a   *Not* so the wicked   3

b   rather, they are like chaff that the wind blows away.

5a   Therefore the wicked will *not* survive judgment,

b   and the sinners will *not* [survive] in the assembly
        of the righteous.

6a   For Yahweh knows the way of the righteous,

b   but the way of the wicked is doomed.

The poet's moral preferences are made clear by the fact that he grants the short middle strophe to the righteous, and honors him by speaking figuratively. The long strophes flanking the center, however, show a remarkable reciprocity: the first strophe "defines" the righteous by contrasting him with the wicked, and the opposite happens in the third strophe. This is a balance of mutual exclusion. With this symmetry the composition as a whole reveals that the good/bad antithesis has a basis: one solid set of values that is firmly oriented toward the "law" (*torah*, strictly speaking "teaching") of God. The opposition between bloom and destruction is traced back in the final verse to the judgment of one person, the deity. The poem is an arena where the forces of inclusion and exclusion engage in battle, but the conclusion of the song is to opt for the Torah.

Thus, the antithesis did not have the last word. If we look at the concluding bicolon from a more verse-technical point of view, we also notice that there is not only opposition: both versets employ the same word "way" and subject it to a subtle change in syntax*. In v. 6a, the way is the object of God's care; in 6b it is promoted to the function of subject. This, however, is a last piece of irony directed against the wicked, as their paths will lead them to destruction.

The conclusion of this first exercise in radical criticism must be: in every case of synonymous parallelism differences remain visible between cola that partner each other, and in every case of antithesis or rivalry between adjoining versets there is a common basis, or we still see elements that the cola have in common.

Recent scholarly efforts in the United States have produced a second avenue of criticism against Lowth's triad, more linguistic and literary than the first type. "Biblical parallelism is of one sort . . . , or a hundred sorts; but it is not three."[7] It would be wise to use the term "parallelism" as a very broad category, and then make subdivisions within this wide concept. Contemporary research into the factors contributing to parallelism of versets has uncovered so many different linguistic devices at the poet's disposal that Lowth's division into three has become outmoded: it is arbitrary, and far too rough.[8]

On the level of the poetic line alone, at least four layers, or gateways into the poem, may be distinguished. Parallelism may be based on phonological or morphological, lexical or semantic text data. To put it in plain English: the poet may create parallelism by means of the tools of sound and grammatical form, and by means of vocabulary and meaning. Surprisingly enough, we can already see this in the six short syllables by Walpole. "Here lies Fred; he is dead." Phonology is represented by the poet's acoustic tools: alliteration, assonance*, and rhyme; the balance of the syllables is also a factor. Morphology, or the study of linguistic forms and structures, analyzes the poet's choice of grammatical forms: the lines are opened by words with a fully or partially demonstrative function (*here/he*), after that we get intransitive verbs in the present tense (*lies/is*), and finally two nouns indicating the man and the main predicate to be applied to him: *dead*. These aspects are implied in the vocabulary, and the word order also provides parallelism. The circle is closed when the established parallelism invites us to semanticize, to ponder whether there is any difference left between "Fred" and "dead."

In the next chapter, these various linguistic layers will also be discussed, on the basis of poetic lines from the Bible. Here I will note only how limited Lowth's model turns out to be: it neglects or ignores the contributions of phonological or grammatical factors, and concentrates almost exclusively on the level of vocabulary and word meanings.

Noting these defects takes us to the third approach of radical criticism, which will uncover even more serious defects. This line of criticism originates from my own structural view of poetry, as demonstrated in almost every chapter of this book. I hold that for any poem there is much more to be probed than just the layer of words and their meanings, and that a complete ladder of parallelisms should be climbed if we want our attention and emotion to cover the possibilities and effects of poetry in a satisfactory way.

I purposely use "parallelisms" in the plural here: there are parallelisms at virtually all levels of the text, and they require detailed elaboration in the following chapters. To put it differently: the text is a hierarchy of layers, each layer having its own characteristics and rules and making its own particular contribution to the overall effect of the work of art on the reader.

This textual hierarchy consists of eight layers in the case of short and medium-length poems, and nine in the case of long poems as Deuteronomy 32 or Psalm 89. They may be represented as a series of steps:

levels in the poem	step no.
the poem as a whole	9
sections	8
stanzas	7
strophes	6
verses	5
versets	4
words	3
syllables	2
sounds	1

The five lower levels constitute the traditional field of linguistics and style analysis. I have inserted a blank line to show the boundary with the larger textual units. Levels 6–9 have only recently become available for systematic research, thanks to the fast developments in linguistics and the study of literature during the twentieth century. For the poets of ancient Israel, it was a standard part of their craft to work at perfect expression and form on all these levels.

A new, comprehensive definition

The poet sets out to write a verse. There is a more than 95 percent chance that it will be bi- or tri-partite.[9] To fill that space, and to remain within the poet's own cultural environment and its literary rules (which will then be understood by readers), the poet thankfully exploits parallelism as a means to balance the members of the verse and control the subject matter. The poet creates *equivalence* by introducing "parallelism of members."

At this point in the first stages of the poet's creative work I will switch to the domain of sentence structure, and describe in syntactic terms the four possibilities the poet may choose from:

1) An attractive and obvious decision is to fill the verset (colon) under construction with one short sentence of two to five words. The compactness of expression of the Hebrew language makes this easy. In this case, *clause* (a simple, non-compound sentence) coincides with colon. When the poet repeats this and creates a discernible cohesion with the aid of sound, grammatical form, or word meaning, a complete verse has been born, a bicolon that in characteristic Hebrew fashion realizes "equivalence" by the parallelism of its members. This situation occurs thousands of times in the Hebrew Bible.

2) The poet may also decide to employ a compound *sentence*. This is a syntactic complex consisting of a main clause and one or more subclauses. If the sentence is compact enough, it may fit into one colon, but this is rarely the case. What the poet usually does is neatly allocate one colon to every part of the compound sentence, and because the same term *clause* is used to indicate the parts of a compound sentence (or *period*), situation 2 is often just another instance of the equation "one clause = one colon." A simple example of this arrangement is the opening of Psalm 1. The poet immediately starts his main clause, which is nominal (i.e., does not contain a verb): "Happy the man"—fortunately, most translations manage to avoid inserting "is" or "be" (subjunctive mood). This main clause is v. 1a, and it completely coincides with the sentence core (subject plus predicate). The poet continues with an adjectival clause in order to tell us what sort of man he has in mind, and uses this clause to fill the B-colon. Next, however, a spectacular decision follows: the poet adds more adjectival

clauses. There are no less than four, two negative followed by two positive clauses:

v. 1a   Happy the man
   b   who has *not* followed the counsel of the wicked,
   c   who has *not* taken the path of sinners,   strophe 1
   d   and has *not* joined the company of the insolent;
v. 2a   but finds his delight in the teaching of Yahweh,
   b   and studies that teaching day and night.

Thus, this one move on the part of the composer creates many forms of equivalence or balance: each of the three full lines contains equivalence of the versets, and there is also equivalence at the level of the verse as a whole. Moreover, in the same move, this syntactic design creates a higher textual unit, as the three poetic lines in vv. 1–2 form a ready-made strophe. Three lines about scum in the plural are framed by three positive lines (1a and 2ab) about the man (singular) who remains on course thanks to "the teaching of Yahweh" (two more singular forms). In this way, the shape of the strophe suggests an encircling: the scum are kept in check.

3) The poet may also decide to write a long—not compound— sentence that exceeds the boundary of a single colon. In that case, the poet will usually arrange the material so that the sentence core is in one colon, possibly accompanied by a direct object, and any further adjuncts occupy the other colon; this happens, for instance, in the tricolic verse that depicts the "raging of the peoples" in Psalm 2:

v. 2a   The kings of the earth take their stand
   b   and regents intrigue together
   c   against Yahweh and his anointed.

Cola a and b contain the first main clause (again: *clause* = colon) and the core of the second main clause, after which the C-colon is filled up with the adjunct that concludes the second sentence. The poet, by the way, thinks of more than just syntax, and at the end even manages to effect a form of balance: he places two people in the C-colon, the deity and the king, and this pair is intended to counterbalance the word pair kings/regents. How do God and king fare in the rest of Psalm 2? If we read on, we find that the first strophe (vv. 1–3) prepares the reader for a harsh confrontation, and that the bosses on earth are in for some hard knocks.

4) The independence of the colon is not affected if the poet includes two different predicates. In that case, the verset contains two short sentences. This situation is not uncommon;[10] take for example the B-colon of a tricolon from Psalm 2:

> v. 7   Let me tell you of Yahweh's decree;
>   He said to me: You are My son,
>   I have fathered you on this day.

Here, the king is being addressed by God, and what he hears is that God has elected him "today." To this end, the poet puts terms of elementary kinship in God's mouth: the words "son" and "fathered" are metaphors that vividly and "physically" express proximity. The pronouns me/my and I/you effectively serve to link the sentences 2–3–4, a nice touch that again expresses proximity and reciprocity.

To recapitulate: the versemonger has four possibilities to fill a colon. The poet can use a phrase (usually a syntactic adjunct); a short independent sentence; often two short sentences; or a part (*clause*) of a compound sentence. What I described as option 1 may now safely be called the central option because, of the four possibilities, a simple (main) clause coinciding with the colon is the representative situation: a complete sentence is finished within a single colon. Labeling the simple sentence (the only case of sentence = colon) the central option or starting point of verse making also receives support from statistics: this type of simple cola constitutes the majority of cases. Options 2 and 3 both imply that the syntactic unit extends beyond the boundaries of a single colon. This means that the sentence continues across the caesura, a form of border crossing that is our first acquaintance with enjambment*.

It is time I presented an adequate definition of a Hebrew poem. In my book *Reading Biblical Narrative,* the counterpart to this volume, I have explained how the narrator uses more than one ingredient: not only language, but also time. Every sentence in a story has a complex relationship with time, if only because the tension discourse time/narrated time is always there. A similar circumstance applies to the poet, who is not only engaged in shaping a complex message through a subtle selection of linguistic tools, but is also constantly watching the proportions of the textual units. The cola fit a specific verse model, the poet keeps the verses within the prescribed boundaries of the strophe, and the strophes, too, follow an articulation whose extent is controlled by the poet.

This last statement may be put differently, using the vocabulary of equivalence and parallelism. Parallelism is not restricted to the level of the versets; we also observe it in verses, strophes, and stanzas. In the same way that equivalence provides cohesion for the cola and knits the verse together, this is also the purpose of the composition—literally "putting together"—of the higher textual levels. Equivalence of verses guarantees the internal cohesion of the strophe, and by creating a specific balance between strophes the poet is able to shape stanzas. In all these forms of articulation, however, time again plays a part.

The sentences of a story take up discourse (narration) time—the time it takes to recite or read them—and refer to narrated (story) time. Analogously, we might now say of the poet (who historically speaking was often a singer, for instance during worship, and whose transmitted text makes the voice of the poet-singer audible even for us): the verses take up singing time—the time it takes to recite or read them—and the proportions of cola and verses, of strophes and stanzas lend structure both to this singing, and to meaning and content of the song = poem. Time is present here in the form of proportionality. The measures of all textual levels together, from syllables through to stanzas or sections, I summarize in the word *prosody*.

This Greek word originally means the "progress of the singing." In practice it is often reduced to metrics, but this betrays rather sloppy thinking. In my view, the concept of prosody deserves a broad definition which takes into account the various levels of the text, i.e., covers its hierarchical structure. In that case, prosody implies that the poet watches and controls the dimensions of the textual units, and as such means regulating and controlling *quantity*, at all levels of the text.

I will now link this up with the word *quality*. This word may be used effectively to refer to the poem's main task: conveying meaning and sense. It is the poet's job to relate quality to quantity. However, since this sentence may equally well apply to the running of a supermarket, we need to narrow down this statement and apply the abstract concepts of quality/quantity in a truly literary way. We are approaching the definition of poetry.

Such a definition will work only if it takes into account both ingredients used by the poet: language and prosody, or observing proportion during the creation of meaning and sense. My definition of a Hebrew poem, then, is as follows:

> A poem is the result of
> (on the one hand) an artistic handling of language, style and
>   structure, and
> (on the other hand) applying prescribed proportions to all
>   levels of the text,
> so that a controlled combination of language and number is
>   created.

I will end this chapter in the same way as I began it. Where poetry is concerned, literary sensitivity and an open mind are more valuable than constructing definitions. Love and concentrated attention are far superior to theories. Nevertheless, it will be a challenge in the following chapters to show how many insights and tools may be gained from a view of the poem as a well-constructed hierarchy.

3

A text model and how to use it

Language and number (continued)

A model of the biblical poem

Poetry is primary literature; poetics, being a scholarly discipline, produces secondary literature. My decision to give priority to literary sensitivity over theorizing about poetry remains valid when I construct a model of the Hebrew poem. The three main collections of biblical poetry are the books of Psalms, Proverbs, and Job. The advantage they offer over the poetry in the books of the Prophets is that with these three, we know where we are: there are hardly any instances where the boundaries of the literary units are uncertain, as almost all the poems have been correctly demarcated by the tradition.[1] In these collections, the following model applies; these rules are also useful when reading poems from the Prophets, even though the model is employed less rigidly there. A poem has:

> 2 to 4 beats/stresses per colon
> 2 or 3 cola per verse
> 2 or 3 verses per strophe
> 2 or 3 strophes per stanza

These characteristics need some clarification. The model should not be viewed as a closed system, and cannot be taken as an absolute standard. There is no call for mathematical rigor in the playful world of poetry.

My discussion starts at the beginning, with the verset. If, like me, you have the courage to believe in metrics in Hebrew poetry you may continue to use the term "beats" to indicate the length of a verset. Should you consider metrics nonexistent or improbable, however, there should be no problem; after all, the words still have stresses, and these can be counted. According to the model, each colon has two to four stresses, but this is not an absolute limit. It does apply to the overwhelming majority of cases, but every once in a while we come across a verset with only one main stress or beat, or, conversely, we find a verset containing five stresses.[2] All this applies only to the original Hebrew text, and is consequently of no great importance for this book; the reader may file it away in a footnote.

The next layer is that of the verse in the literary sense: the full poetic line. The verse almost always consists of two or three cola, never more. Sometimes, however, we encounter a verse that consists of only one colon.[3] The book of Psalms contains twenty-one of these versets functioning as verses. There are none at all in Job, and almost none in Proverbs. Such monocola are literally marginal phenomena, usually functioning as markers at the beginning or end of a higher-level textual unit such as a strophe or stanza.

Of much greater importance is the proportion of two-part to three-part verses. The vast majority of verses are bipartite, i.e., bicola. This is clear from the percentages of tricola: almost 12.5 percent of the verses in the Psalms are tricola, in Job only 8 percent, and in Proverbs even less, 4 percent, which means many of the poems it contains are completely bicolic.[4]

We ascend to the level of the strophes. These usually consist of two or three verses, but some shorter or longer strophes do occur. The Psalter contains forty-one one-line strophes; a few examples are: the hymnic verse that opens Psalm 8 and returns at the end, or the "verses" (here: biblical verses) 7 and 16 that articulate Psalm 50 in three parts; the ending of Psalm 90 (v. 17, a tricolon), or the refrain verses 57:6 = 12 and 59:7 = 15. I estimate that Job contains some ten strophes consisting of only one poetic line,[5] and Proverbs even less.

Every now and then an extra-long strophe materializes. I could point to five four-line strophes in the Psalms, and Job 3 contains three.[6] At the top of the list we find two strophes consisting of as many as five verses; these are Psalm 18:21–25 and Psalm 115:4–8; the latter is a passage about the gods outside Israel, which I will quote here:

v. 4   Their idols are silver and gold,
             the work of men's hands;
v. 5   they have mouths, but cannot speak,

```
                    they have eyes, but cannot see,
v. 6                they have ears, but cannot hear,
                    they have noses, but cannot smell,
v. 7                their hands—but they do not touch,
                    their feet—but they cannot walk,
                    they can make no sound in their throats.
v. 8     Those who fashion them, shall become like them,
             all who trust in them.
```

The indentation of the B-cola (and the surplus in v. 7 with its remarkable C-colon, which is not there for no reason) here represents the typography as offered in several translations. I have, however, added something extra by having "verses" 5–7 indent one more level. As a threesome they are clearly distinguished from v. 4 and v. 8, since they are an obvious enumeration, and with all these nonfunctioning body parts constitute attractive polemics*. The surrounding verses have clearly been synchronized. All refer to people and contain the point: who would be so naive as to worship their handiwork? The C-colon of v. 7 concludes the central series with a slightly different pattern, and together with (the "mouths" in) v. 5a makes a frame around the core of the evidence. At the last moment, it seems as if the poor wretches want to cry out in distress after the merciless trouncing by the poet, but they cannot manage this—they really are dumb.

This core of three verses relates to the framing verses 4 + 8 in the same way that an example relates to a general rule. We may therefore also view the frame as a split-up short strophe, the halves of which now function as an envelope, while the enumeration (vv. 5–7) is a regular three-line strophe. Something similar applies to Ps. 18:21–25. Viewed in this way, these five-line strophes are exceptional and creative applications of the standard dimensions for the strophe (two or three poetic lines), rather than breaks in the pattern.[7]

I will now leave the exceptions—the frayed edges that put the strict rules of the model into perspective—and again look at the bulk of the strophes. It seems sensible to adopt labels for the two-line and three-line strophes. From now on I will call the main group S(hort)-strophes, and the small group of strophes containing three verses L(ong)-strophes. These abbreviations enable us to record the structure of a poem in shorthand: Psalms 1 and 113, for instance, which have already been quoted in their entirety, may now be written as LSL and SSSL, respectively. We now see at a glance that the short and metaphorical strophe that forms the center of Psalm 1 has a symmetrical frame, and that Psalm 113 places its only L-strophe at the end, by way of climax. An example from Job, where the biblical verse usually coincides with the poetic line, looks like this (ch. 9):

	L	L	L	S	/	L	L	L	L⁺	/	S	L	L	L
cola	6	6	6	4		6	6	6	7		4	6	6	6
syllables	47	51	44	33	/	48	50	48	50	/	32	46	48	51
	98		**77**			**98**		**98**			**78**		**99**	

I have added the number of cola per strophe, and the figures for the strophes (the numbers of their original, i.e., pre-Masoretic syllables). The slashes in the diagram indicate that this poem of thirty-four verses consists of three parts. The notation in capital letters immediately shows that the text has a completely symmetrical structure, and that the only two S-strophes frame the center. The twelve strophes have been grouped in pairs, so that the three sections contain six stanzas. The precision of the prosodic design is revealed in the stanzas when we count the original syllables; these totals are given in bold typeface.

Let us return to the components of the model. It is a great pity that our Bible translations achieve precious little in the way of indicating strophes. People just did not realize they existed, in the old days, and then of course nowadays there is the dying-out breed of scholars who do not wish to know. In the many translations dating from the middle of the twentieth century the demarcation of strophes by means of blank lines is utterly arbitrary and even absent most of the time; often a blank line has been inserted to mark a stanza boundary, i.e., a higher textual level. More recent translations are little better, sometimes worse if on verse level they do not indent B-cola and C-cola. Only in the very rare instances where the text really is completely straightforward do the translations manage adequately. In the so-called *Bible de Jérusalem*, a translation supervised by the Dominicans of the *Ecole Biblique* in Jerusalem, the translators were obviously on the lookout for strophic units, but they nevertheless often get it wrong.[8]

Finally, we climb up one more level, to the stanza. This high-level textual unit is usually a collection of two or three strophes. Here, too, the dividing line between strophe and stanza is not a firewall: at times, one long strophe will coincide with a stanza. An example of this is the middle strophe of Psalm 10, v. 9–11. These verses depict the absolute nadir for the harassed poor and consti-tute an L-strophe, and hence, a stanza. This unit is part of the highly regular structure of Psalms 9–10, which together form one poem, and apart from this strophe consist exclusively of stanzas of two S-strophes (= four poetic lines) each.

At the other end of the standard dimensions we find stanzas containing four strophes. Do we really? I know of some: stanza IV of Psalm 69, for instance, comes immediately after the center (= stanza III, the prayer for salvation of vv. 15–21) and distributes its verses 22–29 over four S-strophes in which the poet asks God to punish his enemies; this stanza is in part a curse. And lo and behold, there is one single stanza in the Psalter (none in Job or Proverbs) containing as many as five strophes: this is Ps. 18:8–16, a passage known as the theophany*. This text is a good example of the thesis that recognizing the structure is the instant proof of the correct strophe division:

v. 8a	Then the earth rocked and quaked,	
b	the foundations of the heavens shook,	
c	rocked by his indignation.	
v. 9a	Smoke went up from his nostrils,	strophe 4
b	devouring fire came out of his mouth,	
c	live coals blazed forth from him.	

v. 10a	He bent the sky and came down,	
b	darkness was beneath his feet.	strophe 5
v. 11a	He mounted a cherub and flew,	
b	gliding on the wings of the wind.	

v. 12a	He made darkness his screen:	
b	dark thunderheads, dense clouds of the sky.	
v. 13a	Out of the brilliance before him	strophe 6
b	fiery coals blazed.	

v. 14a	Then Yahweh thundered from heaven,	
b	the Most High gave forth his voice.	strophe 7
v. 15a	He let fly his shafts and scattered them,	
b	he discharged lightning and routed them.	

v. 16a	The ocean bed was exposed,	
b	the foundations of the world were laid bare	strophe 8
c	By Yahweh's mighty roaring,	
d	at the blast of the breath from his nostrils.	

Here we have five S-strophes, but the first one has been weighted down: the verses are tripartite, so that the unit contains six rather than four cola, the same length as a regular L-strophe elsewhere. The strong cohesion within this spectacular passage may be sketched in a few strokes. Strophes 4 and 8 show how the entire cosmos is in disarray as a result of God's anger, and strophes 5 and 7 present him as a warrior descending in order to intervene on earth, on behalf of King David. It is David who is the speaker in this long Song of Thanksgiving, and he is so focused on the intervention of the God who has affiliated himself to him that he does not even grant his enemies an antecedent*: he quickly disposes of them by means of the short "them" in verse 15, at the moment when they enter the picture as the target of God's missiles. In the center we find the mystery of the light that should be surrounded, if not protected, by darkness in order to describe the appearance of God. In short: the strophic structure in this stanza follows an ABXB'A' pattern, and this concentric design is the best possible guarantee for the unity of the stanza.

The ABXB'A' pattern is a concentric design: anger and earthquake constitute the correspondence A-A', war and God's movement from heaven to earth are B-B', and X is the unique pivot with its paradoxical view on God. This first climax of the song inspired the poet to create even more rings with which to surround the theophany:

v. 7a	In my distress I called on Yahweh;	
b	cried out to my God.	
c	In his temple he heard my voice,	strophe 3
d	my cry to him reached his ears.	

[here vv. 8–16: the theophany = strophes 4–8]

v. 17a	He reached down from on high, he took me,	
b	he drew me out of the mighty waters.	
v. 18a	He saved me from my fierce enemy,	strophe 9
b	from my haters, who were too strong for me.	

We do see two strophes here, but they belong together as inextricably as answer belongs to question, and neither corresponds to preceding/following strophes. I therefore see them as the result of (again) a splitting-up: together, strophes 3 and 9 constitute the stanza of distress and salvation. Not until after God's intervention is finished does David bother to use some verse space to refer to the victims in words: "my fierce enemy" together with "my haters" form an obvious word pair in v. 18. The balance between the two strophes is reflected in the subject of the action: in strophe 3, David is the "I," addressing God, whereas in strophe 9 God as the powerful agent is the subject, while David is object and beneficiary.

As a stanza often contains six to ten verses—and two or three stanzas will in this way quickly add up to a poem of fifteen or twenty verses—there are few poems that contain a textual unit on the level between the stanza and the poem itself. Of the 148 poems in the Psalter, about 120 can be printed on one page (in Hebrew, where a complete verse fits on one line). There are,

however, a number of much longer poems, for instance, Deuteronomy 32, Judges 5, and Psalms 18, 68, 69, 78, and 89; these in
turn group their stanzas in (what I call) sections. Thus, the Song
of Deborah accommodates its fifty verses in twenty strophes,
which together form seven stanzas; the latter units are arranged
into three sections.[9]

At this point, a critical reader would be perfectly justified to object
that this model is a product of modern scholarship, being forced
on to the text like a straightjacket. It is a pleasant surprise, therefore, to find this poetic model neatly borne out by the so-called
alphabetic acrostics of the Bible.

The Hebrew alphabet consists of twenty-two characters denot-
ing consonants. The vowel and accent signs we now find in the
Bible were added by the Jewish tradition one or two thousand
years after its composition, in order to ensure an exact recording
of the correct classical pronunciation (in the synagogue). The first
four consonants are called aleph, beth, gimel, and daleth, words we
recognize through their Greek corruptions alpha, beta, gamma, and
delta. Sometimes, poets—and also writers from Ugarit, three centuries before David—regarded constructing a text based on the
letters of the alphabet in order as a challenge: the first verse had to
start with an aleph, the second with a beth, etc., right down to v.
22, which would start with the last consonant taw and conclude
the poem. In this way, an alphabetic acrostic has been created.
(Such acrostics were written in English by Lewis Carroll and
Edgar Allan Poe.)

There are a dozen of these acrostics in the Bible, and their dimensions reveal exactly the contours of the text model. They differ
widely as regards length, and precisely because of this they demonstrate that the poets did indeed work with cola, verses, strophes, and
stanzas. The alphabet provides an acrostic arrangement:

- per colon, in Psalms 111 and 112,
- per poetic line, in Psalms 25, 34, and 145, and also in
  the concluding poem of Proverbs, the praise of "the
  capable wife," 31:10–31,
- per strophe in Psalm 37, and in four of the five poems
  which make up the short book of Lamentations,
- and per stanza in the longest psalm, 119.

This is a remarkable group of poems, and incontrovertible proof that the poets knew exactly what constituted a colon, a verse, a strophe, and a stanza. Psalms 111 and 112 are adjacent in the Bible, which is no coincidence, as they have been completely synchronized. Their themes are complementary: Psalm 111 praises God's uprightness, and Psalm 112 mirrors this by placing the upright man alongside it. Both poems end with a double tricolon as the final strophe, and they are so perfectly twinned that they have exactly the same length: both have 168 syllables in twenty-two cola.

The poems in Lamentations have been constructed in such a way that the letter from the alphabet at the top (Greek *acro-*) of the strophe always opens an L-strophe in chs. 1 and 2 and an S-strophe in ch. 4. Chapter 3 also contains L-strophes, but the special situation here is that the acrostic consonant appears three times in every strophe: at the beginning of each verse in the strophe that it governs. The first strophe opens all of its three verses with an aleph, the fourth strophe contains the daleth three times, etc.

Finally, on stanza level there is the acrostic Psalm 119—a rather special text, which at first sight seems fairly indigestible as it is so very pious. Read in the original language, however, the poem is very stimulating, a multicolored pyrotechnic of variations and other formal devices glittering against the background of a baffling synonymy. With its 176 poetic lines, this Psalm is the longest in the entire Psalter. The lines have been grouped into twenty-two octets and are almost all bicolic. In each stanza (i.e., always eight verses), every line starts with the acrostic consonant in question. Of the twenty-two octets, nineteen have a rigidly binary structure in halves of 4 + 4 verses, which we may call substanzas and which themselves may be divided as 2 + 2 verses. Thus, the substanza consists of two S-strophes.

I will now draw two conclusions from the presentation of the model and its illustrations. First, *the numbers two and three prove all-defining on the four central levels of the poem as a hierarchical structure: colon, verse, strophe, and stanza,* i.e., on all levels above that of the word and below that of the poem as a whole, or its sections. These are the very layers where language acquires its literary added value from the poet. Second, the model also reveals that *three building blocks are fundamental:*

- the colon (to prosody),
- the verse (to semantics* or meaning),
- and the strophe (to the rhetorical or argumentative design).

The verset or colon is already fundamental, as in general it is the smallest independent text unit by virtue of having a predicate (= it contains a verb, states something): it is a unit of meaning that may be understood in itself. To the poet, attempting to control proportions, it is also fundamental as a first building block of prosody, since it is exactly colon length (= the number of syllables) that received particular attention from the Hebrew poets—see below.

The verse is fundamental to poetic semantics, as this is the level where for the first time a systematic exploitation and application of parallelism takes place, the "parallelism of the members." This phenomenon will be discussed in detail in the next chapter.

A poem is at the same time, however, a particular form of persuasion or argument: not the sort of argument that allies itself with logic, or a discourse governed by a plot, which arranges events thematically—these are characteristics reserved for narrative prose—but nevertheless a string of language acts in a particular order (often not immediately clear), the aim of which is to persuade. This last word ties in with the classical definition of rhetoric: the art of persuasion (by means of language). In their own way, poets are just as concerned with this as the philosopher, the writer of a newspaper article, or a Speaker of the House of Representatives.

The Hebrew poet produces lyrical (in the Psalms and the oracles, and in the snatches of poetry that lard the long story from Genesis through to Kings) or didactic poetry (in the representations of the Wisdom literature, Proverbs and Job). The Hebrew poet, too, wants to persuade, by means of poetry, by the condensing of language. Rarely, however, does the poet leave this to one single verse; hence the scarcity of one-line strophes. The poet shores up the verse with one or two more verses, and combined into a strophic unit these represent a step or phase in the poet's argument. This is eminently clear in the book of Job, which of course is one long debate, first between four and later between six speakers, about the most profound existential questions. The poet of Job has his characters present their arguments by strophe. An example of this will be discussed in chapter 9. Elsewhere, too, the strophe serves as the rhetorical building block—as may be confirmed by rereading the texts already discussed from Psalms 1, 2, 18, and 113 (and Ps. 114 further down) or David's Lament.

The perfect tool to forge verses into a strophe that will work as a unit is offered by semantics*: applying parallelism on verse level, i.e., one level higher than Lowth's parallelismus membrorum. In the next chapters we will see how the poet uses this device.

I have pointed to three building blocks, thus distancing myself from the unfruitful discussion that sometimes erupts between scholars, about whether the basic component of the Hebrew poem is the colon or the verse. This shows that these scholars are looking for only one component; actually, there are three, each on its own level.

Going back to the basic level of the verset we meet *a second series of crucial numbers.* As these are found by counting the syllables in the original, pre-Masoretic Hebrew from the first millennium BCE, I can offer no more than a cursory discussion of them in this book. *The numbers 7–8–9 are also essential, and demonstrate that the colon is the fundamental building block of Hebrew prosody.* This is proved by a surprising circumstance occurring in no fewer than eighty-five psalms (eighty-three poems): these poems score an integer for the average number of syllables per colon; this is usually eight, sometimes seven or nine. This highly remarkable finding can be explained only by assuming that the poets themselves counted syllables.[10]

As we have seen, a simple example is Psalm 1, with 144 syllables in sixteen cola; the average (number of syllables per colon) here is the integer 9, instead of the fraction that would be likely to occur had the poets failed to count their syllables and left their numbers to chance. We arrive a fraction if a poem has for instance 168 syllables in twenty-two cola: this division yields 7.63, the fraction that applies to Psalms 111 and 112. The 9 that we have just discovered to be the norm in Psalm 1 is at the same time a signal for the complete Psalter. The 9 is the ceiling: no psalm exceeds 9, although there are a dozen that score exactly that.

If the number of syllables in the Psalter (the actual text, not including inscriptions and the like), i.e., a total of 45,725, is divided by the total number of cola (5,712), the result is also 8—deviating only from the integer in the third decimal (i.e., 8.005). Job and Proverbs even exclusively aim for the 8 as the norm figure. Some of their poems score exactly 8; the average number of syllables per colon in the others is always close.

All this would seem to indicate that the number 8 deserves the title of "central norm figure of prosody." This is the beacon that the poet bears in mind when constructing the cola. It completely dominates the longest psalm by linking up with the alphabet and the acrostic arrangement, so that this technical *tour de force* (as we have seen) consists of twenty-two octets.[11]

It is totally unnecessary for poets to give all their cola the same length (= number of syllables); it is equally unnecessary that a large number of cola actually realize the norm figure. Rather, in practice poets employ a wide range of colon lengths, but at the same time take care to have an exact average (i.e., an integer instead of a fraction).

This range of figures (indicating the number of syllables per colon) may be beautifully demonstrated by Psalm 97; it is an example of the precision with which the poets worked—a precision they did not need to maintain on syllable level, but which they occasionally liked to realize, as a challenge. If we read v. 5 of Psalm 97 as the tricolon that it actually is, this song contains twenty-eight cola, with 224 syllables, and thus realizes the norm figure 8. The way in which this happens is rather unusual:

> 1 colon has 5 syllables
>   2 cola have 6 syllables
>   4 cola have 7 syllables
>   *14 cola have 8 syllables,*   *i.e., a total of 112*
>   4 cola have 9 syllables
>   2 cola have 10 syllables
> 1 colon has 11 syllables

This concentric regularity is built up of seven symmetrical layers. On the axis we notice that exactly half of the total of twenty-eight cola realize the norm figure 8. These fourteen cola contain exactly as many syllables as the other fourteen together. Meanwhile, the number 7 is also active in various ways. To name only two: the number of cola on either side of the normative axis is 7 + 7; if we multiply 7 by the norm figure, we get 56—a figure of which 112 and 224 are multiples. This figure is the total on both sides of the axis.[12]

I have drawn two conclusions, establishing the prominence of the numbers 2 and 3, and the fact that there are three building blocks. I will draw a final conclusion from these two: that the poets paid meticulous attention to the numerical aspect of their work, and that component II will prove to be essential—the figures for the main textual levels, or rather the care taken about the correct proportions, which these figures represent and constantly exude.

The reader's contribution; basic tools

Poets spend great care and love on their work. Who are we not to follow their example? We are the readers—but what exactly is reading? Reading is not a passive business; while we read, we do not merely undergo something. Even the description "receptive" for this activity is inadequate, as we do more than just receive. Whether they realize it or not, readers, when engaged in the act of reading, are extremely involved: they infuse a text with meaning.

Our interest is part of the living text; in our capacity as readers—i.e., through our reading activity—we are a part of the structure of the work of art, however strange this may sound. Our involvement as conferrers of meaning may be given its due recognition as follows. A text that is not read is a cluster of latent meanings. It cannot exercise any influence; its meanings cannot have any effect. The unread text leads the life of a ghost in the underworld. Not until it is read does the text become a "work" in the full sense of the word. It needs readers in order to come alive; as soon as we start listening to a text, but only then, it starts to speak.

Imperfect listening leads to bad articulation and erroneous interpretation; good listening leads to correct understanding. The reader who is unfamiliar with the rules governing the text will produce an incompetent reading, preventing the text from attaining its full potential. Competent readers know how to handle the conventions and techniques employed in the text, and manage to do full justice to it. The meanings that lay dormant in the text-not-yet-read are activated by the act of reading. What was latent becomes patent in a mysterious process: a fusion between the meanings hidden in the text and the meaning being conferred during the act of reading—or, not to put too fine a point on it, conferred by the reader. The poem comes to life only through us, and in no other way. This saddles us with a great responsibility for the soundness and life of the text.

Because of their semantic density, poems are often hard to understand. We as readers would therefore do well to exercise some patience. We need not set ourselves the goal of understanding everything in a single sitting, or even of getting "the message." It is better still if we manage to rid ourselves of the modern desire for instant satisfaction. The poem suffers if we focus our reading on determining one main point, preferably within a short time. We will, however, reap its rewards if we manage to discard the image we have formed of the text after a few reading sessions and start afresh, looking for new meanings; these will certainly appear, in proportion to our openness and alertness to surprises.

In our quest for meaning we do well to accept the basic components in their proper value; in the case of literature this means understanding, and profiting from, the fact that the raw material here is language. The language aspect is basic, and we will be more flexible if we know how to use the simple instruments that demonstrate or explain the workings of language. We really cannot do without the basic terms of grammar, as verse after verse we will be confronted with the dialectics and tension between sentence and verse structure.

In the following, I will need grammatical terms every now and then to be able to describe efficiently what is happening in a verse. Many readers will know these terms; they may skip the next paragraph. Those readers, however, for whom grammatical analysis is not a part of their daily routine also deserve to be enlightened; I will refresh their memories by means of a few simple examples.

Take for instance a sentence such as: "I have listened to you." In a syntactic analysis, "I" is called the subject, "have listened" the predicate, and "to you" is the object (governed by a preposition). In the Hebrew text, this is a direct object (no preposition here) and the entire sentence occupies just one word, but otherwise the syntactic functions remain the same. The subject-predicate combination I call the sentence core. This core is often explained or modified by an adjunct: of time, place, or mode. Adjuncts may refer to various sentence components. In "Anna eats cornflakes with sugar," the adjunct "with sugar" qualifies the object: the cornflakes. But in "Anna eats cornflakes with a fork," the adjunct refers to the predicate: it explains how she eats—in this case, which implement she uses.

Grammatical analysis can be very useful. Its instruments enable us to discover how sentence and verse (or colon) are related, and we become much more sensitive to the rhythm and character of the sentences: are they long or short, do they describe or report, beg, command, or complain? Grammatical analysis sharpens our observation of discrepancies and transitions. In this way, we learn to recognize strophe boundaries, and sometimes we are even able to correct the verse division in our Bible translation. The conclusion of Psalm 69 is a good example. Both the original text and most modern translations represent vv. 36–37 as a tricolon plus a bicolon:

v. 36a	For God will deliver Zion
b	and rebuild the cities of Judah,
c	so that they may dwell there, and inherit it;
v. 37a	the offspring of his servants shall possess it,
b	and who cherish his name shall dwell there.

The Masoretes (the rabbis responsible for the transmission of the biblical text) and the translators have here let themselves be fooled by the transition by means of "so that" and the word "there," which refers back to Judah; and even more by the position of "the offspring of his servants." This subject does not appear until the fourth line, but is actually already active in 36c. I will first switch the order to bicolon + tricolon, and then make some minimal adjustments to the English:

v. 36a	For God will deliver Zion
b	and rebuild the cities of Judah,
c	So that they may dwell there, and inherit it:
v. 37a	the offspring of his servants shall possess it,
b	and who cherish his name shall live there.

For my defense of this adaptation I use such elementary tools of linguistic study as the differences between singular and plural, and between subject and object. Two lines have been devoted to God and his transitive actions: 36a + b. These are the only two lines to contain proper names. Next, number and subject are turned around: there are now three lines dealing with the people, and their status as beneficiary is raised to that of subject. A quick switch from linguistics to literature proves the decisive factor: we observe the effect of parallelismus membrorum, and note a neat pattern in the verbs of the tricolon: two intransitive verbs frame two transitive ones. This is an AB-B'A' pattern, and it governs the series dwell–inherit / possess–live. The intransitive verbs "dwell" and "live" are an official word pair, as are the transitive verbs "possess" and "inherit."

We also need to be aware of linguistic aspects when we observe the contest between sentence and verse structure. In Deuteronomy 32, Moses recites an awesome didactic poem and starts off straight away with a well-wrought L-strophe containing the opening exhortation:

v. 1a	Give ear, O heavens, let me speak,
b	let the earth hear the words I utter.
v. 2a	May my teaching come down as the rain,
b	my speech distill as the dew,
c	like showers on young growth,
d	like droplets on the grass.

The core is simple and consists of two short sentences: the command "Give ear, O heavens!" and Moses' wish that "my teaching may bear fruit." We are not, however, meant to smother poetry in such simplifications, but we should analyze and enjoy how the core has been worked up, unfolded, and decorated—so that we may then discover that this elaboration opens up all sorts of windows and dimensions through which we may catch sight of the added literary and spiritual value of the poem.

In the first poetic line, the elements of the half verses have been arranged according to an abc // a'b'c' pattern. What under c was still a verb, "let me speak," has already in the second colon become nominal, "words." This in turn enables an inclusio of the verse by parts of the body: 1a starts off with ears and thus straightaway anthropomorphizes the heavens; 1b ends with Moses' mouth. In this way, a balanced communication also has been achieved: the man speaks, and the surrounding world listens.

Parallelismus membrorum enables the poet to divide the world into two areas, i.e., the merism "heaven and earth." Rereading the verse, we realize that these represent the domains of God and of man, respectively, and that here already the question is implied whether there will be harmony between the two. Their "vertical" relation is still effective in 2a and 2c, since the rain comes down from heaven. In this way, Moses suggests at the same time that his lesson is of heavenly quality. This is not arrogance on Moses' part, since in the preceding chapter, Deuteronomy 31, we have been prepared for the song by some explanatory prose telling us that God himself has composed it, and that he also commanded Moses to do something that is uncommon in ancient Israel: record the text in writing.

Verse 2 starts with two more lines/cola containing verbs, i.e., the new sentence core (two parallel lines, because of duplication), but 2cd no longer contains any verbs. We notice that the sentence runs on and reaches a broad conclusion in an (again double) adjunct. After this initial excitement the strophe lands, as it were, in the quiet of green pastures. This is also the result of considerable enjambment: the sentence transcends not only a colon boundary, but also a verse boundary. The cola of 2ab constitute not only the numerical center; they are a sort of anchor or point of attachment for two prominent quartets arranged along vertical lines: the terms for the didactic poem, and the fourfold application of simile*. The interlacing of the two quartets in the middle makes for a tightly constructed first strophe:

I speak					
my words					
my teaching	>	>	<	<	rain
my speech	>	>	<	<	dew
					showers
					droplets

The first two terms (rain/dew) appear at the ends of their lines, and are the objects of the act of listening; their synonyms, the next two terms (showers/droplets), open their lines and are the subjects of the act of distilling, coming down = making fertile. The first two cases of simile, "rain" and "dew," appear at the ends of the same two lines (2ab), but are upgraded to the plurals "showers" and "droplets," which then occupy front positions in lines 2cd, and also acquire the "addresses" ("targets") young growth and grass. Thus, v. 2cd is filled to the brim with the terms of the comparison. The two poetic lines of v. 2 also show the following structure:

my teaching	*rain*	
my speech	*dew*	
	showers	young growth
	droplets	grass

In the pair "rain/dew" we again see the above/beneath contrast implied in heaven/earth, but our feet move closer and closer to the ground in the final verse 2cd. This concluding verse also harbors a covert suggestion: Moses, at that moment addressing the nation in a subtropically warm spot, quietly hopes that his audience may be as receptive to his words as the young growth and grass are to the rain.

In our interaction with the poet's language, another set of elementary distinctions is also very effective: the various grammatical persons. More differentiated than English, Hebrew has at its disposal the first, second, and third persons in singular and plural; there are ten different forms in all, as gender is indicated not only for the third, but also for the second person:

| *singular* | I | you (m) / you (f) | he / she |
| *plural* | we | you (m) / you (f) | they (m) / they (f) |

and there are forms for my/our, "you" as object/your (singular and plural, m and f), his/her, and "them" (direct and indirect object, m and f). Furthermore, the conjugated verb forms largely reflect the same distinctions, by means of prefixes or suffixes.

When Israel or Jerusalem are addressed by the prophets as a lady, and sometimes as beloved or whore, the second-person feminine is used; we find this in passages from Hosea, Jeremiah, Ezekiel, Lamentations, and the occasional psalm. The Song of Songs consists of constantly alternating speeches by a boy and a girl, two lovers, addressing each other. The girl speaks slightly more verses than the boy. When he speaks to her instead of about her, the same second-person feminine is again used.

The distinction between the grammatical persons is of great help to us for the articulation of the poem. In the Song of Songs it is by far the most important signal, as the speaking voice changes rapidly: more than forty times in this small collection of love poetry. When someone says "Flee!" in the imperative masculine (8:14), the reader of the Hebrew immediately knows that the girl is speaking. The verb form is the same as that in 2:17: "turn around, my beloved, swift as the gazelle," etc. (The Song of Songs will be discussed in more detail in ch. 10.) When we hear a feminine form, the boy is speaking. A translation should indicate the changes of voice correctly by always announcing the speakers by "He" or "She" in the margin.

In the Psalms, too, the change of persons is an important signal which often helps in distinguishing the strophes. There are rather a lot of poems that cover a triangle: the lyrical I (the speaker or poet)—his God—the enemies. An obvious structure is then for one strophe to say: I am complaining; the next one: they vilify me; and for another strophe to implore: save me; and this variation in persons is accompanied by other differences. In the strophe about the enemies we would expect the speaker to report in the past tense, and in the strophe about his own misery to describe his pain and anger in the present tense, while the verb will have the form of a wish or command in the strophe addressed to God. These lamenting psalms come in two types: the complaint of a single person— for instance, Psalm 71—and the complaint of the people—for instance, Psalm 44 or 74. In the latter case, the poem will not be about calumny or illness, but about disaster on a national scale, such as war and destruction. Contrasted with this genre are the

songs that praise or thank God, and in which the lyrical I (sometimes a "we") usually faces only one other character. This is, of
course, God, mostly addressed in the second person, but in the case
of a song of praise he may also figure in the third person.

The benefit of a bit of grammatical analysis, and paying attention to grammatical persons, immediately becomes clear when we
look at this short poem:

verse	Psalm 114	strophe

1a	When Israel went forth from Egypt,	
b	the house of Jacob from a people of strange speech,	
2a	Judah became his sanctuary,	1
b	Israel his dominion.	

3a	The sea saw them and fled,	
b	the Jordan ran backward;	
4a	mountains skipped like rams,	2
b	hills like sheep.	

5a	What alarms you, O sea, that you flee,	
b	you Jordan, that you run backward?	
6a	Mountains, that you skip like rams,	3
b	hills, like sheep?	

7a	Earth, shake at the presence of Yahweh,	
b	at the presence of the God of Jacob,	
8a	who turned the rock into a pool of water,	4
b	the flinty rock into a fountain!	

This text has a strictly binary structure: 1 poem, 2 stanzas (halves),
4 strophes, 8 verses, 16 cola. The first half speaks about history and
contains only third-person forms of the verb, in the past tense. The
second half, conversely, is determined by the second person of the
address, and by its questions and commands represents a dynamic
present. These changes in tense and person already suggest a division into two stanzas. Yet, more is needed to confirm this. We
should start looking for the demarcation of the strophes—is the
above division correct?

Possibly the most striking aspect of Psalm 114 is the fact that the
third strophe uses almost the same words as strophe 2, albeit in the
interrogative. This duplication is a very broad, and hence crass, form

of repetition. In both units, we meet four "characters" from nature (vv. 3–4 plus 5–6). These are framed by two S-strophes referring to a miracle. Thus, we may easily establish that the poem as a whole is one big chiasm, since its strophic units follow the AB-B'A' pattern.

The poem sings of the exodus, the moment in history that saw the birth of the people of Israel as a political and spiritual entity. It is, however, preferable to speak of a period rather than a moment, as the song presupposes a broad "definition" of the exodus, in three stages:

- phase 1 is the journey out (from the hard labor in Egypt),
- phase 2 is the journey through the desert (forty years, according to the tradition),
- phase 3 is the journey into the promised land (called Canaan at the time, later Palestine).

This series of three phases is subtly reflected in the poem. The transition from phase 1 to phase 2 is pointed out on the map, as it were, by the reference to the sea; this is the (northern tip of) the Red Sea, whose bed ran dry when the Israelites left Egypt, and which shortly afterwards buried the pursuing Egyptian cavalry under its waters (as narrated and sung in the book of Exodus, chs. 14–15). The transition from phase 2 to phase 3 is demonstrated by the exact North–South course of the Jordan. The choice of sea and river in v. 3 not only is very precise, but also implies that the poet cleverly connects the dimensions of time and space. As a pair, sea and river evoke the complete three-stage structure of the exodus, thanks to their position on the continuum of space and time.

I will briefly survey the strophes. The cohesion of the first strophe is already guaranteed by the sentence structure: this verse pair constitutes one compound sentence. The strophe is also remarkable because it connects the beginning and the end of the journey: v. 1 describes the actual departure; v. 2 mentions the settlement in the promised land. By immediately pointing to the two extremes of the expedition, the poet has already presented the whole of the three-part event in the first strophe, in the line of a merism. This leaves the other three strophes free to occupy themselves with moments from the middle phase, the journey through the desert.

The song has been meticulously constructed in other ways, too. In the "outer" strophes, the device of double duty is applied once per verse: the predicate of the A-colon is also active in the B-colon. We see this in each pair of lines; the predicates "go forth" and "become" also apply to vv. 1b and 2b, and "shake" and "turn into" are also effective in vv. 7b and 8b. The "inside" strophes, however, do something exceptional by both more than duplicating the use of a virtual predicate! What in v. 3a is first said of the sea—i.e., that it saw the crossing—applies just as much to the river in 3b and to the mountains in 4ab. And the lively question opening v. 5, which may be freely rendered as "What on earth is wrong with you?" is of course also asked of the Jordan, etc. The question is given only once, but applies to four subjects—what density and efficient use of language! The following diagram again notes how carefully this one device has been applied throughout verses and strophes; an "o" indicates a virtual predicate, and an "x" the visible (I am tempted to say, physical) presence of the verb:

strophe 1	strophe 2	strophe 3	strophe 4
x o x o	x o o o	x o o o	x o x o

Let us look once more at the cohesion of the strophes. The correspondence between the "inner" strophes (2 and 3) as a B-B' pair is crystal clear: it is an instance of perfect mirroring. The combination A-A' for the "outside" strophes (1 and 4) is ensured not only by the fact that they both refer to a miracle, but also by the presence of two characters that are missing from strophes 2–3: God and Israel, in their qualities of powerful savior and chosen people. The name Jacob (1b and 7b), and the Israel of 1a, represent the entire people (ideally consisting of twelve tribes). Things are slightly different in v. 2, where a rare form of parallelism is employed in which both members are explicitly meant to include each other:

> v. 2a   Judah became His sanctuary,
>   b   Israel His dominion.

Here, Judah represents the southern kingdom, which was the domain of the Davidic dynasty, and Israel in v. 2b refers to the northern kingdom (of the ten tribes, after the schism). Of course, the verse is not saying that only Judah has become hallowed ground for God, to the exclusion of the ten tribes, or that God wanted to be the ruler of the northern kingdom only. What actually happens here is that the two names infiltrate each other, although the division into cola seems to pull them apart. The verse mentions two dimensions: politics (power) and religion. To all the people of Israel (albeit torn into two halves after Solomon), both areas remain active and important. With its unique technique of an inclusive alignment of cola, the verse proclaims that God is the creator and sovereign of both dimensions, but the subtle construction also suggests that the sovereignty of this Savior and God of the covenant far exceeds the schism and is a crucial uniting factor. The dichotomy of the poetic line implicitly and lovingly relativizes the schism within the nation: the parallelism poetically restores unity, and forcefully defends the view that Israel as a spiritual unity was a whole, and should remain a whole—a truly paradoxical relationship between verse form and the intention of the poem.

Strophes 2 and 3 are masterpieces thanks to metaphorics, anthropomorphism, and personification: the poet has equipped sea and river, mountains and hills with eyes in order to see, and they observe so well that they acutely realize what is happening here: a ragged bunch of semi nomads are trekking through the cruel desert, and no one dares to lift a finger against them. The eye-witnesses understand that there is only one explanation: the overwhelming power of the only true God. They want to do an about-turn in numinous dread, and rear up in fright—all perfectly reasonable. In strophe 3, the liveliness of this anthropomorphic treatment of the landscape is raised another notch when the poet addresses sea and mountains: they are even promoted to conversation partners! This type of personification, however, at the same time implies that the poet changes the dimension of time with a magic wand. What thus far has been represented as history (in the first half), reported in the past tense, now becomes, by the questioning of sea and rocks, the present—not only for the speaker, but also for that other character silently involved, the reader. And this means that the miracle of the liberation from Egypt is not really finished; it is not a closed book, but living reality for the poet and his audience.

In the final strophe the awe for the Savior is still prominent. The speaker commands the earth to "shake." The choice of this word, for which I am responsible, is a not totally convincing attempt to preserve a salient ambiguity in the original text. The command employs homonymy: two roots in Hebrew that sound the same, but of which the one means "writhe, shiver in fear or agony," and the other "perform a round dance." Poets like these ambiguities, and so did the maker of Psalm 114. The earth has to tremble in awe, as well as perform a chorus dance "at the presence of the God of Jacob." Together, these actions are the best acknowledgment of God. The term "earth" is an extension of the words that have been used earlier for the landscape: it summarizes sea and river, mountains and hills. The magic of the poetic word has turned all of nature into an eyewitness of miracles, from which it should now draw the consequences: adoration and worship.

The final strophe recollects how it was possible to survive a forty-year trek through the desert: on the water that God allowed to be struck from the rock. The opposition rock/water expresses the miracle, and the close-knit symmetry of the cross construction AB-B'A' invites us to make a metaphoric link with the opening of the poem. The fact that life-giving water may be drawn from unsympathetic rocks also serves as an image for the chosen people, who will live by leaving harsh Egypt and the chains of slavery behind it. The one is just as much of a surprise as the other.

4

Parallelism: cola and verses

The poet's main strategy for shaping his verses is of a semantic
nature. It is a special kind of repetition-and-variation which we
have met before, and which is called parallelismus membrorum.
The clarity of Bishop Lowth's description of it has, for two centuries, also had the negative effect of encouraging people not to
look further than their noses (i.e., the verse). Scholars looked at
the poetic line, asked themselves whether the semantic links were
based on correspondence or opposition, and called the result synonymous or antithetical parallelism. All analysis was, however,
"horizontal," i.e., it considered only the parts of a single verse,
hence mostly the bicolon. Yet, we quickly discover that this view
is far too narrow. Take for instance the following three popular
verses from Psalm 137, the song in which "by the rivers of Babylon, there we sat down, and wept, and hanged our harps upon the
willows":

v. 5	If I forget you, O Jerusalem,
	let my right hand wither;
v. 6	let my tongue cleave to the roof of my mouth,
	if I do not remember you,
	if I do not set Jerusalem
	above my highest joy.

This is the slightly old-fashioned English from the RSV. Together,
these poetic lines form an L-strophe. It is immediately obvious that
the four cola of vv. 5–6b have been arranged chiastically, because
"forget" is identical with "do not remember," and the center of the
quartet has become a closely knit pair because of the three body
parts in uncomfortable situations. The poet feels himself becoming physically ill at the very thought of giving up his roots. The

conclusion of the strophe is a climax resulting from a sort of spatial collision. In 6c the speaker tries for the third time to express
the inexpressible by means of the conditional conjunction ("if"),
and for a moment his subclause seems to drag us down with it in
"do not set above," but that is it: the positive terms of v. 6d propel
him and us in the other direction, upwards. This final colon unambiguously reveals what the capital of his homeland Judah really
means to him: it is his supreme source of inspiration. The poet is
writing a "song of Zion," whereas he has just refused to submit to
the pressure from the Babylonian victors and has answered their
request for a song with "How can we sing a song of Yahweh / on
alien soil?" Thus he manages effectively to sing of his situation of
not-wanting-and-not-being-able-to-sing—we run into another
paradox.

The cross construction AB-B'A' for the quartet of cola in vv.
5–6b demonstrates that the "parallelism of the members" as a principle of repetition and ordering is certainly not restricted to the
single verse, and easily transcends the verse boundary. It is also
obvious that the bicolon in v. 6cd is inextricably linked to the previous two verses, on the basis of semantic repetitions (i.e., again
parallelismus membrorum). With respect to the parallel ordering
of versets, this means that this alignment may just as easily demarcate a textual unit of a higher level: a complete strophe. We have
now shaken off a few Lowthian chains and gained unrestricted
access to the phenomenon of parallelismus membrorum.

Yet, we have not finished with the bishop entirely. It was he
who pertinently observed that the parallelism of cola may already
be established by one single word pair. When we read about the
destruction of Jerusalem (on which Lamentations looks back):

Lam. 2:17ab   Yahweh has done what he purposed,
                    He has carried out the decree that he ordained,

little practice is required to see that every element of one verset
has a counterpart in the other. Here, parallelism is based on the
maximum number of word pairs, as was also the case in David's
lament. Lowth, however, observed that one pair is already enough
to establish parallelism. A bit further on in Lamentations the poet
says of God:

3:7   He has barred every exit for me,
            he has chained me in heavy brass chains.

The repetition of "he has . . . me" is a part of the verb form in the original language, and this predicate is the only element that has a counterpart in the other colon. Once we have made the connection—with considerable support from prosody: the suggestion of cooperation emanating from the lengths of the two clauses—we find that there is another, antithetical relationship. The word "exit" betrays not only the speaker's position (he has nowhere to go, see also v. 9), but also his desire to escape. This longing to move is now thwarted by solid matter: he is chained up!

Going one step further, I quote another verse of which the halves have, at first sight, only one element in common:

Ps. 3:5   When I cry aloud to Yahweh,
             He answers me from His holy mountain.

We quickly notice, however, that there is a simple but effective reciprocity in "I . . . Yahweh" plus "he . . . me." It often happens that a reader first sees one such peg to hold on to, and then finds that there is more going on, noticing more subtle or hidden points of contact between the cola. Thus, we may listen to old Jacob who, on his deathbed, blesses all his sons one after another, that is, gives them strength for the future. In Genesis 49:5–7, however, the formula he utters about Simeon and Levi—*about* them, i.e., he uses the third person, an option that already betrays distance—changes into a real curse:

Gen. 49:6b   For in their anger they slay men
             and in their wantonness they hamstring oxen.

In the original language the verse has exactly 8 + 8 syllables. Normally, men and oxen would not constitute a word pair, but here they do. This is because the opening words of each verset straightaway establish the parallelism. The poet has placed the adjuncts disqualifying the sons in front, a syntactic decision for the sake of expressiveness. The synonymy of "their anger" and "their wantonness" is evident, thus making men/oxen a pair of complements. Outside the context of the poem, no clear connection exists between slaying and cutting hamstrings either, but now that the parallelism has already been established these two verbs become obvious partners in violence.

   Another, simple example of parallelismus membrorum becoming active and visible on the basis of one obvious word pair is the repetition of the word "way" in the concluding verse of Psalm 1:

Ps. 1:6   For Yahweh knows the way of the righteous,
               but the way of the wicked is doomed.

The duplication of "way" is immediately obvious, but straight after that we see that the opposition righteous/wicked also produces a word pair, and we next enjoy the subtle difference between the transitive verb representing care and contact, and the intransitive predicate in the final colon, which contains one character less.

The relation word pair—parallelism

Some twenty to thirty years ago the "word pair" was the center of scholarly attention. As it is the principal component in the creation of parallelism between versets, an extensive hunt was started to build up a collection. This collector's mania suited a period in which scholars followed largely atomistic methods. Researchers sifted through separate words, sunk their teeth into grammatical details, or focused on textual criticism, all because of the many flaws in the transmitted text. The exegetes did not realize at that time that outside the world of biblical scholarship, research into productive theories with respect to the textual whole, communication processes, pragmatics, the text-reader interaction, etc. had long since begun. Biblical texts were primarily studied diachronically: one hypothesis after the other was drawn up concerning the origin of the texts, their previous forms, the history of their transmission, and so forth. A valiant search also was conducted to discover "the writer's intention," as if it were even remotely possible to ascertain this if the text itself did not make it fully implicit. All this effort was based on the misguided conviction that a correct understanding of the text could not be achieved without first knowing how it originated, and that such a detour through the reconstruction of the text's history even constituted the principal access to its meaning. Scholars also speculated about the poet's methods: his predecessors were supposed to have accumulated a complete stockpile of word pairs, from which poets then drew in order to assemble their lines. The theory was that during this process of tinkering and fiddling with words, parallelismus membrorum arose by accident or as a kind of by-product.

In short, the illusion was as follows: parallelismus membrorum is the result of (using) word pairs, and writing poetry becomes possible only after a linguistic community has scraped together or thought up a sizeable collection of word pairs. This line of thought in turn stimulated the exegetes to continue their hunt for word pairs ("another one for my list!").

These lists of collected word pairs do have some function, but only if we radically turn the theory that "word pairs make parallelism" upside down. Actually, the situation is exactly the reverse: parallelism attracts word pairs,[1] and these need not be taken from some artificially created inventory; the vast majority are simply available in everyday language. Even if you are not a poet, you will still be able to conjure up a plentiful array of word pairs: father/mother, light/dark, good/evil, above/below, left/right, arms/legs, and so on; and then there are such nice combinations as "hide nor hair" or "all and sundry." This radical reversal consequently means that the whole (of the verse or strophe) controls the parts and allocates their functions to them, rather than the other way round. Of course, it is true that the parts contribute to the whole, but these have been chosen and arranged from the start with an eye to the overall structure. The whole is more than the sum of its parts, as hermeneutics (the art of explaining) has known for centuries.

Parallel and concentric arrangements

After this short excursion, I will further explore the possibilities of parallelismus membrorum. Within the demarcation lines of prosody—and here I mean especially the limited dimensions of cola and verses—there are two ways to arrange word pairs or other obvious correspondences: a parallel pattern, which we may note down as abc/abc, or a concentric arrangement, which would be abc/cba. This could result in tedious monotony, were it not that language offers many forms and devices on different levels, and the poet is their prime manipulator.

For instance, the poet could write: "he led me in darkness, / brought me in gloom," a neatly parallel bicolon; each half-verse has its own sentence core, and the structure is ab/a'b'. The maker of Lamentations apparently thought this yielded too much synonymy, and wrote the line as follows:

3:2   He has led me and brought me
     in darkness and gloom.

This solution, which repeats the verb in the first half-verse and renders the darkness inescapable by duplicating it in the other half-verse, makes God more of a conspirator. The pattern here is aa'/bb', which implies that the parallelism is now already active within the colon. In 3:56, too, the predicate is doubled in the first half-verse, with the adjunct being varied in the other:

    You have heard my voice: do not shut your ear
     to my groan, to my cry.

Compare this with the following variant, one verse further on in Lamentations, in which the "I" of the A-colon is transformed into a second person, thanks to an embedded speech in the B-colon:

3:57   You are near the day that I call upon you,
     You say: fear not.

In these examples the components have been arranged in a parallel structure. The other obvious order is, conversely, concentric (abc/cba) or chiastic (ab/ba). This is a form of mirroring that occurs often and may have varying effects. Three of these effects have to do with balance created by symmetry—for instance, the cycle of nature (a), a tightly closed unit, finished and perfect (b), or its opposite: contrast or irreconcilable difference (c). Some examples follow; let me start in our own age, with the following lines from T. S. Eliot's *Four Quartets*:

    What we call the beginning is often the end,
    And to make an end is to make a beginning

In the overture to Ecclesiastes we find the following observation, not meant to cheer:

(a)
Eccl. 1:5   the sun *rises* and the sun sets,
         and panting hurries to the place where it *rises.*

It is clear that the poor creature—the "panting" turns it into a person—does not have a moment's rest and like the Black Queen in *Through the Looking Glass* is hurrying nowhere fast.
    In 1:7, we read:

         all streams flow to the sea,
           yet the sea is never *full.*

a chiasm that depicts half of a cycle, and especially the pointlessness of it. There is an attractive similarity with 1:8ab, which should perhaps be classed under "being tightly closed." The verse should have the refractory quality that a very literal translation brings out, but this is unfortunately absent in the existing translations:

(b)   All words/things are wearisome,
           man can not state them.

The closure of the ab/b'a' pattern can work out favorably or unfavorably. The actual word order in Psalm 22:13 is as follows:

Ps. 22:13   Surrounded I am by many bulls,
         buffaloes of Bashan have encircled me.

The animals are a metaphor for the poet's enemies; shortly afterwards, in v. 17a, they are dogs. Another example of a chiasm in a minor key occurs a bit further down in this psalm, which starts with the well-known "My God, my God, why hast thou forsaken me?"

Ps. 22:16   Like a shard my vigor dries up,
         my tongue cleaves to my palate.

Being encircled, however, also may mean being protected, of which a chiasm is the perfect expression in a major key. Thus, David says of God "who girded me with might" in Psalm 18:

Ps. 18:34   who *made my feet* like a deer's
            and on my heights has *made me stand*

an image of power and sovereignty that is the exact opposite of
that in 2 Samuel 1:19, where (as we heard) the mighty have fallen,
"your gazelle/jewel [disguise and metaphor for Jonathan], O
Israel" lies slain on the heights of the land.

God is a shield, the lady called Wisdom says in Proverbs 2,

Prov. 2:8a   guarding the paths of justice,
            the way of those loyal to him he protects.

In Psalm 89, a poet loyal to David's dynasty addresses the following words to God, about the power of chaos:

Ps. 89:10   You rule the swelling of the sea,
            when its waves surge, you still them.

A concentric structure is eminently suited to show compelling
coherence. The prose narrative of the paradise story is illuminated
by a poetic line (Gen. 2:23) that has a lot to say about the balance
between man and woman—words that in Hebrew sound roughly
like *'ish* and *'isha*. After the woman has been created, the man
expresses his recognition and concurrence in these words:

this one | shall be called | *'isha* | because| from the *'ish* | taken was |
this one,

in an abc x c'b'a' pattern that revolves around the hinge of the
motivating conjunction "because." (The | separates the various
components, as in the next example.) The symmetry represents
balance and reciprocity. The same symmetry, this time without the
pivotal "x," in Genesis 9 declares that murder may be avenged only
by the life of the killer. For the sake of structure I will translate
literally:

Gen. 9:6   Whoever sheds | the blood | of a man
           for that man | his blood | will be shed.

The symmetric precision shows that the "man" who is the victim
in the first half-verse is identical with "that man" in the second

half-verse. This means that no additional group or individual is introduced in the second colon, as implied by the standard translation, which runs: "by man shall his blood be shed." As soon as we start wondering by whom else (an ant? an elephant?) we realize that the rendering "by man" is a stopgap, which in an erroneous translation has been placed in front in the B-colon. Another drawback is that in this way a third party is suddenly introduced. The translation "for that man," meaning as a compensation for the life taken, is as part of the abc–cba symmetry a perfect expression of *talio* (retaliation): the legal principle that by the symmetry of "an eye for an eye" says that unrestrained revenge is sinful; the punishment should fit the crime.[2]

Case (c), a chiasm expressing opposition, also requires illustration. In Proverbs 8, Wisdom says:

Prov. 8:7   For truth is uttered by my palate,
            abhorrent to my lips is wickedness.

The abstract nouns, representing totally non–abstract behavior, encircle the parts of the body; they cannot be united and thus have been driven to the edges of the poetic line, as far apart as possible. Another sharp contrast is expressed by the prophet who despairs of his life and his mission, since no one is willing to listen to him. Jeremiah 20 contains grim words, strongly reminiscent of the prologue to Job:

Jer. 20:14   Accursed be the day that I was born,
             the day my mother bore me, let it not be blessed.

We also come across a chiastic distribution of the curse/blessing opposition in Genesis 12:3, where God provides Abraham with a new life by sending him away from his familiar surroundings. The deity employs poetry to protect Abraham from the great insecurity that might prove daunting:

Gen. 12:3   I will bless those who bless you,
            and whoever curses you, I will curse him.

The people who prove forthcoming are presented in the plural; the wicked are described in the singular. What about Abraham? If

we consider him for a moment, we find that he is implicitly honored as the norm: he is promoted to the standard which God will
observe. Three biblical books further down, God has not forgotten his own poetic line. He forces a prestigious diviner—called
Balaam and contracted by the king of Moab to curse the people
of Israel who are passing through—to do the very opposite of
what he had been ordered, the result being that the man speaks a
poem full of blessing some three or four times: Numbers 23:7–10
and 18–24, 24:3–9 and, in a slightly looser connection, also vv.
15–24. On behalf of the God of Israel who subjugated him, Balaam says of the people:

Num 24:8a	God who brought him out of Egypt
b	is for him like the horn of the wild ox.
c	He shall devour enemy nations,
d	crush their bones,
e	and pierce them with their arrows.

9a	He crouches, he lies down like a beast of prey,
b	yea, like the lion—who dare rouse him?
c	Who bless you: blessed
d	and who curse you: cursed!

The verse of curse and blessing, reminiscent of God's blessing for
Abraham, now has a parallel structure: the 2 + 2 words of the original Hebrew text are neatly aligned as ab/a'b'. In v. 9ab, on the
other hand, we observe a chiastic construction, where the devouring beast is framed by the polar expressions of lying down and
being roused. The relationship between vv. 8c and 8de is also
expressed in a crosswise construction, but this time it is mainly sentence structure that is responsible. The king of Moab can no longer
get a word in edgewise, as his position, between wild oxen and
lion, is not exactly enviable. The poet leaves us readers with a
puzzle: who exactly is the subject of vv. 8c–9b, God or Israel? The
schoolmaster wants a definite answer; the lover of poetry is happy
to leave both options open.

The rigorous design often discerned in the poetic lines sometimes yields an unexpected bonus: it enables the specialist to repair
the occasional mishap. In Psalm 44:2–3 most translations meekly

follow the verse division as handed down in the rabbinical tradition. Below, I quote two complete strophes from the RSV, and would like to draw attention especially to the transition from v. 2 to v. 3:

Ps. 44:2a   We have heard with our ears, O God,
    b   our fathers have told us,
    c   what deeds thou didst perform in their days,
    d   in the days of old:

    3a   thou with thy own hand didst drive out the nations, but
                 them thou didst plant
    b   thou didst afflict the peoples, but them thou didst set free.
    4a   for not by their own sword did they win the land,
    b   nor did their own arm give them victory
    c   but thy right hand, and thy arm, and the light of thy
                 countenance
    d   for thou didst delight in them.

    5   Thou art my King and my God;
            who ordainest victories for Jacob.

The subject is the promised land, and the point is also clear: it is a gift from God, and Israel should not regard taking possession of it as a military feat on which it can pride itself. The first strophe looks far back into history, the second strophe draws the lesson and concludes with an appeal for renewed support.[3] The conclusion of v. 2 is suspiciously short—only three syllables in the original Hebrew, which is not enough—and the opening of v. 3 seems too long. This impression is correct: if we look at v. 3ab closely, we observe a strictly regular abc//a'b'c' pattern, and the striking fact that each colon has a predicate consisting of *two* verbs. The element "with thy own hand" belongs to the conclusion of v. 2—I am not the first one to make this observation. Translated extremely literally, this is the text of v. 2cd + 3ab:

    2c   what deeds thou didst perform in their days,
    d   in the days of old, thou, with thy own hand.
    3a   thou didst drive out the nations, but them thou didst plant
                   a   b   c
    b   thou didst afflict the peoples, but them thou didst set free
                a'   b'   c'

This arrangement honors not only the strict design of v. 3ab, but
also that of v. 2cd. We may now observe how beautifully the contents of v. 2cd have been balanced: a striking duplication of the
root "do, perform" broadens the predicate in the A-colon, and
another, expressive repetition answers this device by also expanding the subject: "Thou, with thy own hand." The reverse of this is
that the B-colon does not need a predicate. The decisive factor,
however, is the circumstance that the two cola now show the compelling structure of a chiasm: subject and predicate frame the two
temporal adjuncts, thus forming a perfect conclusion to the verse.

Finally, the short motif "with thy own hand" anticipates strophe
2, where it is meticulously worked out by means of the opposition
"not by your own sword, but by his hand." The connection in itself
creates a new parallelism, this time on strophe level, and this form
of alignment is also brought out much more clearly if we repair the
verse boundary and move God's hand back to the end of v. 2.

In English we sometimes hear the expression "a voice crying in
the wilderness," which we assume is from the Bible. Well—yes and
no. The words occur in the New Testament, in Mark 1:3 and John
1:23. The Gospel writers took these words from Isaiah 40 and
applied them to John the Baptist, but they treated the quotation so
freely that the dividing line between the cola was lost. The
prophet—a poet now called Deutero-Isaiah, as he lived two centuries after the actual (first) Isaiah and had lived through the entire
exile (which ended in 538 BCE)—immediately in his overture (Isa.
40:1–11) proclaims to the Judaeans a message of comfort and
return from exile, and says: "Hear, a voice cries" (v. 3a). This is an
introductory colon, which remains outside the highly regular strophe design, but this is of less importance than what it is the anonymous voice (an exile? an angel?) has to say in 3bc. This is a bicolon
of 4 + 4 words (and the same number of beats, for supporters of
scansion, like myself), in which I have indicated the two phrases per
colon by a | ; I have retained the original word order on purpose:

Isa. 40:3bc   In the desert prepare | the way of Yahweh,
                make straight in the desert | a highway for our God.

We have here a maximum parallelism of the members, based on
four word pairs. Before the break, the correspondence is chiastic

(ab–b'a'), after the break it is parallel: cd–c'd'. Consequently, the correct translation of the verse is:

Isa. 40:3   A voice cries:
"In the wilderness prepare the way of Yahweh,
make straight in the desert a highway for our God."

Thus, there is no "voice crying in the wilderness" at all in the original poem! As it was not Mark's and John's business to write a textbook on verse structure, they took the poetic license to introduce a new connection between two adjoining words. This sort of liberal adaptation of the Scriptures was certainly not uncommon among their Jewish contemporaries.[4]

The appearance and function of saying things twice

The vast majority of verses are bicola, and it is useful to keep the bicolon in mind when pondering the question of the actual function of parallelismus membrorum. The old approach, which goes back to Lowth and was until recently the exclusive preserve of theologians, betrays a hint of intellectualism and a Western sense of superiority: why should things always be stated twice? Isn't that a bit primitive? This attitude is incorrect, and can be weeded out only if we take the poetic aspect of poetry seriously and cease to make it subservient to historiography, theology, or other disciplines that feel slightly uncomfortable with literature.

The bipartite design that a verse often shows is rarely an example of mathematical balance. Often, verses will have their center of gravity in the A-colon, but equally often the focus is on the B-colon of a verse. I will explain both situations. The main point of a verse is clearly in the A-colon if (a) that verset contains the sentence core, and the second half-verse does no more than complete the information in the verse by means of an adjunct, or—a slightly less obvious strategy—if (b) the poet applies *gapping:* he constructs two sentences coinciding with two cola, but places a predicate only in the A-colon. In that case, the verb is still virtually present in the B-colon but does not take up any space. The slot reserved for the predicate there may then be filled with something new, or with a word repeating another component (subject, object, or adjunct). We have already seen this in

2c   what deeds thou didst perform in their days,   (case b)
d   in the days of old, Thou, with thy own hand.

Since the predicate has been left out of the B-colon (= v. 2d) there is room for a bit more attention to the subject. And because those words (Thou, with thy own hand) take up only four syllables in Hebrew, the adjunct "in their days" may be expanded to "in the days of old." A simpler application of (b) is the following:

Lam. 5:2   Our heritage has passed to aliens,
                 our homes to strangers.

In v. 6, however, where the predicate has also been left out of the B-colon, we see the gap filled, not with a merely decorative term, but with an object:

Lam. 5:6   To Egypt we hold out a hand,
                 to Assur, for our fill of bread.

Case (a), only an adjunct in the second colon, is less exciting. There are two examples a bit further down in the same chapter from Lamentations; these are verses that together make up an S-strophe:

Lam. 5:9   We get our bread at the peril of our lives
                 because of the sword of the wilderness.
    10   Our skin glows like an oven
                 with the fever of famine.

It is not the desert that is the oven here, but our own skin. And the word "famine," elsewhere a recognized word pair if combined with "pestilence" or "the sword" to depict the disasters of war or damnation, here does double duty as the counterpart to both "sword" and "bread"—which at the same time serves to frame the strophe.

In other cases, the center of gravity of the verse is placed in the B-colon. For this, a neat formula has been devised, saying: "A, what's more, B." In other words: the first colon states (describes, demands, complains of) A, but the second colon says something even stronger.[5] This is an important rule of thumb that has all sorts of applications. Competent readers use it in order to determine in each case the exact relationship between the second half-verse and the first. The B-colon can do all sorts of things with the statement, contribution, or information of the A-colon: expand it, intensify it, underline it, embellish it. These are all variations within a process of amplification, and there is a whole range of devices at the poet's disposal to lend shape to this intensification in the B-colon. A number of examples are listed below, and I invite the reader to start pondering straight away whether the B-colon is "more" than the A-colon:

(a) Prov. 2:14 (about bad company)
who rejoice in doing evil,
    and exult in the treacheries of evil men.

(b) Prov. 3:7 Do not be wise in your own eyes,
    Fear Yahweh and shun evil.

(c) Song 2:3 Like an apple tree among trees of the forest,
    So is my beloved among the youths.
I delight to sit in his shade
    and his fruit is sweet to my palate.

(d) Ps. 37.21 The wicked man borrows and does not repay,
    the righteous is generous and keeps giving.
    22 Those blessed by him inherit the land,
    but those cursed by him shall be cut off.

(e) Ps. 61:5 That I might dwell in your tent forever,
    take refuge under your protecting wings.

(f) Ps. 18:42 They cried out, but there was none to deliver,
    to Yahweh, but he did not answer them;
    43 I ground them fine as windswept dust,
    I trod them flat as dirt of the streets.

These are six examples out of thousands, and they require little comment. In (a) we see how doing evil is expanded into the concrete plural "dirty tricks" (translated freely), and especially that the perpetrators are as bold as brass: they are actually cheering. In (b), the verse grows from one to two predicates, and the B-colon gives chapter and verse (figuratively speaking): it places God's proper name opposite the "evil" that would result from "being wise in one's own eyes," if the warning was not heeded.

In (c), the strophe from the Song of Songs, the first bicolon is occupied by one long sentence, a comparison. The rule "A, what's more, B" is active in v. 3cd, since the desire to sit in his shade is surpassed by the indicative, the concrete elements "fruits" and "palate," and the sensory/sensual aspect of the second colon. The S-strophe I have given under (d) arranges its quartet of cola chiastically according to the difference of good/evil. In v. 21 a subtle moral assessment takes place. To return what one borrowed is only to be expected; no special merit is attached to it. A "righteous man" (*tsaddiq*), however, who goes on giving, does far more than is asked or expected of him. In v. 22 a pleasant rule is followed by an extremely harsh one. In example (e), "take refuge" is much more specific than "dwell," and the singular "tent" is overtaken by "your wings," not only because these are plural, but also because they follow the explicit "protecting," and contribute to the connotation of shelter.

In (f) we have a full S-strophe, in which the established King David speaks of the war, his enemies, and God's support of him. The crying out of v. 42a is also present in the B-colon, but (only) now accompanied by an address: God himself, by way of his proper name. The anonymous "there was none to deliver" of the A-colon is replaced by the much more painful non-reaction of the deity. In the next verse David can reap the rewards: the B-colon of v. 43 is even more humiliating than the A-colon.

Every once in a while we are able to understand how poets went about their work, and how they combined pleasure in variation with amplifying and intensifying meaning. In David's lament we soon hear what obsessed the speaker: the fact that the Philistine home front was celebrating the great victory of its army over Saul and his troops. David finds the very idea unbearable, and he tells the messengers who he is at that moment imagining, but who in reality have long since reported the victory to the Philistine cities:

2 Sam. 1:20   Tell it not in Gath
             do not proclaim it in the streets of Ashkelon,
         lest the daughters of the Philistines rejoice,
           lest the daughters of the uncircumcised exult.

This is a full S-strophe where in both verses the rule "A, what's more, B" is active. "Exult" is stronger (louder) than "rejoice," and the name "Philistines" is replaced and explained by "uncircumcised," a pejorative term suggesting uncleanness. We immediately notice the sharp differences in length: the line about Ashkelon is much longer than that about Gath, also in the original language. This time, it is especially the two prohibitions (v. 20ab) that enable us to track the options the poet had at his disposal, by asking ourselves: Why did the poet (the historical David, or the author who centuries later portrayed the character David in the books of Samuel) choose the names Gath and Ashkelon?

The enemy lived scattered over five cities, the names of which we all know: Gath, Gaza, Ekron, Ashdod, and Ashkelon. (Three of them still/again appear on the map of Palestine.) The names in the middle of this list have two syllables, but the surrounding ones have one and three syllables. The difference in length between Gath and Ashkelon in David's verse is a first and very simple application of the "A, what's more, B" principle and does not yet add any literary quality to the verse. We also notice, however, that Ashkelon beats Gath by having "streets" granted to it by the poet, and that the verb in this verset describes the contents of the message more explicitly: instead of merely "telling," the B-colon commands to "proclaim" (= "bring good tidings").

These are already three points in favor of the Ashkelon-verset, which is enough. But this does not mean that (the colon containing) Gath has lost! This name, the only name of one syllable, was chosen for at least two reasons. The sounds of "Gath" exactly mirror the veto on "proclaiming" (in the original Hebrew *taggidu*). And then there is the political angle: at the moment David is reciting the poem, three days after the battle, he is still vassal to Achish, the king of . . . Gath! Thus, in a sense, he starts with his own position, and the prohibitions and curses that then follow betray a turning point in his life. Their negativeness is a signal of distance; by commemorating Saul and Jonathan in this beautiful song, David separates himself from his embarrassing position and opens up for himself the way to the throne of Judah. Our conclusion must be that although the line about Ashkelon realizes the "A, what's more, B" principle on three counts, the choice of Gath is a striking instance of polyvalence which keeps the verse balanced: the name is here a node of meanings thanks to (another) three aspects, i.e., the prosodic (the minimal single syllable), the euphonic (via strong alliteration), and the political (David resigns).

This simple exercise makes thoroughly clear that the old perspective—parallel half-verses were assumed to "really only" say the same thing twice—falls far short of the mark, and blocks our view of all the subtle details. We have now reached the point where we can formulate what exactly parallelism achieves.

The function of "parallelism of the members"

The first thing a parallel construction does is to introduce a form of repetition. As a result, the reader immediately notices or recognizes a correspondence between the cola—whether this connection is based on antithesis or synonymy does not concern us now. Noticing the correspondence between the A-colon and B-colon, however, is only the beginning. This form of repetition and equivalence serves as a foundation for observing and enjoying differences. The similarity becomes the background against which disparity announces itself: the folds of difference in the half-verses. If we let our attention penetrate into these folds, we find ourselves on the track of new meanings.

The dynamics and surprises of parallelismus membrorum may also be expressed in a metaphor. This way of constructing verses is like a pair of binoculars. Some centuries ago, the lenses of a field glass were set in cylinders which could be slid in and out but which remained a single tube—the watch on a ship looked through it with one eye. Today's field glass is a binocular: we look through two cylinders, with both eyes, so that we have the advantage of seeing depth. Our eyes, with or without binoculars, see "in stereo." The effect results from the fact that one eye has a slightly different angle of incidence than the other and hence produces a minimally different image; these two pictures are easily super-imposed and assembled into one image inside our brain.[6]

Parallelismus membrorum does something comparable: this shaping device creates two subtly different images on one line (the full poetic line). As this is done with the tools of language, we have every opportunity to consider both pictures separately and let them sink in. This is where the metaphor ceases to be appropriate: the point of the similarity between A and B is their very difference! Only those who look closely and have patience will discover and savor the role played by dissimilarity, its surprises, and its richness of meaning.

These dialectics of the equal and the dissimilar, of similarity and difference, make us realize the limitations of such old labels as "synonymous or antithetical," and especially how they may lure the reader into the trap of an either-or situation. In Proverbs 2:13 is a two-part verse in which Wisdom warns us against the wrong company:

Prov. 2:13   of those who leave the path of rectitude,
              to follow the ways of darkness.

Is this is a case of synonymous or antithetical parallelism? Some followers of Lowth will opt for the antithetical, pointing to the opposition of the straight paths and the dark ways, and of leaving (= not treading on) and following. Another follower, however, will maintain that both cola say the same thing: are they not "merely" variants of each other? A third will latch on to the word "to" and point out that the verse indicates an about-turn in behavior. A pity only that the original Hebrew phrase be rendered just as easily as "by following" or even "and follow."

The reader would do better to withdraw from this yes-no contest. There is equivalence here, and this balance fits the poem as a whole beautifully. Proverbs 2 is a poem of twenty-two verses, exactly the number of consonants of the alphabet, although it is not an acrostic. These twenty-two verses are divided exactly into two; the first half, eleven verses, strikes a positive note, the second eleven are in a minor key. The positive half consists of two stanzas, vv. 1–6 and 7–11 (four strophes: one SL and one LL combination), which constantly recommends the reader to follow Wisdom's counsel;

those who do this will be under God's protection. The negative half
intends to do the same, but is full of apotropaic and cautioning
terms: one should turn against evil. This part consists of five strophes, arranged as SS plus SSL, in two stanzas, vv. 12–15 and 16–22.
The L-strophe at the end returns to a positive tone. The stanzas run
parallel, because of their complementary openings:

Prov. 2:12   to save you from the way of evil men,
          from *men* who *speak* duplicity

(in vv. 13–15 expanded into a series of plural forms)

  2:16   to save you from the *strange woman*
          from the alien woman whose *talk* is smooth

(after which vv. 17–19 expound on her unfaithfulness, and the
accompanying dangers).

    It happens only rarely that a sentence transcends and ignores a
strophe boundary (in typographical terms, a blank line). It is even
more rare for a sentence to run across a stanza boundary. Yet,
Proverbs 2 is a spectacular example of exactly this. The entire poem
is an extreme instance of talking in synonyms, separated into positive and negative terms. Just about every verse is a variation on
the theme of "look for wisdom," or conversely, "avoid evil." As this
synonymy goes on and on, the text may be read as one large syntactic unit, and a simple adjunct consisting of a preposition and an
infinitive, "to save you," may become the marker of a new stanza.
Still, it is exactly the duplication of those words, i.e., the parallelism
between vv. 12 and 16, which encourages us to place the stanza
boundary immediately before it, although the adjunct appears to
be separated from the sentence core by this blank line.

Linguistic forms, and variation in repetition

Reading and experiencing the articulation of complete verses
becomes easier if we are aware of the linguistic foundation of the
variations. Poets explore all the nooks and crannies of their native
language system, and adroitly exploit the many contrasts and differences for their parallel constructions. I have collected some

examples below, on which I will comment briefly. The first series (a through f) contains instances of the poet's using differences in grammatical form.

(a) Ps. 34:2   I bless Yahweh at all times,
                   praise of him is ever in my mouth.

(b) Ps. 34:19   Yahweh is close to the brokenhearted
                   and he delivers those crushed in spirit.

(c) Songs 1:2   let him give me of the kisses of his mouth,
                   for your love is more delightful than wine.

(d) Prov. 1:8   My son, heed the discipline of your father
                   and do not forsake the instruction of your mother.

                   (It is I, Yahweh, who have made everything . . .)
(e) Isa. 44:26   who confirm the word of my servant
                   and fulfill the prediction of my messengers

(f) Deut. 32:7   Remember the days of old
                   consider the years of generation after generation;
             ask your father to inform you,
                   your elders, to tell you.

In (a) and (b), the main difference is that the one colon uses a verb to express what in the other colon is expressed by a noun: "I bless" versus "praise," and "close" versus "he delivers." In the first verse from the Song of Songs (c) we see that the grammatical person shifts straight away: the "him" of the A-colon is the second person in the B-colon. The girl manages to maintain the distance of the third person for only one colon, and then she "has to" become more personal: she wants to start addressing her lover as soon as possible. The semantic point of contact of the two sentences is not expressed, and is a subtle one: the oral activity of kissing becomes the tasting of wine in the second half-verse, and as a result of the comparison drawn by the girl, the wine is a half-metaphor.

In (d), the man/woman difference is exploited ingeniously so that the synonymy does not degenerate into monotony. The words "discipline" and "instruction" are masculine and feminine in the original Hebrew, and in gender correspond to father/mother. Furthermore, the half-verses relate to each other as plus

to minus: the positive advice is in the B-colon underlined
by the two-minuses-make-a-plus formula. In (e), the singular
"servant" becomes the plural "messengers," while "word" is nar-
rowed down to "prediction," so that we as readers dare to conclude that the messengers God mentions in this oracle are
prophets. In (f) we see a double application of "A, what's more,
B." The days become years, the father is accompanied by the elders
(plural).

	(about evildoers:)
(g) Ps. 73:11	they say: how could God know;
	is there knowledge with the Most High?

(h) Prov. 3:1	My son, do not forget my teaching
	and let your mind retain my commandments.

We now reach the domain of sentence structure and syntactic
variation. Example (g) offers an alternation of verb and noun
(both from the root "to know"), and the simple word "God" is
replaced and colored by one of his titles. The verse contains an
embedded speech consisting of two sarcastic questions, a lively
direct quotation of these unsavory types. Example (h) reveals a
minus-plus order and two transitions: from second to third person, and, in the case of the object, from singular to plural. Old
Isaac's blessing of Jacob starts off as highly synonymous (i), but the
poetic line 29cd smartly switches the positions of subject and
object around and places Jacob (in the second person) chiastically
around the brothers (plural, a collective); they are encircled by
their boss:

(i) Gen. 27:29a	People will serve you,
b	and nations bow to you;
c	be master over your brothers,
d	and your mother's sons will bow to you.

(j) Ps. 6:6	No, there is no praise of you among the dead,
	who would acclaim you in Sheol?

	(about the fall of those in power:)
(k) Job 5:14	By day they encounter darkness
	and at noon they grope as in the night.

(l) Ps. 33:10   Yahweh frustrates the plans of nations,
                    he brings to naught the designs of peoples;
      11   what Yahweh plans endures forever,
                    the designs of his heart from generation to
                    generation.

(m) Ps. 125:1   Those who trust in Yahweh are like Mount Zion,
                    that cannot be moved, enduring forever.
      2   Around Jerusalem there are mountains,
                    and Yahweh enfolds His people
                    now and forever.

Example (j), from Psalm 6, not only switches from noun to verb in its predicate, but also shifts mode: the first colon is a statement, and the second is a rhetorical question. Example (k) is a complicated mixture of lexical and semantic word pairs. The lexical pair is the duo day/night, which frames the verse as a whole in an inclusio. On either side of the caesura this couple is chiastically replaced by another pair of opposites, darkness/noon. At the same time, however, two parallel pairs semantically support each other: day/noon at the beginning of each colon, and darkness/night at the end. Thus, the verse appears to offer us an intricate puzzle, which it does not do for nothing. The confusion it threatens to land us in reflects the confusion that will seize the "bigwigs" as soon as God strikes them: they even lose their grip on the elementary distinction between light and dark.

Example (l) contains an ab–a'b' series in two verses. This parallel construction, however, also contains the opposition between the peoples, whose plans are frustrated, and God's plan, which will endure; this contrast is further illustrated by the juxtaposition of two transitive verbs (of destructive action) with the quiet and more nominal character of the intransitive predicates in Psalm 33:11. The opening of Psalm 125, example (m), presents four proper names in a chiastic alternation: Yahweh + Zion-Jerusalem + Yahweh. This crosswise construction already betrays how inextricably the capital on Mount Zion—itself a metonymy for the Judaeans—is linked to God. This is outdone, however, by the mere contiguity (in a paratactic arrangement via the conjunction "and") of cola 2a and 2b. This design creates a simile (comparison): in the same way as the mountains encircle the city, God's protection surrounds the people. On this basis the poet concludes that people who trust in God are as solid as the mountain—a conclusion he moves to the front.

In this chapter we have already seen more than a dozen passages which are longer than a single verse, and which even constitute whole strophes. This abundance of examples makes clear that parallelism works not only on the level of the colon, but also on that of the verse. The definition of parallelismus membrorum should certainly be expanded to include verses as well. As a textual unit, however, the verse is not covered by the term "member," so that in addition to "parallelism of the members (= cola)" we should also grant full recognition to "parallelism of poetic lines (= verses)." This figure also has a valid claim to a place in the model of the Hebrew poem. I will conclude this chapter with a few examples.

We have just read v. 7 from Moses' long didactic poem, Deuteronomy 32. The biblical verse itself was an S-strophe arranging its full lines in parallel, in which the audience was encouraged to go and ask their father/the elders about the lesson from the past. The poem goes on to provide its own panoramic answer to this question, and looks back to the beginning of history in three strophes, two long and one short (vv. 8–12):

Deut. 32:8a	When the Most High gave nations their inheritance,	
b	and set the divisions of man,	
c	He fixed the boundaries of the peoples	strophe 5
d	in relation to Israel's numbers.	
v. 9a	For Yahweh's portion is his people,	
b	Jacob his own allotment.	
v. 10a	He found him in a desert region,	
b	in an empty howling waste.	
c	He engirded him, watched over him,	strophe 6
d	guarded him as the pupil of his eye.	
v. 11a	Like an eagle who rouses his nestlings,	
b	gliding down to his young,	
c	so did he spread his wings and take him	
d	bear him along on his pinions,	strophe 7
v. 12a	Yahweh alone did guide him,	
b	no alien god at his side.	

The three verses of strophe 5 are governed by a threefold "peoples/people" in the A-cola, and a threefold "inheritance/portion/allotment." The number of the sons of Jacob, which at the end of Genesis amounts to seventy, will be the measure for the division of the world. The climax of the first L-strophe is the election of one people, which becomes God's own property. This is the reason why the six cola are balanced as 3 + 3: the first three refer to the masses, and the second series deals with the one people. This latter series stands out by containing proper names—another threesome.

The short strophe 6 progresses like a narrative. Half of it is about finding, and terrifies by three fearsome terms of space. After this, the care taken of the foundling is all the more comforting; there are also three verbs that take God as their subject. Thus, the halves of this unit, two bicolic verses, also have been well synchronized and justify the demarcation of the strophe by their cohesion.

The long strophe 7 can immediately be identified as a unit because it is an elaborate metaphor. The image of the eagle fills no fewer than four cola, which by Hebrew standards is quite a lot, and then proves to be part of a simile. The comparison takes up the complete strophe with its "just as . . . so . . ." structure, and in v. 12 lands, as it were, on the uniqueness of Yahweh.

The whole of vv. 9–12 deserves a title along the lines of "the stanza of the election." Moses continues his didactic poem a moment longer as if it were a story by means of a stanza in which God strengthens and pampers the people (the nine cola of vv. 13–14). Then we reach the lowest point: the luxury leads to corruption, or worse, to idolatry (a new stanza, vv. 15–18).

In the stanza of the election, the verses reveal a parallelism that articulates the three strophes; their concluding lines form a series that brings out God's intervention and commitment:

v. 9a	For *Yahweh's portion* is *his people*,
b	Jacob his own allotment.
v. 10c	He *engirded him*, watched over *him*,
d	*guarded him* as the pupil of his eye.
v. 12a	*Yahweh* alone did *guide him*,
b	no alien god at his side.

The first of these three verses is static; the second full of action and of a narrative character. The third concluding verse already looks back again, and makes the stanza end on the exclusiveness of this deity called Yahweh. There is, however, a snake in the grass: the last colon denies that an alien god helped him, and with this the poet anticipates the drama which will be unfolded four verses further down (idolatry and punishment), and which will almost lead to the total destruction of Israel (in vv. 22–25). The only thing that will eventually stop God from totally annihilating the people is the realization (vv. 26–31) that if he does so, his enemies in the area will brag, and foster the illusion that Israel was destroyed by them and their strong arm. This prospect revolts God so much that he abandons his original plan and eventually takes pity on the afflicted people (vv. 36–42).

The concluding verses of strophes 5–7, which I have here written out again, are also interesting, since they demonstrate that the "A, what's more, B" rule is also active on the level of verses and strophes. The intensification that the poet so often achieves in consecutive cola may be achieved just as well by means of poetic lines. Finally, this whole chapter may be reread with an eye on prosody: all the material discussed here also demonstrates that parallelism, both of cola and of verses, is a powerful mechanism for regulating proportions. The poet employs such maneuvers as parallelism, inversion, word pairs, and binary differences in linguistic forms while never for a moment losing sight of proportions. Language obeys number, and number intensifies language.

5

The strophe

The word "strophe" comes from Greek and means "turn" or "twist." It is by no means obvious that a Greek term should offer an appropriate label for textual units in the Semitic languages of the ancient Near East. In our case, however, it does. There are plenty of twists in classical Hebrew literature, and the technical term "strophe" is eminently suited to biblical poetry, which is characterized by rapid shifts and changes. Tone, verb tense, grammatical person, genre, subject material, or mood all constantly vary, and all these changes are reflected in the structure of the strophe. We are able to discern these shifts by means of the strophic characteristics of the text.

The isolated strophe does not occur in the poetry books of the Bible, but it does appear in the prose passages. Along the route from Genesis through Kings we come across medium-sized poems every now and then—for instance, the Song of Hannah in 1 Samuel 2 or David's lament in 2 Samuel 1—and we occasionally even discover a very long poem, such as Deuteronomy 32, Judges 5, or 2 Samuel 22. This type of poetry is articulated in the same way as the psalms into strophes and stanzas. I also note two verse-filled chapters that I would rather call a chain of strophes with the occasional stanza: the blessings for the tribes of Israel in Genesis 49 (spoken by Jacob, shortly before his death) and Deuteronomy 33 (spoken by Moses, shortly before his farewell). Most poetry within a prose setting, however, is short: just one or a few verses. We are then confronted with a short or long strophe which at the same time is a complete poem. Thus, Genesis 2:23 is an S-strophe, and Genesis 9:6–7 and 12:1–3 are both L-strophes—I have already discussed a verse from each of these passages. Lamech's song of revenge, Genesis 4:23–24, also consists of three verses. And

the oracle that Rebecca receives in Genesis 25:23, which describes
the tumult in her womb (an alarming pregnancy), consists of two
bicola in a design that quickly becomes clear to the reader:

Gen. 25:23   Two nations are in your womb,
                    and two nations will issue from your body.
               One nation will be mightier than the other
                    and the older shall serve the younger.

This is the announcement of the arrival of the twins Jacob and
Esau. As they will be ancestors, they are here presented under the
guise of two collectives—the people of Israel versus their neighbors from Edom. The first verse promises the mother a numerous
progeny, but the second verse carries a message of inequality by
specifying a master-servant relationship. And the surprise has been
saved for the end, when the natural order is reversed. Like a stinger
in the tail, this last verset not only presents the point of the oracle,
but by its choice of the adjectives "older" and "younger" also
reveals that the difference will already manifest itself in the
individuals.

Various instances of such short but complete poems may be
found in Numbers, Joshua, Judges, and Samuel. They obey the
rules I have already discussed, and they do their work alone—
albeit in interaction with the surrounding prose, which they interrupt in order to illuminate. In this chapter, however, I will focus
on strophes from those biblical books that wholly or largely consist of poetry.

A strophe from Psalms, Job, Proverbs, Isaiah, Jeremiah, Lamentations, or Song of Songs never speaks and works on its own. This
is because in such cases the strophe is always a building block of a
greater whole, just a part of a poem, which for those books means
part of a text that consists of several strophic units.

The question now arises: How may a textual unit that is no
more than part of a whole nevertheless be observed and be distinguished from its surroundings? What makes a strophe a strophe?
My answer requires two sections: one in which I analyze the strophe from the inside and indicate how it holds its own, and a second section that looks carefully at how the strophe stands out from
its surroundings without being left to fend for itself. The strophe

has internal as well as external cohesion. Finally, I will examine the relationship between these two forms of unity. The reader may already suspect that this will turn out to be variable.

The private life of the strophe

In the textual model the numbers two and three are normative. At verse level, we have seen that they are applied disproportionately: there are many more bicolic verses than tricolic verses. This discrepancy disappears on strophe level, where the dimensions two and three have much less unequal status. Poems consisting exclusively of two-line strophes are rare.

To give the reader an idea of the distribution of these numbers, I offer some statistics that I myself have collected from the largest collection of poetry, the book of Psalms. Its 148 poems together contain 1,193 strophes, which in turn may be divided into 855 short units (S-strophes, usually two verses) versus 338 long units (L-strophes, almost always consisting of three verses). Converted into poetic lines, this means that the S-strophes (including several dozen one-line strophes!) govern almost 1,700 verses, and the L-strophes, sometimes consisting of four verses, are responsible for almost 1,100 verses. In percentages this would be roughly 60 percent for S versus 40 percent for L.

The strophe is so essential to the structure of the poem that its internal cohesion deserves to be analyzed first and evaluated. This cohesion may come about in various ways. The strophe may

- constitute one syntactic unit, for instance, one compound sentence or a sentence extended in a different way,
- formulate or explain one thought,
- present its cola as a clear series,
- be an embedded speech, for instance a quotation,
- present or work out a metaphor or simile,
- demarcate itself by means of inclusio.

I will discuss these possibilities on the basis of some examples, starting with the cohesion that arises from syntactic structuring. Psalm 18 starts with a hymnic strophe (vv. 2–4), which is the counterpart to a stanza full of thanks and praise (vv. 47–51, an

L- plus an S-strophe). These exalted opening and closing passages
form an inclusio in a major key, framing the long Song of Thanksgiving spoken by the established King David. Inside this frame, we
find a wide range of dynamics, and we accompany David on a
journey through fear and distress. As we remember from the discussion in chapter 2, the special stanza of the theophany (God
comes down and goes to battle, five S-strophes) is enclosed by the
stanzas of distress and salvation (vv. 5–7 and 17–20, both consisting of two S-strophes). In vv. 5–6 the poet constantly varies
between a verb in the past tense and a phrase containing a noun
in the plural and one in the singular. I give 18:5ab + 6ab below,
each on a separate line, with the slash indicating the caesura
between the A-colon and B-colon. The hyphen indicates that a
particular word group is either one word or one phrase (a combination of nouns) in the original language. In Hebrew, there are
exactly twelve words, evenly distributed over the cola as 3 + 3 and
3 + 3. I have indicated the subject by NW (Nominal Word group)
and the predicate by vP (verbal Predicate); the word "ropes" in the
first colon in 2 Samuel 22 appears as "breakers" = waves (the same
poem, with a lot of variant details), which I have here adopted.

Surrounding-me-were	waves-of-death	/	torrents-of-corruption	terrified-me,
vP	NW		NW	vP
NW	vP		vP	NW
ropes-of-Sheol	encircled-me	/	before-me-yawned	snares-of-death.

The numerical perfection proves to go hand in hand here with a
cast-iron syntactic design, and with the maximum use of word pairs.
We see a quartet of cola, and note that the strophe has been constructed on a total of five (!) chiasms. First, each poetic line follows
the AB-B'A' pattern, i.e., on the horizontal level we immediately
observe two crosswise constructions. Reading "vertically," we find
an all-governing chiasm on strophe level, which going from the first
verse to the second moves the outside members inward and the
inside members outward. Finally, both A-cola form a cross in which

the verbs encircle the nouns, and the B-cola together also form an X (Greek *chi*), this time with the nouns encircling the verbs.

This is an extreme example of semantic, syntactic, and numerical density, as well as concentric symmetry; there is no arguing against it. It proves very little about the mode of existence of other strophes, but it does show what level of precision is possible and feasible, and also that the poet can create remarkable forms of cohesion when he wants to. This should prevent us from taking verse and strophe structure too lightly; we never know beforehand what we are going to encounter, so it is good to be prepared for the impossible.

Is there really no arguing against this interpretation of the structure of this strophe? I turn the image inside out, because of the meaning which the strophe offers through its multiple chiastic construction: there is no chance for the "I" to escape. The AB-B'A' structure is perfectly suited to depict and symbolize confinement and encircling, and the poet here seized his chance to make this prison unassailable for David on three levels: the half-verses, the poetic lines, and the strophe itself chain him up in their very design, that of concentric symmetry. In semiotics* (the theory of signs) this sort of situation would be called an "iconic sign." The verse and strophe here are designed to be an icon, i.e., an image that is to represent incarceration. The question that remains for David is, Who in heaven's name is going to get him out of this multiple confinement? Nobody, except . . . and here the poet intervenes with his super-stanza: the five strophes about God's appearance from heaven constitute his final solution.

The strophic unit may also be the result of an extended or compound sentence. We have seen this several times already. In his Lament (2 Samuel 1), David forbade the messengers to report the outcome of the battle to Philistia. The sentence core consisted of the prohibition, which was followed by subclauses starting with "lest." The first strophe of Psalm 1, after the "happy," consists of little else besides a chain of adjectival clauses. Psalm 114—as we have also seen—starts with a temporal clause, and completes its first strophe with the main clause that proclaims Judah-and-Israel to be the dominion and temple of God. The S-strophe at the end is also a syntactic unit consisting of one sentence.

Psalm 13 consists of three strophes, and according to general scholarly opinion has twelve cola. This is wrong, and comes from an erroneous division of v. 4, where there is actually a chain of three subclauses starting with "lest." The correct articulation is:

13:2a	How long, Yahweh, will you ignore me forever?
b	How long will you hide your face from me?
3a	How long will I have cares on my mind,
b	grief in my heart, all day?
c	How long will my enemy have the upper hand?
4a	Look at me, answer me, Yahweh!
b	My God, restore the luster to my eyes,
c	lest I sleep the sleep of death,
5a	lest my enemy say "I have overcome him,"
b	lest my foes exult when I totter.
6a	But I trust in your faithfulness,
b	my heart will exult in your deliverance:
c	I will sing to Yahweh, for he has been good to me.

Thus, there are actually thirteen cola, which by their total of 117 syllables in the original language realize the exact norm figure 9. The first strophe is one of impatience and despair, presented in a two-line and a three-line verse. The cola form a chain because they are all questions; they ask "how long" four times, and also employ a temporal adjunct in v. 3b. This is an instance of the strophe being demarcated by an obvious sequence. The middle strophe has the same rhythm of bicolon-plus-tricolon. There is a positively worded verse (4ab) containing two commands and two vocatives for God, which thanks to a clever arrangement proves to be a neat chiasm, after which a tricolon occurs, fending off negative events. Thus, this strophic unit is defined by sentence structure and a plus–minus relationship. The transition to the first person and a positive outcome mark off v. 6 as the third strophe.

A strophe also may derive its unity from the fact that it is a quotation or embedded speech. This happens twice in Psalm 132. In vv. 3–5 David swears an oath to God, and in vv. 11cd–12 God answers by in turn swearing an oath to David; these are both L-strophes. Their function will be discussed when I consider the composition as a whole, in chapter 7.

A strophe may be shaped by a metaphor; the eagle from Deuteronomy 32 is an example. Below, I quote six verses from the book of Job; these are strophes 3 and 4 from the poem Job 14:

Job 14:7   There is hope for a tree;
            if it is cut down, it will renew itself,
               and its shoots will not cease.
     8   If its roots are old in the earth
           and its stump dies in the ground,
     9   at the scent of water it will bud,
           and produce branches like a sapling.

    10   But mortals languish and die;
           man expires; where is he?
    11   As water evaporates from a lake
           and a river dries up and is parched,
    12   so man lies down, and will not rise;
           until the heavens are no more, he will not awake,
             not be roused from his sleep.

The third strophe of the poem is determined exclusively by figurative speech: each line contains a vegetative image. Verses 10–12 offer us a negative image, this time that of man. The first verse is very bare, as if the poet wants to say: forget all metaphors, just look death straight in the eye. Verses 11–12, however, do contain another image, this time in the form of a comparison. The connection with the strophe about the tree trunk is well maintained, as we again have water here. The water in strophe 3, however, was life-giving, whereas in vv. 11–12 it becomes an image for the evanescence of our lives, and as such serves death. The concluding tricolon contains as many as four negations, and uses these to strike out the euphemism "sleep."

A strophe may very well be kept together by a frame; this is a phenomenon which takes us to the boundaries of the unit and hence to the next paragraph, where we shall consider how the strophe is distinguished from its surroundings. Yet, such an inclusio will have its points of contact with the words it encloses, i.e., with the "contents" of the strophe. The L-strophe opening Psalm 69 is built on the image of mud and water into which the "I" is sinking, vv. 2–3. The L-strophe vv. 4–5 becomes even more physical, and already speaks of the hatred that is felt for the speaker. The

L-strophe vv. 6–7 already starts a prayer. Another two strophes follow, again in L-format, about the position of the "I":

Ps. 69:8	It is for your sake that I have been abused,	strophe 4
	shame covers my face.	
9	I am a stranger to my brothers,	
	an alien to the sons of my mother;	
10	my zeal for your house has consumed me,	
	and the abuse of those who revile you	
	have fallen upon me.	
11	When I wept and fasted,	strophe 5
	I was reviled for it.	
12	I made sackcloth my garment,	
	but I became a byword among them.	
13	Those who sit in the gate talk about me	
	—I am the taunts of drunkards.	

The keywords here are "abuse" and "taunt," and in both strophes the "I" is confronted with a collective. The most painful circumstance is the fact that these are not enemies from outside, but his own people. The gate is the spot where the community meets and sits in judgment, but now it is a scene of debauchery, at the cost of the "I." In the original Hebrew, strophe 4 is marked by a frame consisting of the 3 + 3 words of vv. 8a and 10b. The translation can show only half of this, in the correspondence between "for your sake" / "upon me," and especially in the keyword "abuse."

The word "consumed" from v. 10a literally means "eaten." This knowledge puts us on the track of a beautiful, associative connection between the two strophes. The "eating" that the speaker experienced in v. 10a is followed in v. 11a by fasting. At the end of strophe 5 we discover its counterpart, the act of "drinking," presented negatively as drunkenness. This new inclusio, however, is the imaginative variation of a well-known word pair, eating and drinking, and stretches both activities in a direction which is detrimental to the speaker. The three cola about abuse (8a, 10b, 11b) are supported by three cola about taunts (12b–13b), so that the "I" has totally lost his bearings.

I have also mentioned that the unifying factor within a strophe may be a single idea. Any concept of "idea" should be treated with extreme caution, as in the Western world the Bible has been studied for so long by intellectuals whose research has been either damaged or threatened by their worship of concepts, hypotheses, and theories. That is not the fault of the concept itself, however, and of course there were plenty of ideas in ancient Israel. As an example I have chosen a sequence of strophes spoken by the first pedantic prig who confronts Job in the long debate of the eponymous book. Eliphaz opens the debate in Job 4. He first notes that the man who was such a support to others in times of trouble is now himself unnerved (strophe 1 = vv. 2–4 and strophe 2 = vv. 5–6)—not a particularly compassionate beginning. The fifteen poetic lines which fill strophes 3–8 are all bicolic except for two verses, and this is what the hero has to listen to:

Job 4:7	Think now, what innocent man ever perished,	strophe 3
	and where have the upright been destroyed?	
8	As I have seen, those who plow evil	
	and sow mischief, reap them.	
9	By a breath from God they perish,	
	by the blast of his nostrils they perish.	
10	One lion roars, the other one growls,	strophe 4
	the teeth of the cubs are broken.	
11	The lion perishes for lack of prey,	
	and the whelps of the lioness are scattered.	
12	A word came to me in stealth,	strophe 5
	my ear caught a whisper of it	
13	in thought-filled visions of the night,	
	when deep sleep fell on men.	
14	Fear and trembling came upon me	
	causing all my bones to quake with fright.	
15	A spirit passed by me,	strophe 6
	making the hair of my flesh bristle,	
	like a wind.	
16	It halted; its appearance was strange to me,	
	a form before my eyes;	
	I heard a murmur, a voice:	
17	"Can mortals be acquitted by God,	strophe 7
	or man be cleared by his Maker?	
18	Even his servants he does not trust,	
	and he finds error in his angels."	
19	"How much more in those who dwell in houses of clay,	
	whose origin is dust!	
	They are crushed like moths,	strophe 8
20	shattered at daybreak or at night,	
	unnoticed, they perish forever.	
21	Is not their tent cord pulled up?	
	They die, but not in wisdom."	

Strophe 3 starts with a question and ends with a vengeful God. The point of this unit is the inescapable pattern linking guilt and annihilation. A speaker starting verses with "Think now" and "As I have seen" increases the pressure on the addressee. If the "you-

and-I" tone suggests intimacy, this is a manipulative strategy. It obscures the fact that Eliphaz is uttering a threat; what else could the function of the metaphor governing strophe 4 be? The translator runs into problems here, as the Hebrew poet cleverly uses five different words to indicate lions of various rank and type, whereas English offers only one; I have had to improvise.

Strophes 3 and 4 together constitute the second stanza of the poem. The third stanza recounts a nocturnal revelation (strophes 5–6), and the fourth quotes its content, a message in words (strophes 7–8). By introducing this revelation Eliphaz gives a new twist to the business of impressing Job, and he is not going to hurry: he uses four strophes this time. Strophe 5 is still seemingly neutral, offering such "hard facts" as night, sleep, and whispering, while strophe 6 presents the accompanying emotion, and the figure that will become the envoy of the revelation. The cohesion of strophe 5 is easily guaranteed by the sentence structure: the sentence has not finished after v. 12b, and so enjambment occurs. The murmur of 16c and "the word" of v. 12a together form a neat inclusion of this narrative stanza. The unifying factor of strophe 6 is the numinous character of what is being described.

All this is an attempt to make Job receptive to a view of God and man that would be repulsive to all but the staunchest Calvinist. The negative tone of strophe 7 almost noticeably reeks: God is presented as a being totally poisoned by suspicion. As if that were not yet enough, Eliphaz employs a special argumentative technique as the poem moves from this strophe to strophe 8. The rabbis call this model *qal wachomer* ("from light to heavy"), and in rhetoric it is known as *a minori ad maius*; it is indicated by the pivot "how much more."

If we listen closely, Eliphaz's "how much more" really means its opposite, "how much less"—a disingenuousness that is characteristic of his mind. He argues: God does not trust his angels (v. 18), *how much less* does he trust the creatures on earth! Consequently, this "how much less" is a negative *a fortiori:* how much stronger is his distrust of people? The question in v. 17 is again manipulative, and as the opening of the fourth stanza it is the perfect counterpart or successor to the verse that opened the second stanza, v. 7. Because of their form (a rhetorical question presupposing a negative answer) and content (the guilty or unclean person), these poetic lines belong together so that we also recognize their correspondence within the stanza design.

But look who's talking: what Eliphaz proclaims in strophe 7—that total distrust is part of God's character—is a projection of his own innermost attitude to life, and he even tries by means of verbal fireworks to grant this doctrine official status by presenting it as a revelation.

Let us take a brief excursion into prosody. Job 4 has been composed in meticulous fashion: the eight strophes constitute four stanzas, which mirror each other two by two. A great regularity may be observed on three levels, demonstrated below by the capitals S and L, and also by the syllable totals for the strophes and stanzas. The figures for the stanzas have been given in bold type below the figures for the strophes:

Job 4

strophes	L	S	L	S		S	L	S	L
cola	6	4	6	4		4	7	4	7
syllables	51	39	53	32		34	54	33	54
	90		**85**			**88**		**87**	

If we now add the stanza totals, both halves of the poem turn out to have exactly the same number of syllables, i.e., 175; this results in a round figure 350 for the poem as a whole.

The strophes exist by being distinguished from each other

From the preceding section we may conclude that the strophe can easily fend for itself. This section will demonstrate that it does not have to. The poet has many devices at his disposal to grant the strophe internal cohesion, and the reader will do well to learn to recognize these tools. Our poetry manuals teach us, however, that a strophe is never alone, but always works together with its colleagues, the textual units surrounding it. The strophe always functions in relation to the other strophes, which offers new possibilities to the "composer," the poet who assembles them.

Let us first think back to the figure of the frame. An inclusio such as we have seen in Psalm 69 looks inward, as it were: as a border it draws attention to the strophe itself and what is inside it. There is a reverse side to this obvious statement, however: because of the inclusio, the strophe is also distinguished from its surroundings. It seems to withdraw upon itself, as if saying to adjoining units: this area is mine, not yours.

Internal cohesion thus may be viewed from the other side. We must now take a step backward, to create some distance and to ascertain how the strophe behaves within the tissue of relations that make up a poem. In doing so, we encounter properties of external cohesion: although the strophe remains identical with itself, it also owes its existence to differences, to its quality of being a "twist." The strophe is marked out by being different from its surroundings.

The poet marks the differences between strophes by always introducing new twists. What do these changes look like? Here, too, the poet can employ all sorts of linguistic, stylistic, and structural devices to make the reader experience transitions. We enter a new strophe if there is a change in

- the characters who populate the unit;
- verb tense;
- the mode of the sentences (do they report or describe?; are they wishes or commands?);
- grammatical person;
- language: from verbal (reporting or desiring action) to nominal (static, describing properties) language;
- subject matter;
- tone or genre.

Furthermore, the boundary positions in the strophe are sensitive: especially the beginning may be clearly marked, for instance, by a striking adverb such as "Therefore," a form of address (the vocative, in the Psalms often "O Yahweh" or "My God!"), or an imperative such as "Hear me" or "Save me!"

It is not difficult to illustrate each of these possibilities by dozens of examples. This would, however, also entail quoting several connected strophes for each option, which would take up a lot of space. There is another method that makes this unnecessary. I have chosen a substantial passage from Isaiah and a lament from Psalms, and as I discuss each strophe briefly, most types of "twist" or transition will pass under review.

The powerful opening speech of the book of Isaiah

The book of Isaiah is named after a Judaean prophet who was active in the second half of the eighth century BCE. He lived through the rapid expansion of the most powerful nation of his time, the Assyrians, in Syria-Palestine; saw the demise of the northern kingdom (Samaria fell in 722 BCE); and also saw the tiny state of Judah attacked. After the war has completed its destructive course through the land, Isaiah pronounces God's part of a dispute: the argumentative speech we now find in Isaiah 1:2–20 (a *rib* or lawsuit, as it is called by scholars); this is an indictment. In his text he hardly mentions any name, historical detail, or concrete fact of the kind historians love to hear, but focuses mainly on quality. This characteristic has—we may suppose—made the text so valued that it has survived the ages and has received a place in the canon. I will discuss the poem roughly per stanza. The first stanza comprises vv. 2–4; the next two occupy vv. 5–9.

Isa.1:2	Hear, O heavens,
	    and give ear, O earth,
	        for Yahweh has spoken:
	"I reared children and brought them up,
	    but they have rebelled against me.
		strophe 1

3	An ox knows its owner
	    an ass its master's crib,
	but Israel does not know,
	    my people takes no thought."
		strophe 2

4	Ah, sinful nation,
	    the nation laden with iniquity,
	brood of evildoers,
	    depraved children!
	They have forsaken Yahweh,
	    spurned the Holy One of Israel,
	        they turned their backs.
		strophe 3

The first strophe is also the pretentious opening of the book. The poet calls upon the entire cosmos to be his witness, in about the same way as Moses did in his didactic poem in Deuteronomy 32. After the exhortation to listen, the floor is given to a character who for the moment plays the part of the plaintiff in a trial. It is God himself who without delay takes on the part of the father and thus justifies his expectations of the other party, whom he has raised. Developments move so fast that already in the second poetic line we hear the friction between claim and complaint. Nevertheless, the speaker still has not told us exactly who it is he is so unhappy about.

The identity of the other party is indirectly revealed in the second strophe. This unit differs from the preceding one in that the subject matter has changed. The first half sounds like a proverb, and in v. 3cd the accused is rather exposed; translated literally: "Israel does not know, my people do not understand." There is no direct object, i.e., the verb is here used absolutely (as the technical term goes), and not without reason. What this omission (ellipsis*) makes clear is that the ignorance described is not related to something specific and is therefore unlimited: their stupidity is boundless.

Changes of grammatical person and genre mark strophe 3. This is a so-called "woe"-exclamation in which God is now a third person, and the prophet specifies the indictment: iniquity and corruption, culminating in a turning away from God, which also explains the criminal actions. This ending (v. 5c) is the elaboration of v. 2e, a connection which also creates a parallelism between strophes 1 and 3 that in turn keeps the stanza together.

Corruption breeds corruption. The poet-prophet abandons the original depravity, and in stanzas II-III speaks of the resulting degeneracy as the manifestation of underlying evil. Stanza II (vv. 5–6) employs the language of the body; stanza III (vv. 7–9) is couched in military-political terms.

Isa.1:5   Why do you seek further beatings,   strophe 4
                that you continue to offend?
            The whole head is ailing,
                and the whole heart is sick.

     6   From the sole of the foot to the skull   strophe 5
                no spot is sound:
            all bruises, and welts,
                and fresh sores,
            not pressed out, not bound up,
                not softened with oil.

     7   Your land is a waste,   strophe 6
                your cities burnt down:
            your soil, before your eyes—
                strangers consume it,
                    a wasteland, as overthrown by strangers.

     8   The daughter of Zion is left   strophe 7
                like a booth in a vineyard,
            like a hut in a cucumber field,
                like a city beleaguered.

     9   Had not Yahweh of hosts   strophe 8
                left us a fugitive,
            we should soon be like Sodom,
                and seem as Gomorrah.

The strophes are marked by a shift in subject and tone, as well as by
the introduction of the second-person plural: the prophet addresses
his audience as separate persons. First, there is a unit which sounds
almost medical: strophes 4–5 about pus and festering sores (= stanza
II). This image of an ailing body serves as an excellent metaphor for
the corruption of the nation: the people are critically ill. Strophe 4
addresses the people as "you," and covers the whole person via
metonymy by mentioning head and heart. After that, the form
"you" disappears to make way for the almost clinical description in
v. 6. Again, the whole person is dealt with, this time by a merism,
"from head to toe" (as we would put it).

   This physical manifestation of decay is followed by a new twist,
which offers images of war and its effects, so that strophe 6 represents the political effects of corruption: destruction of the land as

a punishment for the entire nation. This stanza (the third) ends with a form of desolation that nevertheless offers a glimpse of hope. Verses 8–9 present an image from horticulture, and by means of a counterfactual* ("Had not . . . , we should . . .") end in a distant past: Sodom and Gomorrah have been proverbial for depravity since the primeval age which Genesis tells us about. They should be viewed as mythical-literary places rather than as names from a historical reality.

We have now looked at eight strophes. They contain many cola that are all the more intense because of their shortness and that leave us with little hope. In the seventh strophe, however, the city of Jerusalem appears under the name of "daughter of Zion," and in the shape of the wretched structure of branches and leaves that has been relinquished by the farmer. This image is clarified in the eighth strophe as "a fugitive, a survivor." The names of Sodom and Gomorrah convey the message that Judah has escaped total annihilation only by the skin of its teeth. This does seem to be a positive statement, and the prophet suddenly even uses the pronoun "we" in order to get closer to his audience and to give them a feeling of adversity shared, and of a new beginning. This concludes the first section of the long oracle.

The Judaeans have listened to all this with mixed feelings, but breathe somewhat more freely thanks to the first-person plural. This is, however, a mistake; the poet has wrong-footed them. He has inserted a hook linking the end of the first section to the beginning of the second, by repeating the names of Sodom and Gomorrah. In v. 9, the reference seems comforting, locked inside the counterfactual mode and the message that "we" escaped after all. In v. 10, however, Isaiah deals his audience a blow by addressing them as the "chieftains of Sodom": a major insult that certainly keeps their attention from drifting. . . . Again, the shift in grammatical person is the strophe marker:

Isa. 1:10   Hear the word of Yahweh,
    you chieftains of Sodom!   strophe 9
  give ear to our God's instruction,
    people of Gomorrah!

   11   "What need have I of all your sacrifices?"
      —says Yahweh.
    "I am sated with burnt offerings of rams, strophe 10
     suet of fatlings,
      and blood of bulls;
    lambs and he-goats
     I do not delight in."

   12   "That you come to appear before me—
      who asked that of you?   strophe 11
    Trampling my courts,
     do not continue it!
   13a Bringing vain oblations,
     offensive incense it is to me.

   13c New moon and Sabbath, proclaiming
      of solemnities:
    assemblies with iniquity I cannot abide.
   14   Your new moons and fixed seasons
     I hate with all my soul;   strophe 12
    they are become a burden to me,
     I am exhausted carrying them.

   15   And when you lift up your hands,
     I will turn my eyes away from you; strophe 13
    even when you pray harder,
     I will not listen.
    Your hands are stained with blood!

   16   Wash yourselves, clean yourselves,
     put your evil doings   strophe 14
      away from my sight!
    Cease to do evil,
   17 learn to do good,
      devote ourselves to justice!
    Aid the wronged,
     Uphold the rights of the orphan,
      defend the cause of the widow!"

Strophes 9–16 may, two by two, be accommodated in higher textual units, stanzas IV–VI, but the stanza boundaries are not very conspicuous this time, except for the line dividing v. 15 from v. 16.

The cola of strophe 9 are varied according to the AB-A'B' pattern. As a plea for attention, they form a strophic unit. At the same time a parallelism is created two levels further up, as this exhortation is the successor of the first strophe. There is also a pertinent/fitting variation in the repetition: it is not the cosmos that is addressed here, but "you," and "you" had better listen very carefully to a pronouncement, an "instruction" (*torah*) from God. By phrasing this as "our God," Isaiah for a moment retains the common ground that has enabled him to reach his obstinate audience, but this is the end of the familiarity indicated by "our." Strophes 10–11 now present the contents of the lesson; we know exactly how far this instruction to the community extends, thanks to the use of the first person for God, which runs through to v. 15. As God continues to say "you" even after v. 15, we also may see him as the speaker of the last strophes, vv. 16–20.

A shift of speaker and subject marks the transition to strophe 10, a unit that focuses exclusively on a graphic component of worship: all forms of sacrifice. A frame provides the rounding-off: "what need have I" becomes "I am sated," which is chiastically completed by "I do not delight in." In strophe 11 we see the place that should be one of sincere communication, i.e., the temple court, while strophe 12 covers the cultic calendar of the visitors. The underlying tone remains one of disgust, since the persistent criticism is that the people care only about outward forms, and the "I" (i.e., God) castigates this hypocrisy.

The unity of strophe 13 is already suggested by a new AB-A'B' design. Two compound sentences neatly coincide with the two verses, and their components exactly cover the half-verses. This arrangement is varied by a chiasm, hands-seeing/hearing-hands. Furthermore, there is a surplus: line 15e about the hands being stained with blood, an extremely incriminating monocolon, is the final blow.

We gradually move from the corrupt "yesterday-and-today" toward "tomorrow," as God now uses the future tense: he prefers to close his eyes and ears. He even rejects prayer, a much more

direct and honest form of contact than the mumbo-jumbo of sacrifice and ritual.

Strophe 14 is marked by the change to new linguistic forms,
and finally reveals the exact nature of the corruption: social injustice. God bursts into a chain of commands that occupies three
times three cola. It is the sharp staccato that at the beginning of
this book acquired its proper form. These commands are very
direct, and they make sense only if God is convinced that it is possible to continue together after all. The circumstances that will
ensure this are the subject of the concluding verses 18–20 (stanza
VII). The escapee will be given one more chance:

Isa. 1:18a	"Let us go, let us have a tribunal,"	
b	Yahweh says.	
c	Be your sins like crimson,	strophe 15
d	they will turn snow-white;	
e	be they red as purple,	
f	white as fleece they will become.	
19	If you agree and give heed,	
	you will eat the good things of	
	the land;	strophe 16
20	but if you refuse and disobey,	
	you will be devoured by the sword!	
	The mouth of Yahweh has spoken.	

It does not matter much any more who is speaking. The first
line of v. 18 is spoken by God, but after that the prophet's point of
view practically coincides with that of his superior. The very last
colon mentions Yahweh in the third person, so that we are inclined
to allot this line to the prophet. What is essential, however, is to see
that this straightforward sentence concluding the long oracle is the
counterpart to v. 2c, the pivotal line of the opening strophe. In this
way, the passage as a whole has acquired a formal inclusio, as the
entire text begins and ends with a tricolon that concludes with
"Yahweh has spoken."

Strophe 15 in turn has a vocabulary of its own. The first verse
reveals the status of this oracular speech: God has all the time
played the role of plaintiff in a court of law, and has expounded his
views as part of a lawsuit. Thus, the long poem has a formal-legal

aspect. The strophe is characterized by a fourfold comparison built on neat chiasms, in both 18cd and 18ef. I have retained the original word order so that the crosswise construction remains visible: the verbs are on the edges, whereas the colors red and white surround the caesura in both bicola. The phrase "Be [your sins] . . ." has the same meaning as the conjunction "if" in the final strophe, so that a parallelism is created between the units 15 and 16. In the same way as the color red reminds the listener and reader of the hands stained with blood, "the land" and "devouring" remind us of the aftermath of the war, when strangers came and razed the land.

The bodies of both these strophes have been constructed on an opposition. In strophe 15 (v. 18cd + ef) the two cola in each verse cover the two halves of a radical turn, while the message of the two poetic lines remains the same. Strophe 16 contains only one such turn, and here the complete verses each express half of an opposition: goodwill in v. 19ab versus obstinacy in 19cd. The quartets 18cdef and 19abcd are framed by one line asserting that God has spoken; this is an inclusio that unites the strophes into a final stanza.

This poem constitutes the powerful opening of the book of Isaiah. It is long, but its vigor and passion are reflected in and conveyed by proportions that are surprisingly modest. Even in translation the cola are still very short; there are many terse strophes, and five stanzas consist of only two strophes. The vocabulary is extremely varied, since the poet draws from a multitude of domains, the most important of which are law, war, horticulture, and the cult—not to mention the language of a distraught surgeon in stanza II. The imagery is very apt: the crib, the wounds and their bandages, the wine grower's hovel, the racket around the temple, and the contrast between red and white. There are seven stanzas and forty verses—very biblical figures. In the statistical summary below I have indicated the separation between vv. 1–9 and 10–18 by a double slash. This boundary contains the concatenating device (the "hook"), which makes sure that the faraway names Sodom and Gomorrah suddenly creep unpleasantly close to the poet's audience.

stanza *nos. of:*	I	II	III	//	IV	V	VI	VII
strophes	3	2	3		2	2	2	2
verses	7	5	6		5	6	6	5
cola	16	10	13		11	12	14	11

In the original language, this formidable disputation takes up no more than 234 words.

In the darkest places, in the depths: Psalm 88

This psalm is a lament of exactly forty cola. Verses 9 and 10 are tricolic; the rest are bicolic. The articulation in seven strophes is inescapable, and I am filled with vicarious shame to have to report that not a single translation or commentary presents the correct division. The only remedy for this sort of omission is subjecting the poem to a sound poetics. As always, the first step in the analysis is to read the text over and over again, and try to cover the ground exhaustively by noting everything of any literary value. Nothing short of checking the complete range of stylistic and structural devices will do. In the case of Psalm 88, the next step is to examine the relative effects of the various formal characteristics. We shall see that the strategic placement of keywords has far-reaching consequences here. First, however, I will start looking for "twists," referring to the list of characteristics I have given earlier. The text of vv. 2–7 is as follows:

Ps. 88:2   O Yahweh, God of my deliverance,   strophe 1
                by day and night I cry out before you.
     3   Let my prayer reach you,
                incline your ear to my cry.

     4   For my soul is sated with misfortune,   strophe 2
                I am at the brink of the realm of
                    the dead.
     5   I am numbered with those who go down
                    to the Pit,
                I have become like a man without strength.

     6   Among the dead released,   strophe 3
                like bodies lying in the grave,
            of whom you are mindful no more;
                and they, they have been cut off from your hand.

v. 7   You have put me at the bottom of the Pit,
        in the darkest places, in the depths.

The speaker marks the opening by a vocative: God's proper name. He supplements this by an apposition mentioning that quality of God's to which he wants to appeal:"God of my deliverance" (JPS). This sounds positive, but unfortunately it is both the first and the last fragment in this song on the brink of the grave that indicates any hope. Verse 2b contains the merism of day and night, which tells us that the poet has time for little else but crying for help. In the second poetic line, the speaker himself furnishes a label for his text: it is a "prayer." The half-verses combine the visual with the auditory—another aspect suggesting totality, just like the merism of the temporal terms in v. 2b.

The transition to strophe 2 is clear, thanks to the shift from presence to absence and the change in verb tense and mode. The commands of v. 3 are followed by four cola in the past tense, with predicates, moreover, in the passive. The wishes expressed in strophe 1 have been replaced by a description of "my" unpleasant situation: I am about to topple into the grave any minute now. And where has God gone?

Next, the presence of the "I" in the text also becomes doubtful. The personal pronoun is conspicuous by its absence in the very first colon of the third strophe (v. 6a). This omission is too much for most biblical scholars, so that they start tinkering with the Hebrew. Even without the visible presence of the word "I," however, it is clear that the speaker is talking about himself, and actually I consider the ellipsis of the pronoun—in linguistic terms: a zero-morpheme*—a meaningful signal, part of a clever play on the contrast presence/absence in this poem. By dropping the form "I," the poet shows us that he is done for. The absence of the pronoun is another example of an iconic* sign. The "I" surfaces only at the end of the strophe, but it is the object, even the victim, of "your" cruel treatment. This "me" anticipates strophe 4.

The poet is very ironical about his fate by representing himself as "released among the dead." God has returned to the text, this time as the "you" who is held responsible for "cutting off" the poet—who fills the rest of the strophe with terms for the underworld (*sheol* in Hebrew) that leave nothing to the imagination. He chooses, for instance, the word "Pit," and since he had also used this in v. 5a, he has now created a parallelism on strophe level.

The poet continues with two massive units:

> 8   Upon me your fury lies heavy,   strophe 4
>   with all your breakers you afflict me.
> 9   You make my companions shun me,
>   You make me abhorrent to them;
>   [I am] shut in, and cannot go out.
> 10   My eye pines away from affliction;
>   I call to you, Yahweh, each day
>   I stretch out my hands to you.
>
> 11   The dead—do you work wonders for them?   strophe 5
>   Do the shades rise to praise you?
> 12   Is your faithful care recounted in the grave,
>   your constancy in the place of perdition?
> 13   Are your miracles made known in the darkness,
>   Your justice in the land of oblivion?

Strophe 4 is the middle unit of the composition and, with its eight cola, the weightiest. Four lines are devoted to God and his repressive actions; four lines explore the misery and despair of the speaker, who eventually returns to the position he took at the beginning, i.e., praying and crying for help. The "I" is complaining of the total isolation into which he has been cast by none other than his God. He does not complain about enemies, but about something much worse: he has been robbed of his friends, to the extent that they are disgusted with him. The words of v. 9c turn this alienation into a prison. The strophe progresses from "upon me" to "to you." These pronouns form a thin border around the whole.

The real cohesion in this loaded center comes from the outside rather than from within. The boundary with strophe 5 is beyond doubt, as this new unit, vv. 11–13, is instantly recognizable as a chain of three verses asking six rhetorical questions. The speaker impresses upon God that it is not a good idea to push him into the grave, as in that case he (God) cannot expect him (the poet) to put in a word for him, let alone a word of praise—an attractive and spirited manipulation of the addressee. Furthermore, the argument is the most powerful application of the contrast between present and absent: the "I" is not present at all in strophe 5! The ego has now completely evaporated, so to speak, and the poet talks in strictly general terms of the dead and their deafening silence.

14	As for me—I cry out to you, O Yahweh,	strophe 6
	in the morning my prayer reaches you.	
15	Why, Yahweh, do you reject me,	
	do you hide your face from me?	
16	I have been afflicted and near death from	
	my youth,	
	I suffer your terrors, I am at my wits' end.	
17	Upon me your fury descends,	strophe 7
	Your terrors dumbfound me.	
18	They swirl about me like water all day long,	
	they encircle me together.	
19	You have put friend and neighbor far from me,	
	and my companions are total darkness.	

The threshold of the final stanza is indicated by the fact that the same "I" that was so notoriously absent in strophe 5 has been emphatically placed in front position in strophe 6. Verse 14 is the counterpart to the very first verse, which creates a parallel on stanza level. Next, a double why-question follows that certainly does not ask for information, but is, as elsewhere, the vehicle of great indignation: v. 15 is a reproach, and by its choice of words again holds God responsible for the speaker's isolation. In v. 16 he frankly states his distress. Thus, a verse in the second person (15) is surrounded by verses of cause (distress, 16) and effect (cry for help, 14). These lines all have "I" as subject, whereas the final strophe repeats the object form "me," in order to demonstrate consistently the extent to which the speaker is the "fall guy."

This final strophe (vv. 17–19) is characterized by a remarkable aspect which at the same time guarantees its cohesion. In the three successive cola 8a–8b–9a we saw, respectively, God's anger, threatening breakers (as an image of anger), and alienation caused by God; the first words of that strophe were "upon me." The seventh and last strophe starts in exactly the same way, and again presents the elements of anger, water, and alienation. This time, however, they have been doubled and each receive a complete bicolon of their own.

The duplication, of course, also means that strophe 7 functions as the climax.

I have not yet mentioned the most conspicuous markers in the poem. For once I will permit myself the luxury of repetition, by printing the poem again, this time in its entirety. The phrases I have italicized demonstrate that the opening words of strophes 4–5 refer crosswise forward and backward. The "dead" of v. 6a are "the dead" of v. 11a, which is why I have tried to maintain the original word order as closely as possible in my translation of this colon. The opening "upon me" guarantees the start of a new strophe in vv. 8a and 17a. These crosswise connections make strophes 4–5 the central stanza where the main lines of the poem meet and are tied together.

The demarcation of vv. 8–13 as the center would be even more convincing if it were accompanied by cohesion in the flanks. Can we assume that the first three strophes are stanza I and that strophes 6–7 are stanza III? The poet again provides us with a structural signal. The three-part structure of the poem is itself marked by the strategic placement of a keyword: this is the series dark–darkness–the darkest places, which in the original language also shows minor variations, but always on the same root. This keyword, too, deserves italics:

Ps. 88

2	O Yahweh, God of my deliverance,	stanza I
	by day and night I cry out before you.	
3	Let my prayer reach you,	
	incline your ear to my cry.	
4	For my soul is sated with misfortune,	
	I am at the brink of Sheol.	
5	I am numbered with those who go down	
	to the Pit,	
	I have become like a man without strength.	
6	*Among the dead* released,	
	like bodies lying in the grave,	
	of whom you are mindful no more;	
	and they, they have been cut off from your hand.	
7	You have put me at the bottom of the Pit,	
	in *the darkest places*, in the depths.	

8	*Upon me* your fury lies heavy,	stanza II
	with all your breakers you afflict me.	
9	You make my companions shun me,	
	You make me abhorrent to them;	
	[I am] shut in, and cannot go out.	
10	My eye pines away from affliction;	
	I call to you, Yahweh, each day	
	I stretch out my hands to you.	
11	*The dead*—do you work wonders for them?	
	Do the shades rise to praise you?	
12	Is your faithful care recounted in the grave,	
	your constancy in the place of perdition?	
13	Are your miracles made known in the	
	darkness,	
	Your justice in the land of oblivion?	
14	As for me—I cry out to you, O Yahweh,	stanza III
	in the morning my prayer reaches You.	
15	Why, Yahweh, do you reject me,	
	do you hide your face from me?	
16	I have been afflicted and near death from	
	my youth,	
	I suffer your terrors, I am at my wits' end.	
17	*Upon me* your fury descends,	
	Your terrors dumbfound me.	
18	They swirl about me like water all day long,	
	they encircle me together.	
19	You have put friend and neighbor far from me,	
	and my companions are total *darkness*.	

The articulation of the poem in seven strophes may thus be noted as SSL/LL/LL, with a balance of 14–14–12 cola.

After one paragraph on internal and one on external cohesion, I conclude with a synthesis of these two. Their relationship varies, but they manage to work together very well. If the internal cohesion is considerable or compelling, as was the case with vv. 11–13 in Psalm 88, few or no devices for external cohesion are needed. If, on the other hand, the unity within the strophe itself is not clear or uncertain, as in vv. 8–10, the poet may compensate for this by making the unit stand out sharply from its surroundings. This is indeed what happens in these lines: vv. 8–10 remain together thanks to the fact that the next lines (six questions in three verses) cohere unconditionally, and also because the trio anger-water-alienation starts with the same "upon me" that also opens the final strophe and is itself repeated with double force.

Another example is the boundary at the end of strophe 2 in the same psalm. If no context were given, it would be difficult to separate v. 6ab from vv. 4–5, which also speak of the imminent death of the "I." Suppose, however, that we wanted to incorporate v. 6ab in the second strophe: this would be instantly refuted by two characteristics of the text. In the first place, v. 6ab cannot be separated from its sequel because of a strong linguistic factor: v. 6c is an adjectival clause, and only in exceptional cases and on the basis of weighty arguments can such a relative clause be separated from its antecedent by a strophe boundary. To put it in positive terms: the natural coherence between an adjectival adjunct and the sentence core will in principle be respected rather than broken up by the strophe design. Second, various aspects of v. 6a offer forceful arguments against cutting off v. 6ab. The omission of "I" forms a sharp contrast with strophe 2, and it is especially the opening phrase about "the dead," strategically placed as the counterpart to "the dead" in v. 11a, which ensures that all of v. 6abcd forms a unit together with v. 7, the first of a series of five consecutive L-strophes.

Finally, I return to the middle strophe of Psalm 88. Only now that we see the whole, and are able to appreciate the interplay of the strophes, does the function of this center become truly clear. First, this fourth strophe has become an intersection within the poem thanks to crosswise repetitions linking the center to the extreme ends. The first three cola (v. 8a-8b-9a) point forward to the last strophe; the last three (the members of the tricolon v. 10) point backward to the first strophe. Inside this crosswise connection, however, there are another two cola, v. 9b and v. 9c, which constitute the center of the center. They are the nadir of the poet's experiences, even to the extent that in 9c he again leaves out "I am," before telling us that he cannot go anywhere. This renewed ellipsis links up with the previous one, in v. 6a, and provides a new discovery. The predicates "released" and "shut in" are an opposition, which has been the subject of a curious switch. "Released," "free" (meaning not being a prisoner or slave) is how we feel on earth when all is well, but what follows is permanent incarceration: by death. The poet has switched these states around and made them the subject of his most expressive manipulation of the contrast present/absent. We now notice that, in the same way that God was absent from strophe 2 and the "I" from strophe 5, death is missing from strophe 4: exactly that part of the text that is framed by two detailed explorations of the nether world, strophes 3 and 5 with their markers "among/upon the dead." What can this mean?

This exploration of death has a rather special status, since the journey through the realm of the dead is imaginary: the poet himself is, of course, not dead yet. Consequently, the two strophes are a poetical instance of the counterfactual mode. The verses they encircle, however, do describe the poet's actuality. The poet is stating that in harsh reality, God is destroying him by anger and a frightening isolation. The result is that he is experiencing in the here and now one of the prominent aspects of death, a sense of "being shut in," while his imagination tells him he will able to feel free only after death, when God's grip no longer keeps him in isolation. In this way, the middle strophe, the only strophe to contain eight cola, gathers together everything that was crucial outside it. The center is able to contribute to the whole, thanks to the contrasts with its surroundings.

6

The stanza

Existence, length, and function

Continuing upward through the layered structure of the text, we find a unit one level higher than the strophe. No accepted term exists to label this entity; I use the word "stanza," which is as good a name as any other.

First of all, the fundamental question should be raised: does the stanza actually exist in Hebrew poetry? Although my own answer would be an affirmative one, it cannot be given with as much assurance as in the case of the strophe. As it turns out, the stanza moves on a scale ranging from "hardly visible or meaningful" to "clear-cut and essential."

The first indication that a "stanza" is a meaningful entity is offered by the group of poems designed acrostically according to the letters of the alphabet. As we have seen in chapter 3, Psalm 119 with its twenty-two octets occupies a special position. Almost all of these have a strictly binary structure, so that the eight verses may be divided into two foursomes (substanzas), four twosomes (= S-strophes), eight poetic lines, and sixteen half-verses. In each octet, every line starts with the same consonant: thus, the first unit has the aleph in front position eight times (in the Semitic languages a specific guttural sound, not a vowel), the second has the beth, etc., until the entire alphabet has been completed. Thus, as Psalm 119 is clearly different from the other alphabetic acrostics, which work per colon, verse, and strophe, we must conclude that each octet in this poem is something more than a strophe but less than the whole poem, so that this monumental text of 22 x 8 verses already constitutes proof that the stanza does exist, as the unit following the strophe in the hierarchy of the text structure. This psalm also illustrates the significant status of the number 8.

The existence of the stanza as a real entity is conclusively confirmed by a second clue, provided by the obvious and convincing
structure above strophe level that many poems exhibit. Two examples may suffice here. Anybody who turns to a translation of Psalm
19 can see—possibly even quicker than the exegetes who consult
the Hebrew text—that this poem consists of three parts. The center, vv. 8–11, is all description and shows us the qualities of God's
word. No action in the narrative sense of the word takes place, and
many sentences are static. For example, v. 9c says "The instruction
of Yahweh is pure," and this middle part of the text concludes with
a climax in v. 11. This is an S-strophe, which lavishes a fourfold
comparison on the truth as represented by "the precepts of
Yahweh":

Ps. 19:11   They are more desirable than gold,
                  than much fine gold;
             and sweeter than honey,
                  than drippings of the comb.

At first glance, we readers may think that this simile is based on two
different sensory experiences, which would be a sensible enough
conclusion. The first two half-verses describe a visual experience;
the second pair appeals to our taste buds. Then, however, we see that
there is a connection between tasting and seeing: the color of honey
is no other than that of gold. Four makes two makes one.

This admiring description is flanked by two framing stanzas, vv.
2–7 and vv. 12–15. The first refers to the fact that the heavens
speak, which is all the more telling because heavenly "speech" does
not need words, and grants a superb metaphor to the sun on its
daily run. Conversely, the stanza on the other side of the normative center focuses on the earth. There we find "your servant," who
hopes to become as pure as the precepts given him by God. The
final verse, v. 15, devotes its text to the words of the poet, and thus
provides an inclusio: the conclusion is now the verbal counterpart
of the beginning, where day and night declare the glory of God—
but mutely. The articulation into strophes and stanzas of the complete poem is as follows:

	S	S	L	//	S	S	S	S	//	S	L
vv.	2–3	4–5b	5c–7		8	9	10	11		12–13	14–15

The strophes occupying the middle consist of bicolic verses. They have a prosodic aspect, which even in translation remains visible: each of the four constitutes a quartet of remarkably short cola.

Another example of the stanza convincingly asserting itself is Psalm 24. Looking at the text we immediately see that we have two halves here, and that vv. 7–10 consists of two times two striking tricola, exalting God as "the King of glory." Thus, these two S-strophes each contain six cola, which in fact makes them just as long as the regular L-strophe, which consists of three two-part verses. They are almost identical and constitute stanza II.

If we now go back in the text and consider vv. 1–6, we have no trouble recognizing the regular L strophe. It has been used twice there: vv. 1–3 are three bicola; vv. 4–6 are the same. The first strophe is characterized by spatial terms, which encompass creation, and ends in a question, which is then answered by each verse in strophe 2. Thus, one trio of verses exactly fits on top of the other, and these L-strophes together fill stanza I. This means that the poem as a whole is precisely balanced:

stanza I	*stanza II*
3 + 3 verses = 6 x 2 cola	2 + 2 verses = 4 x 3 cola

At least, that is the impression the reader might get from a first encounter with the source text. Close observation, however, shows that some liberties have been taken with v. 4. This poetic line is a three-part rather than a two-part verse, consisting of three clauses, each with its own predicate. Consequently, the second strophe contains seven instead of six cola, and most translators have avoided the strong pressure of regularization, or the desperate longing to attain the symmetry of 6 + 6 cola for each half of the poem.

Many other poems also articulate their material into stanzas. The reason is obvious. Imagine a poem of some thirty verses, accommodated in six L-strophes and six S-strophes, in whatever order or combination. This would yield a text consisting of twelve strophic units and filling a complete page. I am convinced that because of their large number such strophes would seem mere fragments, and that we would feel a void in the structure above strophe level. Such a concatenation* of twelve little bits requires a structure of its own—for instance, four groups of three strophes. And this is exactly what happens: look, for instance, at Psalm 35 (which accommodates its thirty-four verses and fourteen strophes in six stanzas) or Psalm 71 (thirty poetic lines, twelve strophes, six stanzas), or Job 6 (exactly the same figures).

Now that we have justified the existence of the stanza, we will have to consider its length. According to the text model presented in chapter 3, the stanza usually consists of two or three strophes, of which we have already seen several examples. Yet, as was the case with the strophe, at either end of the range of "regular" stanzas we also find the extreme dimensions of one, four, and five. Just as the strophe will occasionally consist of only one poetic line, or conversely four or five, we also sometimes find a stanza consisting of just one, or as many as four or five strophes. The circumstances in which this will happen are unpredictable, and such cases can be demonstrated only after an in-depth analysis of a poem. The proof can be based only on individual characteristics of the text in question. I will mention some instances, but due to lack of space I will not be able to provide detailed proof in all cases.

We would expect a stanza coinciding with a single strophe to be truly momentous. And such proves to be the case. The type of composition that may best serve to prove that strophe and stanza occasionally coincide is the concentric design, shaped around an axis of symmetry. As an example I will take the ABCXC'B'A' pattern: a seven-member structure, the middle one of which does not have a counterpart. This usually means that the middle part is unique, or for a different reason constitutes a turning point in the composition or argument. We find such a structure in Psalm 28 (see for the correct division in ch. 12).

A comparable situation occurs in Psalm 10, which together with Psalm 9 forms a single poem: a text in which the oppressed man hopes for God's protection against evildoers. This long text consists exclusively of S-strophes, except for one passage, 10:9–11. This is an L-strophe of seven cola, which stands out sharply from its surroundings. Of the other strophes, there are sixteen containing four cola and two containing five cola. The one strophe of three verses is different for a reason. It occupies the exact center of Psalm 10, and refers to the very nadir in the speaker's fortunes: the moment when he looks death in the face, since the enemy is waiting like a lion in its lair and may jump out at him at any moment.

Thanks to the fact that this L-strophe is at the same time also the middle stanza in Psalm 10, both halves of the poem (the ten strophes of Psalm 9 and the nine strophes of Psalm 10) are balanced, each containing five stanzas. Anybody who values consistency will then start to look for the middle stanza in Psalm 9 and is rewarded: the strophes comprising vv. 10–13 are indeed the counterpart of the center of Psalm 10.

Psalm 48 is to my mind the most beautiful of all the songs about Jerusalem. The poem contains nine strophes, forming pairs of stanzas around the single central strophe:

stanza	I	II	III	IV	V
strophe no.	1–2	3–4	5	6–7	8–9
no. of cola	4 + 4	4 + 4	5	4 + 4	4 + 4
verse nos.	2–3b	5–6	9	10–11b	13–14b
	3c–4	7–8		11c–12	14c–15

Stanza I speaks of Yahweh, "our God" and "God," and shows us Mount Zion and its citadels (in strophes 1 + 2). Stanza V speaks of Zion and its citadels, and of "God," "our God" (in strophes 8 + 9), so that we recognize a frame. Stanza II presents hostile kings, their fleet and their terror; on the other side of strophe 5 there is praise for God's loyalty, and jubilation on the part of the allies in Judah. Now what does the middle say exactly? The diagram tells the reader to go and look in v. 9. This central strophe reveals that Jerusalem is "the city of Yahweh of the armies" (in the time-honored language of the KJV "the Lord God of hosts"), "the city of our God," firmly established by God for all eternity.

Thus the poet has given his design an unwavering center. The proper name "Yahweh" and the indications "God" and "our God" appear again, and construct a straight bridge between the opening and the conclusion of the song. The senses of hearing and seeing (v. 9ab) link the terrified watching of the kings in v. 6 to the exuberant vocal activities of the women in Judah, on the other side of the firm foundation, the central strophe. The whole is defined by prosody, as the 4 + 4 strophes on either side of the center contain four cola each, but the fifth strophe is different: it contains five cola and is the only L-strophe, thanks to the fact that v. 9e (the last colon) is a monocolon. It is this monocolon (RSV: v. 9d) that formulates the point by stating what it is exactly that "we" have seen and heard.

I really cannot imagine that the design of Psalm 49 is a coincidence: it also has nine strophes, with an extra long one as the center. Its verses, 11–13, are flanked by two identical series, i.e., four strophes S-S-S-L: vv. 2–3/4–5/6–7/8–10 come first; vv. 14–15b/15c–16/17–18/19–21 follow after the middle. The two L-strophes at the end of both series each contain six cola, but strophe 5, the only strophe to contain two C-cola, towers above this with its eight cola and consists of exactly seventy syllables; apart from this central strophe, the song is strictly bicolic. This time, the center is a low point of disillusion and exposure—let the readers judge for themselves.

My last example of a stanza coinciding with a strophe is the famous Psalm 51, another composition in nine strophes. Here, the poet goes one step further, in the sense that the middle stanza has the dimensions of an S-strophe! Nevertheless, this unit (vv. 12–13) is clearly recognizable as exceptional, this time because of its exalted contents: the pure heart and the steadfast spirit for which the poet asks God. Here, too, there are two pairs of strophes before and after the center: first vv. 3–5/6a–d/7–8/9–11, then 14–15/16–17/18–19/20–21, which means 5 + 5 verses before the middle and 4 + 4 after. A detail here is that vv. 16–17 are not a tricolon plus bicolon, but the other way round, so that 16c moves to the position of an A-colon. This arrangement of 2 + 3 cola also concludes the poem: strophe 9.

There are also stanzas comprising more than two or three strophes. Take, for instance, the luxurious center of Psalm 19, mentioned earlier in this chapter. This is a quartet of quartets: four strophes of four cola each, all combined into one stanza. And the poem that I will now discuss in separate halves also works with long stanzas: Isaiah 44:24–45:7. I wish to deal with each half of this poem separately, but before we begin to read the first half we must look more closely at the background of this poem.

The Cyrus oracle: Isaiah 44:24–45:7

The New Babylonians—who under Nebuchadnezzar had captured Jerusalem in 586 BCE and had demolished Solomon's temple before deporting the Judaean top/upper class—were the last superpower in the Near East to speak a Semitic language, at least for some time. Less than half a century later they were wiped out. The Persian conqueror Cyrus captured Babylon without bloodshed in 538 BCE and established an empire that was to last for two centuries. Within a short time, he issued an edict permitting the exiles from Judah to return to their native land. The great poet who witnessed this is nowadays usually called Second Isaiah (Deutero-Isaiah, cf. chapter 4), and is the author of the texts in Isaiah 40–55. Many of his verses have a positive tone, as he preaches the consolation of the return to Judah.

What the reader also should know is that the division of the Bible into chapters dates from the Middle Ages and is often wide of the mark. The poem I will discuss here is a good (read: glaring) example, since Isaiah 45:1 is not the start of a new poem or chapter but the middle of a literary unit starting in 44:24 and ending in 45:7. Between its tricolic ends (44:24cde, and the entire final strophe), this oracle of salvation is strictly bicolic, which is one of the reasons why, together with many exegetes before me, I have deleted colon 26d.

The first half of the Cyrus oracle

Isa. 44:24	Thus says Yahweh, your redeemer,
	    who formed you in the womb,
	It is I, Yahweh, who make everything,
	    who alone stretch out the heavens,
	        and unaided spread out the earth;
		strophe 1

	[It is I]	

25	who annuls the omens of diviners,
	    and makes fools of the augurs,
	who turns sages back
	    and makes nonsense of their knowledge;
		strophe 2

26	who confirms the word of his servant
	    and fulfills the prediction of his
	        messengers;	

26c	who says in favor of Jerusalem: "Let it be inhabited,	
e	and I will raise up its ruins,"	
27	who says to the deep: "Be dry, I will dry up your floods;	strophe 3

28	who says to Cyrus: "My shepherd!"
	    he shall fulfill all my purposes,
	He shall say of Jerusalem: "She shall
	    be rebuilt,"
	    and to the temple: "You shall be
	    founded again."	

The poem opens with a variation of the formula used by biblical writers to introduce a speaker. This variant is characteristic of the prophets and is known as the "messenger formula." Its significance is considerable: the speaker who is handing over the floor, i.e., the prophet who speaks only the first verse, uses it to indicate that the prophet is only a messenger from God and that the words that follow have the status of a direct quote. Thus, the words spoken by an oracle do not originate in the brain of a man who proclaims himself to be an ethical genius, and who has just thought them up; they are the exact words of God himself, and any "I" in this text refers to the true author: God. This in any case is what the writer pretends; just like a narrator does, the poet—the true creator of the text—establishes a fictional world, in which the claim "this is

God's word" is valid within the boundaries of the lyrical world evoked.

Deutero-Isaiah is a virtuoso in the field of "extension." In his texts, we find a great many appositions, adjectival adjuncts, and various forms of synonymy. In his very first verse, he cannot resist expanding the messenger formula by two appositions that are still his own words. The "your" betrays his own contribution, and straightaway creates an audience. The exiles are immediately represented in the text thanks to this possessive pronoun, and its singular form suggests that the poet condenses this group to "Jacob"—the individual and at the same time the people whose name will emerge further down in the poem, in 45:4.

The poet qualifies God straightaway as the "Redeemer," i.e., he who frees his people from slavery. The word is reminiscent of the birth of the people of Israel, coinciding with the slave labor in the Nile delta and their departure from the "slave camp of Egypt." The Exodus is the emblem of Yahweh's having redeemed the people he has chosen. By using the word "Redeemer," the poet directly joins in his audience's emotions and the outstanding fact in their present reality: they have been set free by the new power.

Next, Second Isaiah links this salvific fact to another beginning. He confronts his hearers with their own, physical beginnings, and points out that they grew in their mother's womb due to Yahweh's creative power. Finally, after having raised all these issues in one poetic line, he devotes his second line (24cde) to an even more fundamental beginning: God is the creator of the world itself, and straightaway it is stated clearly that nobody else was involved—a fact anticipating the poet's theme, which he will gradually and irresistibly unfold in the second half. Meanwhile, the language has shifted to the first person: God is allowed to present his all-encompassing creation himself, and from the second verse onwards is granted the pronoun "I." Only at the end of v. 24b, then, can we put a colon (:). After it, the first person reigns supreme in this oracle, through to the very last verset.

The first stanza consists of a beautiful, ascending series of 2 + 3 + 4 verses. The devices by which the poet keeps this part of the text together are powerful and striking. To mention four: sentence structure, anaphora*, inclusio, and keywords. Syntax here shapes a spectacular *coup d'état* on God's part, since the entire stanza boils down to: I am the only one who works x, y, and z, for better or for worse. The first strophe refers to "beginning" three times, and thus itself becomes the foundation of the literary structure. The second strophe employs a sort of plus/minus pattern by ridiculing the clergy outside Israel during four cola and then devoting two cola to a positive counterpart: the messengers from God himself, possibly his prophets. Strophe 2 opens a long string of forms that lend an anaphoric character to the verses up to 45:1: in the original Hebrew, the lines start with participles, and the translation reflects this long enumeration of qualities by a series of (adjectival) adjuncts starting with "who."

The whole of 44:24–28 is marked by inclusio. The text apparently started with the cliché of the messenger formula, but things are seldom what they seem. We have seen that the added phrases about redeeming and forming were the poet's own, so that the formula acquires an unusual application. The conclusion of the stanza, however, shows something that is even more important and refers back to the beginning. It draws our attention again, and in even more original fashion, to God's speech. Furthermore, God's words are now directed very specifically at the lived reality of the Judaeans. They, of course, have to cross a great river and trek through the desert for days on end before they reach home, where a depressing sight awaits them: the ruins of the capital and the temple. Consequently, it is positively mind-boggling for Deutero-Isaiah's audience to hear that God is giving the responsibility for the reconstruction to the Persian ruler Cyrus. They cannot believe their ears and demand another explanation. They are getting one; it is the second half of the poem.

Two keywords also contribute to the cohesion of the first stanza. First, there is the verb "to fulfill" (vv. 26b and 28b) linking the second and the third strophe. It creates a parallel between the word of God's servant and the God-pleasing work of Cyrus, a parallel that to a true Judaean, i.e., somebody who sees Yahweh as the only God, must appear unseemly: too much honor for a heathen potentate. This Judaean listener demands a more detailed explanation from the poet, and does not know yet how soon this will come; his ears will burn by the time we get to 45:1. The word "fulfill" is from the Hebrew root *sh-l-m,* which will be somewhat familiar to us, as it is also the basis of the word *shalom* (which will appear in 45:7!) and of the second half of the name *Jeru-shalayim*. The root is used in a wordplay: the double "fulfill" is in league with the name of the capital, used twice, and in this way the poet suggests that the fulfillment of God's will would first of all be the rebuilding of the city and the temple. He reinforces this by another keyword, "raise up," which in v. 26a rhymes with "fulfill" (with which it forms a word pair), and which literally becomes active in the next strophe (26e): raising ruins. We conclude that "fulfill" (make whole = *shalem*) coincides with "put upright," and that in all cases Jerusalem is the beneficiary.

Strophe 3 started all of its four verses with "say." As a literary figure, this "four" may be rephrased as 3 + 1. The form "who says" is part of the long enumeration in which God is all the time the powerful subject of adjectival adjuncts, and is given to God three times: in vv. 26c, 27a, and 28a. Next, however, there is a surprise: the fourth time we come across "saying," in 28c, it is an infinitive, which moreover gets another subject: the mortal Cyrus! Again, the Judaean listener raises an eyebrow: Is it not too much honor for such a heathen ruler to have his command placed on a par with the word of God?

The shock and astonishment of the Judaean audience increase only when they hear the second half of the poem, especially its beginning:

Stanza II

Isa. 45:1	Thus says Yahweh to his Anointed,	
	to Cyrus, whose right hand I have grasped	
	to trample nations before him,	
	ungirding the loins of kings,	strophe 4
	to open doors before him,	
	gates will not stay shut:	

2	I myself will march before you	
	and level the ring-walls,	
	I will shatter doors of bronze	strophe 5
	and cut down iron bars;	
3a	I will give you the treasures of the dark	
b	and the riches from secret hoards.	

3c	So that you may know that I am Yahweh,	
d	who calls you by name, the God of Israel,	
4	for the sake of my servant Jacob	strophe 6
	and Israel, my chosen one,	
	I have called you by your name,	
	I hail you by title, though you did not know me.	

5	I am Yahweh and there is no one else,	
	beside me, there is no God:	
	I engird you, though you did not know me,	strophe 7
6	so that they may know, from the rising of the sun	
	and where it sets, that there is none but me:	
	I am Yahweh and there is no one else,	
7	I, who form light and create darkness,	
	who make happiness and create evil,	
	I, Yahweh, make all these things!	

The poet makes a new start in 45:1 by again using the messenger formula. He surpasses himself this time by using the actual formula (v. 1a) like a rack on which to hang a large number of cola (like as many coats), so that one formula now governs three subclauses. The master of expansion manages to produce one gigantic period, without the separate parts losing any of their clarity and power. The reader is always able to replace each colon by an independent clause.

In v. 1b there is an adjectival clause, followed by a chain of clauses (partly final) describing four actions, all clarifying what it means when God grasps your hand as king: the world is all yours.

To our imaginary Judaean listener, the opening means a great shock: God proclaims the Persian his "anointed." This means that he receives the official and sacred title of "King" from the hands of God himself—the sacred title that until now had been exclusively reserved for the king of Israel! This is outrageous terminology, and a break with such rusty religious convictions as: only we have been chosen by God, the office of king is only sacred when an Israelite holds it, and so on.

Strophes 4 and 5 together make up an image by means of which the poet makes Cyrus's great campaign digestible to his audience and makes it fit his own rhetorical purposes. What are these purposes? He has created strophes 6 and 7 to tell us that. Strophe 4 is still "only" an introduction to God's real message to Cyrus, and although the sentence goes on and on we finally reach a colon (:) after v. 1f. Not until strophe 5 do we hear God speak in the first person to Cyrus personally. This is an escalation compared with strophe 3, when God talked to his messenger (the prophet himself) *about* Cyrus.

When you entered a battlefield in antiquity, you hoisted up your long tunic with your belt in order to be able to move and fight freely. The loins that in 45:1d are "ungirded" indicate that "the enemy"—the kings confronted with the fervor of the conqueror Cyrus—has been overpowered and can no longer offer any resistance. The events that in actual time preceded this ungirding are in the text presented later, when God reveals to Cyrus the divine reality behind the scenes of politics and world history. In v. 5c the exact opposite, "engirding," is used as a favorable statement about Cyrus: God himself puts his belt on him. We as readers can, of course, reconstruct that this happened at the start of the vast campaign in which Cyrus established the Persian empire.

After five strophes of preparation, already glittering with poetic brilliance, the point is finally presented in strophes 6–7. This is a revelation offered by God himself, and meant for Cyrus personally. God explains to the king that his power and victories—however vast and numerous they are—are nevertheless mere counters in a far greater plan, and that God's handling of world history has been motivated by his connection with that tiny people from Palestine, almost beneath the conqueror's notice. Cyrus hears that he is only a pawn on the chessboard of the only true God. His existence only serves God's care for "Jacob." To this end, he is called "by his name"—an expression that means that God created him and gave him his identity.

The actual message of the Cyrus oracle is presented by strophes 6–7, and the keyword there is "knowing" in both senses of the word. Small wonder that this verb is placed strategically and that its semantic field acquires weight and structure by a striking contrast:

v. 3c	v. 4d
so that you may know	you did not know me
that I am Yahweh	

v. 5c	v. 6a
you did not know me	so that they may know
	that I am Yahweh

The structure is chiastic. We notice oppositions of plus/minus, of past and present, and of Cyrus and his subjects—the "they" in v. 6a may even be so broad as to mean "humankind." These four sentences about knowing/not knowing have been very cleverly positioned. Two of them provide a frame for strophe 6, firmly demarcating this unit; the other two adjoin each other in strophe 7 and expand the target of God's revelation, the group around Cyrus, to include the full extent of the creation: from East to West, the merism says. Thus, the first pair has been driven apart to the edges of its strophe, whereas the members of the second pair have been pulled together by an opposing, centripetal force, and as a yes/no duo almost clash: v. 5c and v. 6a touch each other on the linear axis, being adjacent cola, or on the temporal scale.

The inclusio of strophe 6, incidentally, includes more elements: the aspect of knowledge is twice accompanied by "calling you by name." As a result, cola 3cd and cola 4cd form an AB-B'A' pattern, and this chiasm has become the demarcation and the strong frame for the strophe. The question that remains is what is inside the frame; answer: the heart of this unit. These are cola 4ab and, as the spearhead of the message, are far more important than their frame. Cyrus is here told who, according to the speaker, are the center of history: the chosen people. The secret of the king's history lesson is the two proper names constituting the hard core of the strophe. Thus, "Cyrus, my shepherd" (44:28a) is surpassed by "Israel, my chosen one" (45:4b).

The concluding verses form a rare 3 x 3 design: this massive, fully tricolic L-strophe is the climax of the message to Cyrus. It has just been explained to him that his political lot was determined by the God of Israel, but this having been established, the speaker focuses his words on . . . himself. The zenith of the revelation is a self-revelation. This seventh strophe has significant expressions in common with the first, so that a border for the poem as a whole has been created. The message conveyed by this inclusion might be summarized in (New Testament) Greek as: God is the alpha and the omega of history. In Hebrew, however, this is expressed by means of other polarities: from East to West; light and dark, as obvious reminiscences of Genesis 1; good and evil, as having been equally created by God. In v. 7b, *shalom* (peace, prosperity) and "evil" are opposed: I assume that for the prophet's audience they first and foremost refer, respectively, to the liberation and the new future in the promised land, and to war and exile, the two-generation period that began with the destruction of Jerusalem and which now, thank God, is over.

Let us look back once more and trace the main outline of the composition. The very first verse, the citation formula in 24ab, proves an advance on the messenger formula in 45:1, which has been expanded to no fewer than six cola; it is truly an advance, as the actual speech to Cyrus does not start until 45:2. Stanza I with its three strophes is a long run-up, in which the speaker addresses the Israelites with an enumeration of his own qualities, perfections that make up the foundation and the springboard for his revelation to Cyrus. The second half starts off by changing the addressee, and after the colon (:) that ended strophe 4 uses the first person throughout. The conclusion, then, of my exploration is that this seven-strophe poem exhibits a balanced construction of 3 + 1 + 3 units. The L-strophe 45:1 is the pivot around which the two threesomes revolve:

strophes 1–3	address Israel	about "Cyrus, my shepherd"
strophes 5–7	address Cyrus	about "Jacob, my servant"

The different addressees and different subject matter turn out to form an extensive chiasm, a design that at this level serves as a neat expression of mutual commitment.

An anti-hymn on Wisdom: Job 28

There is one stanza in the entire collection of Psalms that contains as many as five strophes: the awesome theophany of Psalm 18 (as we have seen in chapter 3). The tight ABXB'A' design of strophes 4–8 (vv. 8–16) proves that they really constituted a single textual unit one level higher up. The poet who wrote the book of Job sticks to the text model, so that his stanzas almost always contain either two or three strophes. Still, in his poetry there is also one poem containing a stanza of five strophes. This is the song about Wisdom—an anti-hymn rather than a hymn—which takes up chapter 28 and occupies a central position in Job's very long, last speech in the discussion with his three friends (Job 26–31, five poems). Here, Job offers a razor-sharp and disillusioning view of the relations between God, man, and the world—a structure of separate circuits, as we shall see.

The poem consists of three parts, since verses 12 and 20, which are almost identical, serve as refrains and by their positions separate the stanzas. They raise an interesting question for us: Do they introduce parts II and III, or do they conclude parts I and II? This is the subject of considerable bickering among scholars. The first stanza, the most colorful picture of mining the Bible has to offer, is as follows:

Stanza I: Job 28:1–11

verse		strophe
1	There is a mine where silver comes to light,	1
	and a place where gold is refined;	
2	iron is taken out of the earth,	
	and copper melted from rock.	

3   Man sets bounds for darkness,   2
          to every limit he probes
             to rocks in deepest darkness.
4   Man opens up a shaft far from where people live,
          forgotten by travelers they dangle,
             far from the inhabited world they hang.

5   The earth—from her, bread appears,   3
          below her, there is churning as of fire.
6   Its rocks are a source of sapphires,
          and there is gold dust.

7   The path that leads to it—no bird of prey knows it,   4
          the vulture's eye does not see it.
8   The proud beasts have not reached it,
          and the lion has not crossed it.

9   Man sets his hand against the flinty rock,   5
          and overturns mountains by the roots.
10   He carves out channels through rock,
          and his eye beholds every precious thing.
11   He dams up the sources of the streams,
          and brings what is hidden to light.

Let me begin my discussion by pointing out a peculiarity of the original text. In vv. 1b, 3–4b, and 9–11 the Hebrew has only a verbal predicate, in the third-person masculine singular, by which I mean that the subject has not been indicated by a word of its own; consequently, those lines do not contain the word "man" which has been used here in the translation. There are good reasons for this.

In the RSV or JPS translations, the verses are given without breaks in the form of white space, so that our first task is to bring some order to this continuous chain: an articulation in strophes. As is often the case, here, too, the distribution of characters is a good instrument to clear up matters. We see straightaway that vv. 7–8 have been reserved for the animals, neatly divided between a few cola for the birds and a few cola for the beasts of prey on the ground. Furthermore, their cola become a close-knit quartet by the power of the repeated negation.

Well, surely the remaining verses are about humankind? Yes and
no. Strophe 1 is strictly concerned with precious metals and gem-
stones, and deals with their location and the action (melting) by
which they are mined from ore. In the Hebrew text there is no
mention of "man," even though he does the searching and melting. All verbs are in the singular. Strophe 2 stands out straightaway
by being the only tricolic unit, and after four cola presents the first
plural forms. Nevertheless, in the original text "man" is still not
mentioned explicitly as the subject. At the end of the strophe we
do hear about civilization/the inhabitants of the world, but only
because it is/they are so far away . . . Society is definitely not a witness to the incessant toil below the ground. We will leave the question why humankind is not allowed any room in the Hebrew for
a moment—it might be a deliberate ellipsis. Furthermore, strophe
2 avoids all mention of metal or gems, and this aspect also contributes to the correct demarcation of the strophes.

Verse 3 turns on the contrast between darkness and ceaseless
searching; verse 4 contains a clever transformation of the darkness
by mentioning oblivion three times. Man seems to be an indefati-
gable researcher who is always successful. Man's investigations
(strophe 2) are contrasted with the inability to see on the part of
the animals (strophe 4). There is no place in this poem for the Dar-
winist view that man is little more than a glorified monkey.

In strophe 3, nature is firmly taken in hand by culture, if man's
ambitious bustle may be called that. This goes so far that v. 5a skips
a few steps. Bread appears from the earth, but there is no mention
of a farmer, crop, mill, or baker. These omissions may have been
intended to suggest the hot eagerness, the ambition and the rush
of man as an engineer. Verses 5 and 6 balance each other as they
take as their subjects the earth and its coveted minerals, respectively. This makes them the counterpart of strophe 1.

Passing over the animals, we encounter the first L-strophe in vv.
9–11. Its length already suggests that this is the climax of the first
part. Its keywords are "eye" and "light," "precious" and "bringing
up." Strophes 1 and 3 have also mentioned "bringing to light,"
which is the purpose of the searching and churning: the minerals
that are found have a high market value. Meanwhile, the poet per-
sists in his avoidance tactics; even now, the original text here does

not contain a word that exactly pinpoints the subject responsible for the hacking and rooting around. Our suspicions of an ellipsis are becoming stronger.

Strophes 1–5 all have a clear-cut direction: their subject matter has been distributed very precisely, and they are distinguished from each other by contrasts. The darkness deep inside the earth and the sharp gaze of the animals (which does not detect the valuables being sought at all) are contrasted with the effective searching and discovering on the part of man. The stanza acquires its cohesion from a tight ABA'B'A" pattern ordering the strophes. The key-word "come/bring to light" is a significant factor in the correspondence A-A'-A." No wonder that it also provides a frame, since it occurs in the first and last lines.

Having dug up all this gold and silver, we now take it to market to see whether it will buy us some wisdom. Money buys everything, does it not?

Stanza II: Job 28:12–19

verse		strophe
12	But where can wisdom be found,	6
	and where is the source of understanding?	
13	No man can set a value on it,	
	it cannot be found in the land of the living.	
14	The deep says: "It is not in me";	
	and the sea says: "I do not have it."	
15	It cannot be bartered for pure gold,	7
	and silver cannot be measured out as its price.	
16	the finest gold from Ophir cannot be weighed against it,	
	nor precious onyx, nor sapphire.	
17	Gold or glass cannot match its value,	
	nor vessels of refined gold be exchanged for it.	
18	Coral and crystal cannot be mentioned with it,	8
	but a flicker of wisdom is better than rubies.	
19	Topaz from Nubia cannot match its value,	
	pure gold cannot be weighed against it.	

Repetition and variation make the beginning of this stanza run parallel to that of the first stanza. Again, attention is given to sources, and again there is reference to a precious "mineral"—an interesting transition to figurative speech. The language, however, now takes the form of a question (v. 12), which may indicate that the vast self-confidence of the clever researchers has its limits after all.

I do not need to explain the theme of this stanza: the punters have come down to earth with a shock, in spite of all the gold and silver they have brought. Strophes 7 and 8 are closely linked because of their economic terminology, and because here in particular the poet employs such richly varied vocabulary. Strophe 6 belongs here for two reasons: the "it" that appears in verse after verse in vv. 15–19 always refers back to "wisdom," so that strophe 6 carries an important antecedent governing the entire stanza. The second link is provided by a keyword: the word "value," not to mention the various synonyms for it, occurs in v. 13a, but also in vv. 17a and 19a.

Strophe 6 offers surprises in all of its three verses. After the rhetorical question that introduces a new character, Wisdom, "man" finally appears in the Hebrew text in v. 13. The singular also indicates the collective: we are talking about the whole of mankind. The cola have been arranged in a chiastic design: the people circle around Wisdom as flies around honey. The "A, what's more, B" rule of thumb is also active here. In the Hebrew text, top and bottom of the verse contain masculine forms; in the middle are two feminine singulars. The omission of "man" in the first stanza of the original text proves to have been no coincidence. This ellipsis stops in stanza II, and the gap is filled in at the moment when the many negations threaten to annihilate "man."

Finally, verse 14 is very dynamic by having its half-verses filled with 2 + 2 clauses that introduce yet more new characters, and even give them the floor. They are allowed in their embedded speech to tell us of their impotence. A nice touch of irony, as they consider themselves to be impressive personalities: they are the mythical characters of Tehom (primeval flood) and Yam (sea), figures which for centuries have had divine status in Canaan.

The entire stanza is determined by an omnipresent "no." The negation occurs 4 + 7 + 3 times in these three strophes (eleven times in the original Hebrew). Man, who sought and found in the heart of the mountain, or deep under ground, is rendered power-less in the marketplace and is not making much progress in his quest for wisdom. Can nothing be done?

Stanza III: Job 28:20–28

verse		strophe
20	But wisdom—from where does it come,	9
	and where is the source of understanding?	
21	It is hidden from the eyes of all living,	
	concealed from the fowl of heaven.	
22	Corruption and death say:	
	"We only have a report of it."	
23	God understands the way to it,	10
	and it is he who knows its source.	
24	For he sees to the end of the earth,	
	observes all that is beneath the heavens	
25	while he fixes the power of the wind,	
	and sets the measure of the waters.	
26	When he made a rule for the rain	11
	and a course for the thunderstorms,	
27	then he saw it and gauged it,	
	he put it in its place and probed it.	
	(But about man, he said:)	
28	See, fear of the Lord—that is wisdom,	
	and to shun evil is understanding.	

Strophe 9 is an exact parallel of strophe 6. Not only does v. 20 say the same as v. 12, but "all living" and the adjective "hidden" in v. 21 are the counterparts to "the land of the living" and the nega-tions in v. 13. Furthermore, v. 22 is a clever adaptation of v. 14. There, we had an AB // AB pattern neatly distributing two speak-ers and their speeches over two half-verses; here we have an AA + BB. Again, these are two prestigious mythical characters, and they, too, have to admit to having no firsthand knowledge.

The poet cleverly exploits the difference between hearing and seeing; these senses are mentioned here and in the conclusion drawn by the hero at the end of the book (42:5), and indicate the contrast between really knowing something oneself, and the unreliability and vagueness of rumors. In the Hebrew original, v. 22b literally says: "with our ears we have heard a rumor about it." Thus, these ears contrast with the eyes of v. 21. The birds of v. 21 remind us of their sharp gaze and the negation accompanying it in v. 7, and "heaven" (the sky that is their element) has now become a complement of "the land" in v. 13b.

Strophes 10 and 11 also have three lines each. For the third time, the middle lines (vv. 24 and 27) are about "seeing," but this time in a positive sense. This is because a new character has been introduced: the only one who is really able to see clearly, and gauge correctly, in heaven and on earth—as it was put so beautifully in Psalm 113 (see chapter 2). And there is always an "it," in v. 23 still referring to Wisdom. Just as vv. 12 and 20 did, this line speaks of the places where Wisdom is found, and also has the synonym "understanding" (this time as a verb). So . . . Wisdom has finally been found, and was even found at the beginning of time, strophe 11 adds. But it is accessible to only one person, God.

With their positive statements, the verses of the last two strophes put an end to the negations that have dominated the field since v. 12. These six verses have been arranged in an ABC–C'B'A' pattern. The wisdom and understanding that in v. 28 are finally described in positive terms are chiastically the mirror image of v. 23ab, and thus create the correspondence A–A'. The synonymy of vv. 24 and 27 is crystal clear: correspondence B–B'. The same holds for the C–C' members in 25–26, where the Creator is organizing the weather. Verse 27 states of God that he measures and gauges, and truly probes the object; he fathoms wisdom. A delicate choice of words, as in strophe 2 we also read about deep probing—but what was sought so eagerly has now amply surpassed, if made downright shameful.

The ending is rather special. To the question where man may now acquire full wisdom, the answer still turns out to be: nowhere. He will have to be content with a simple maxim, which nevertheless carries considerable weight; it is the word of God, who in v. 28 is introduced as a speaking character by the poet, and thus takes his place after Death and the Primeval Flood (a humorous change, again in the final verse of a strophe!). The parallelism of the half-verses ensures that the terms define each other. What is "the fear of the Lord," or, to put it in less old-fashioned terms, "respect for Yahweh"? The answer is practical: refrain from doing evil. Practicing everyday ethics is difficult enough, and it is enough.

Scholars seem unable to agree on whether the refrain verses 12 and 20 begin or conclude stanzas. The application of a clear and unencumbered poetics, however, quickly solves this problem. There are at least five reasons why these two verses should be regarded as opening new stanzas:

- The text model indicates that it is highly unlikely that v. 12 belongs in the fifth strophe, as this unit would then have four poetic lines, which is usually too many.
- Verses 1–11 are exclusively occupied with mining; it is improbable that the poet would have awkwardly slipped in an essentially different entity at the end.
- If placed at the end of stanza I, the rhetorical question of v. 12 would lack all rhyme or reason.
- The word "wisdom" in v. 12 is the antecedent of a long chain of the pronoun "it." If we placed v. 12 in stanza I, the constant referring back to this antecedent (not only the beginning of the chain, but also of a new level of argument and reflection) would cross the stanza boundary, which is unattractive.
- The one factor that supplies the decisive counter-argument comes from structural analysis. Strophes 6 and 9, which both begin with a question about the source of wisdom, are L-strophes whose trios of poetic lines have been precisely aligned with the trios at the end, constituting the L-strophes 10 and 11; in other words, with that part of the text which, after many negations, speaks favorably of God as an alternative, and provides the solution to the problem.

Job has here presented a sound and well-constructed argument. This becomes evident when I give the various factors their proper places in a diagram:

	sharp eyesight	/	knowledge	/	wisdom
animals	yes		no		no
people	yes		yes		no
God	yes		yes		yes

It would seem that the poet is something of a systematic philosopher. Not only has he analyzed this system of almost completely separate circuits, but he also has managed to give it an effective poetic shape by employing three stanzas that cover the labels for both the columns and the rows of the diagram.

In the discussions of stanzas from Deutero-Isaiah and Job, I have tried to demonstrate the importance of demarcating these higher textual units, and the dangers of marking the wrong boundaries. These contours may be essential to the argument, and may thus be crucial to a correct and well-founded understanding on the part of the reader.

7

The poem as a whole

We have looked at the smaller textual units—cola and verses—and have examined the larger entities of strophe and stanza. We now therefore find ourselves on the threshold of the poem as a whole. The questions that now arise, from the perspective of the maker of the poem, are: What is it that makes a text into a whole, and how does the poet control this? The questions that must be answered from the perspective of the reader are: How do we recognize a whole? And which rules govern our interaction with it?

In the twentieth century a growing number of novelists, playwrights, and poets no longer have felt any need to create texts with a definite, finished form. They consider all rounding-off artificial or too slick, no longer realistic, or too dull. Consequently, it has become a normal thing for us, when watching a play or film on television or in the theater, to ask our companions whether this story has "an open ending."

Abandoning or undermining "finished" forms is still a recent phenomenon. It does not occur in the larger part of the tradition—the literary canon—and is even completely foreign to texts from antiquity. A text was thought to deserve what in literary theory is called *closure* (French *clôture*). The question that will exercise us in this chapter is how closure is employed in the biblical poem, i.e., how the text has become a well-rounded whole. I will mention the most important devices at the disposal of the Hebrew poets and will illustrate them with examples—without, however, trying to provide an exhaustive overview. I think it will be enough to make the readers aware of the issue, so that they can find their own way and are alerted to the delicate function of first and last lines when perusing a poem as a separate entity.

The beginning and end of a text indeed require a delicate

touch. We realize this with a shock the moment we ourselves, armed with a pen and a blank sheet of paper, sit down to write a story or poem. The Hebrew poet has trodden this path before us, and has lavished a lot of attention on the boundaries of the whole.

Psalm 8: beginning and end are identical

The most far-reaching option for marking off an entity is to end it in exactly the same way as it started. This phenomenon is rare in the Bible; I myself know of one clear example, Psalm 8. This is a song consisting of ten two-part verses, which opens and closes with one line of (in the original language) 2 + 6 words that already reveal much of the tone and direction of the whole: "O Yahweh, our Lord, / how majestic is your name throughout the earth!" The center of the poem is a classic text of biblical anthropology:

Ps. 8:5	What is man that you have been mindful of him,
	mortal man that you have taken note of him?
6	Yet, you have made him little less than divine
	and adorned him with honor and glory.

These are positive words, which might be a bit too much of a good thing for some modern readers; they may prefer to listen to the gloomier tones of Psalm 144:3–4, where we read:

Ps. 144:3–4	Yahweh, what is man that you should care about him,
	mortal man, that you should think of him?
	Man is like a breath,
	his days are like a passing shadow.

This seems the reverse side of the coin, and we may also include Job 7:17–18 in this series. Returning to Psalm 8, we see that the poem is marked by a repeated verse, which is a refrain and at the same time an envelope, as it provides an inclusio. The sequel to v. 2 has for centuries caused confusion, and in the JPS version still reads:

Ps. 8:2c	You who have covered the heavens with your splendor.
3	From the mouths of infants and sucklings
	You have founded strength, on account of your foes,
	to put an end to enemy and avenger.

Founding strength from the mouths of infants? This utter non-sense, which has driven many a churchgoer to despair, is simply the result of inadequate analysis. Translators have not paid sufficient attention to parallelismus membrorum and the details which constitute this parallelism. Competent readers notice that

> (a) In vv. 2c and 3b there are two abstract nouns (splendor, strength) that are positive and honor God. In the original Hebrew both consist of only one syllable, with the same long vowel -o-, a phonetic aspect which suggests a connection.
> (b) There is an effective opposition between "mouth" and "silence" (as NIV has in 3c).
> (c) "Infants and sucklings" apparently form a word pair within the colon, and are probably meant to be the opposite of the other word pair "enemy and avenger" (also intra colon).
> (d) The three categories of enemies in v. 3bc are eliminated by the two actions of God's (founding, silencing).

The word "covered" in v. 2c is no more than a translator's educated guess. The Hebrew scholar need only change one vowel sign of this word for all the pieces to fall into place—a charge that is supported also by the arguments under (a), (b), (c), and (d):

Ps. 8:2	O Yahweh, our Lord,
	how majestic is your name throughout the earth!
	Your glory is chanted above the heavens
3a	by the mouths of infants and sucklings;
b	You have founded strength, on account of your foes,
c	to silence enemy and avenger.

From the traditional verse numbering, especially the position of 3a, we conclude that already the rabbis were confused; they linked the adjunct in v. 3a to its sequel, instead of to the preceding v. 2c. The correct rendering—already found in the RSV, albeit with a different wording and an unfortunate division into cola—shows that vv. 2c + 3a form a bicolon continuing the positive tone of the refrain 2ab, and that the bicolon 3bc is an antithetical sequel. The treatment of "narrated" time is interesting: chanting God's majesty is, of course, only possible after, and as long as, the opposition is kept under control. [1]

Psalm 8 is a composition of four S-strophes inside the envelope. I cannot resist showing its numerical perfection by giving a diagram of the exact dimensions of the original (Hebrew) text:

strophe no.	1	2	3	4	5	6
verse nos.	2ab	2c–3c	4–5	6–7	8–9	10
size	S–	S	S	S	S	S–
cola	2	4	4	4	4	2
syllables	15	39	41	40	30	15

The envelope contains 15 + 15 = 30 syllables, exactly the same number as strophe 5. Strophes 2-3-4 clearly have the round figure 40 as their norm. The poem has 180 syllables in all, and if we divide this by 20, the total number of cola, we obtain an exact 9 as the average number of syllables per colon. This 9 is the normative figure that at the same time is the ceiling of the Psalter: there are a dozen psalms scoring this exact 9, and none with an average exceeding it.

Other closure devices

Poets can also wrap up their work by using a frame that offers a slight variation on the idea of identical beginning and end: Psalm 103 starts with a strophe that says "Bless my soul, Yahweh" in two consecutive A-cola. The final strophe, vv. 20–22, addresses the same exhortation, three of them this time, to the inhabitants of heaven, and in v. 22c concludes by exactly copying v. 2a.

Psalm 18, the long Song of Thanksgiving by the firmly established King David, starts with one long strophe of praise; David calls God "my fortress, my shield," and uses as many as eight or nine nouns as appositions to the vocative "O Yahweh" in the awesome catalogue in vv. 2b–3c. The poem ends with two units thanking God, the L-strophe vv. 47–49 and the S-strophe vv. 50–51. By repeating some words from the first verse, "my Rock, God of my deliverance," the poet establishes the connection with the beginning. In this way, the lengthy poem is kept together by a strong hymnic frame.

Another device to provide cohesion for the verses of a poem is the use of refrains. In David's lament (discussed in chapter 1), the threefold complaint "how have the mighty fallen!" is distributed in a special way. It appears in the very first verse—as a B-colon and refrain clause—and later—as an A-colon—concludes the two strophes in the final stanza that are devoted to King Saul and to Jonathan, respectively: 2 Samuel 1:19b, 25a, and 27a.

The one poem made up by Psalms 42 and 43 does not have one refrain, as most commentaries would have it, but three: two short one-colon refrains, which both occur twice, and one long refrain, which takes up an entire strophe and occurs three times. The opening of the poem is familiar:

Ps. 42:2   Like a hind crying for water,
           my soul cries for you, O God;
      3   My soul thirsts for God,
           the living God;
        when will I come
           and behold the face of God?

The poet's situation is miserable, "oppressed by the enemy," as 42:10d and 43:2d make clear—this phrase is one of the two short refrains. The other refrain is in 42:4cd and 11cd; it illustrates his pain and even hands the microphone to his adversaries: "they always taunt me with: where is your God?"—a speech full of contempt.

The long refrain occupies strophes 4, 9, and 12 (for the division of the poem into twelve strophes, see the list in chapter 12 of this book). It offers us a glimpse of the soul that thirsts:

        Why so downcast, my soul,
           and why disquieted within me?
        Have hope in God, for I will yet praise Him,
           my ever-present Help, my God!

This pair of bicola, together an S-strophe, appears in Psalm 42:6 and 12, and 43:5.

Other psalms with refrains are 46, 49, 56, 57, 67, and 99. This form of repetition gives the poem a very clear articulation and usually comes at the end of a stanza. Psalm 59 has two refrains, each of which is used twice: v. 7 = 15 and v. 10 = 18.

Closure is first of all established on the edges of the poem: the first and last verses. If these have not been linked by repetition (i.e., inclusio), they usually each have a striking form of their own. Consider, for instance, the first boundary post: the opening lines of the poem. In Job and Proverbs, or in the oracles spoken by Balaam to the King of Moab, in Genesis 49 (Jacob's blessing of his sons), and Deuteronomy 32 (Moses' Song close to the Jordan), the poet begins with some form of recognizable opening. This is often an exhortation to listen. The exhortation is addressed either directly to his audience (as in the case of Balaam and Jacob) or to the halves of the cosmos, which are called as witnesses; we saw this at the beginning of Isaiah and in Deuteronomy 32.

The participants in the debate in the book of Job often use the first lines of their poems (chapters) to dismiss the previous speaker with a critical or caustic remark, before they start on their own themes. In the book of Psalms, many poems start with an imperative addressed to God, asking Him either to listen to a complaint, or to get going straightaway and relieve misery: intervention is urgently requested ("Deliver me, O Yahweh!"). Other songs start with a wish. The poet informs us that he wants to sing a new song, or says "I am going to sing of Yahweh," or exhorts his audience to join in a hymn of praise; we find this in, for instance, Exodus 15 and Psalms 89, 92, 95–100.

The second boundary post is the conclusion of the poem; another moment that requires extra care. The poet now has different tools to finish off his work. As is only to be expected, the conclusion is prominent if it is also the climax. The macabre Psalm 88 (see chapter 5), about death as the realm of freedom now that God has made the speaker's actual existence a prison, ended in an L-strophe which doubled the hostile forces from the middle of the poem: anger, the waters of chaos, total withdrawal of loved ones and friends. The one strophe (six cola) that provided the hymnic opening for Psalm 18 is at the end surpassed by its counterpart, a stanza of two strophes and twelve cola.

If the ending is not the climax, it may be a supplication; this is the case in Psalms 19 and 20. It may be an inference, as for instance in Ps. 1:6 and especially in chapters from Wisdom literature (Proverbs and Job). It may be an answer to a question which the poet asked earlier in the poem (see Psalm 15 and compare Psalm 24, on account of vv. 3–4). It may be a lament which seemed utterly fruitless until shortly before the end (Psalms 6, 17, 59, 73), or a last, urgent appeal (Psalms 38, 39, 80, 82). The number of different possibilities is endless, and I invite the reader to be always on the lookout for, and appreciative of, new forms of closure.

Give them their deserts: Psalm 28

All right, so poets may place a clear frame around their work, but that does not mean they are then at liberty to make a mess of what is inside it—in that case, the poem would have to be consigned to the waste bin after all. To put it in positive terms: poets ensure maximum impact and cohesion for their poem if they order their material in a tight structure from a to z, or perhaps from alpha to omega. A poet may decide to write seven strophes in an ABC X CBA design. This is what happens in Psalm 28; I have given vv. 5, 7, and 9 their proper division into cola:

Psalm 28

1a	To you I call, Yahweh, my rock;	strophe 1
b	do not turn away from me,	
c	lest I, if you hold aloof from me,	
d	be like those gone down into the Pit.	
2a	Hear my loud pleas,	strophe 2
b	when I cry out to you for help,	
c	and lift my hands	
d	toward your inner sanctuary.	
3a	Do not drag me off with the wicked,	strophe 3
b	nor with the evildoers,	
c	who profess goodwill toward their fellows,	
d	while malice is in their heart.	
4a	Pay them according to their deeds	strophe 4
b	and their malicious acts;	
c	pay them according to their handiwork,	
d	give them their deserts.	
5a	Because they do not consider	strophe 5
b	the deeds of Yahweh	
c	or the works of his hands,	
d	He will tear them down, not rebuild them.	
6a	Blessed is Yahweh,	strophe 6
b	for he listens to my loud pleas.	
7a	Yahweh is my strength and my shield;	
b	my heart trusts in him.	
c	I was helped, and my heart exulted	
d	and I glorify him with my song.	
8a	Yahweh is their strength,	strophe 7
b	He is a stronghold of deliverance for his anointed.	
9a	Deliver your people	
b	and bless your inheritance,	
c	tend them and sustain them forever.	

The four cola of strophe 4 are the center; their separate messages are highly synonymous. Together they constitute a request for retribution—those who hatch mischief should catch it. This textual unit is the X around which the entire composition revolves. Strophes 3 and 5 correspond as C and C', since they both show the misbehavior of the adversaries. Strophes 2 and 6 make up the pair B-B' thanks to an extensive repetition, which straightaway catches the eye: they both contain the words "listen to the voice of my pleas" (as the Hebrew text literally says). At the same time this shows their complementariness, and the progress between them: they represent prayer and the answer to it. The "outside" pair of strophes reflects the same relationship of prayer and answer, as the word "my rock" is at the end explained as "the stronghold of my deliverance." The strophes are grouped into stanzas as 2 + 3 + 2 units: stanza I is prayer (vv. 1–2); stanza II stands out because of its subject, being concerned with the enemies (vv. 3–5); and stanza III brings deliverance and the option to sing a hymn of praise (vv. 6–8). Thus, Psalm 28 as a whole is a "ring" composition. Its concentric symmetry automatically ensures an optimum closure. I have marked the three parts by extra blank lines.

An honorable poet: Psalm 26

Psalm 26 also has an obvious center. This is the only L-strophe in the poem, and it is about an altar that lends direction to love and praise—a positive core this time.

Psalm 26

1a	Vindicate me, Yahweh,	strophe 1
b	for I have walked without blame;	
c	in Yahweh I have trusted	
d	without faltering.	
2a	Probe me, Yahweh, and try me,	strophe 2
b	test my kidneys and heart.	
3a	For I am aware of your goodness	
b	and I walk in your truth.	
4a	I do not consort with scoundrels,	strophe 3
b	or mix with hypocrites;	
5a	I detest the company of evil men,	
b	and do not consort with the wicked.	
6a	I wash my hands in innocence	strophe 4
b	and walk around your altar, Yahweh,	
7a	raising my voice in thanksgiving,	
b	and telling all your wonders.	
8a	Yahweh, I love your temple abode,	
b	the dwelling-place of your glory.	
9a	Do not reckon my soul among the sinners,	strophe 5
b	or my life among those who shed blood,	
10a	who have crimes at their fingertips,	
b	and whose right hand is full of bribes.	
11a	But I walk without blame—	strophe 6
b	redeem me and have mercy on me.	
12a	My foot is on level ground—	
b	in assemblies I will praise Yahweh.	

The center is surrounded by the wicked and criminal characters occupying strophes 3 and 5. Around these, however, strophes 1, 2, and 6 make up a positive series A-A'-A." The first strophe is a kind of upbeat; the rest follows a concentric pattern, so that the whole is arranged as an AA'BXB'A" design. The appropriateness of the A labels may be demonstrated by, among other things, the following series of phrases from the same semantic field: "walk" versus "faltering" in strophe 1, "I walk" in strophe 2, and "my foot on level ground" in strophe 6. These are supported by a characteristic of the speaker: his integrity. The inclusion provided by 1b and 11a is obvious.

The silence between storms in Psalm 18

I remarked earlier that a poem acquires a tight structure when the material between the opening and the conclusion is also organized convincingly. This may be demonstrated in a nutshell by mapping out Psalm 18. The list in Chapter 12 of this book shows that this long Song of Thanksgiving is articulated into twenty-four strophes. It consists of 111 cola, which may be rephrased as five times 22 plus one. The surplus colon reinforces the center:

Psalm 18

stanza	content	no. of strophes and cola	
introductory hymn		1 strophe	6 cola
Ia	distress	2 strophes	8 cola
II	theophany = God at WAR	5 strophes	22 cola
Ib	release	2 strophes	8 cola
III and IV	center = CLEANNESS	2 + 3 strophes	23 cola
V and VI	God supports David = David at WAR	2 + 3 + 2 strophes	32 cola
VII	final praise and thanks	2 strophes	12 cola

With its twenty-two cola, the theophany establishes the measure. If we count its immediate surroundings, i.e., the opening strophe plus stanza Iab, we find exactly the same figure: 6 + 8 + 8 = 22 cola. The middle of the poem provides reflection in moral/ religious terms; it offers a focus for meditation. The center of this center is strophe 13, vv. 26–27, which speaks of the symmetry of retribution in both a good and an evil sense. On the other side of the middle we find stanzas V–VII with 32 + 12 = 44 cola, which is the duplicate of the norm figure 22. On either side of the center there are two panels about war, full of noise and battle. First, God personally goes to war, descending from heaven in order to rescue David (stanzas I + II), and after that the rescued king finishes off his enemies in stanzas V–VI.

The promise of a lasting dynasty: Psalm 132

In 2 Samuel 7 we read that the established king David wants to build a temple (Hebrew *bayit*, lit. "house") for God. Through the prophet Nathan God lets David know that he has never asked for a temple and can manage perfectly well without. Next, we get to the real point: God reverses the roles and promises David that he will give him a house (*bayit* = dynasty), and grant great prestige to the city on Mount Zion. David's son then will be allowed to build that temple. This promise of an enduring dynasty is as it were the charter of Zionism *avant la lettre*. The prose text has a counterpart in poetry: Psalm 132.

The song divides into two halves, and almost all Old Testament scholars are of the opinion that it consists of 10 + 10 verses. If this were true, it would yield a pleasing balance, and vv. 1 and 10 would provide the frame for the first half. In the following analysis, however, I will argue that, on the contrary, we have here a case of asymmetry. By means of blank lines I have already divided the twenty verses and forty cola into nine strophes. The unequal halves have two stanzas each. The first half is as follows:

verse	Psalm 132	strophe
1	Yahweh, remember in David's favor	1
	his great self-denial,	
2	how he swore to Yahweh,	
	vowed to the Mighty One of Jacob:	
3	"No, I will not enter my dwelling place,	2
	nor will I mount my bed,	
4	I will not give sleep to my eyes,	
	or slumber to my eyelids,	

5   until I find a place for Yahweh,
               an abode for the Mighty One of Jacob!"

6   We heard it was in Ephrat,   3
               we came upon it in the fields of Jaar.
7   Let us enter his abode,
               let us prostrate ourselves before his footstool.

8   Advance, Yahweh, to your resting-place,   4
               you and the Ark of your strength.
9   May your priests clothe themselves with righteousness,
               and may your loyal ones raise a cheer!

Readers who pay close attention to the shifts of voice and address, and to the phenomenon of embedded speech, will grasp the correct division fairly quickly. The poet himself (and any pilgrim around the temple who speaks or sings the song after him) opens with a prayer to the deity for David, or "David" might here even mean the descendant currently occupying the throne. Verse 2 is spoken by the same voice, and is closely linked to v. 1 as a more detailed elaboration of David's "self-denial." Thus, strophe 1 may be demarcated as an introductory unit. Next, there is a change of voice, for in vv. 3–5 the oath David swore, i.e., to build a temple for God, is repeated. These 3 x 2 cola are one long sentence spoken by David. Thus the structure of that sentence ensures the strophic design: vv. 3, 4, and 5 cannot be separated from another. They are full of synonymous parallelisms, but at the same time there is progression: enter the house, lie on the bed, fall asleep—a chronological series. This tranquillity and the notion of "inside" are opposed to the great hustle and bustle outside that the speaker proposes to start. Strophes 1 and 2 also form a pair because they both end on "the Mighty One of Jacob."

Strophe 3 is spoken by yet another voice. I imagine this to be the religious community, say a group of pilgrims, since Psalm 132 is one of the songs meant to be sung *lamma'alot;* this means "on the way up," in the sense of either the steps leading up to the temple court, or the movement of the faithful toward the capital and its sanctuary. Verse 6 probably refers to the transport of the Ark, which was first kept in Kiriat-jearim (see the end of 1 Sam. 6), and was later conveyed in procession to his new capital by David, the man from Ephrat = Bethlehem, as 2 Samuel 6 relates. The strophe is spoken by a "we": the group that wants to worship, v. 7.

In strophe 4, we hear the first speaker again; although the group may be speaking with him, he is speaking to someone else: to God himself again. God is asked to take action and defend city and temple. Verse 9 rounds off the first half, and later acquires a counterpart that stands out by having the same length, i.e., a complete verse: this is v. 16. The word "righteousness" has been replaced by "salvation," i.e., release, and the cheering is emphasized (below, I have translated it by an adverb, "loudly").

The text of the second, longer half takes up vv. 10–18, and as with the first half, I have indicated the division into strophes:

verse	Psalm 132	strophe
10	Do not reject your anointed one	5
	for the sake of your servant David!	
11a	Yahweh swore to David a firm oath	
b	that he will not renounce:	
11c	"One of your own issue	6
d	I will set upon your throne.	
12a	If your sons keep my covenant	
b	and my decrees that I teach them,	
12c	then their sons also, to the end of time,	
d	shall sit upon your throne!"	
13	For Yahweh has chosen Zion,	7
	he has desired it for his dwelling.	
14	"This is my resting-place for all time,	
	here I will dwell, for I desire it.	
15	I will amply bless its store of food,	8
	give its needy their fill of bread,	
16	I will clothe its priests in salvation,	
	its loyal ones shall cheer loudly.	
17	There I will make a horn sprout for David,	9
	I will prepare a lamp for my anointed one.	
18	I will clothe his enemies in disgrace,	
	while on him his crown shall sparkle."	

The connection between vv. 9 and 16 implies that the poem might well have been finished after the second batch of four strophes, and sharpens our eye: unexpectedly, there are two extra verses, so that the second half is one complete strophe longer than the first half. What does this mean? Or should the psalm be divided into two times ten verses after all?

Verse 10 reveals that David himself now belongs to the past, but also shows that his dynasty is already a household word. This gives us an approximate date for the composition of the song: it fits the cultic and historical situation in the period around 850–600 BCE. (The sixth century BCE saw the traumatic destruction of city and temple by the New Babylonians, and the deportation of the Judaean elite. Psalm 132, however, still attests to an uninterrupted interaction with, and trust in, the Davidic throne.) Verse 11 is a striking parallel to v. 2, but at the same time a reversal, leading to something surpassing David's "self-denial." The reversal is the same as that in 2 Samuel 7. This time, it is God who swears and David is the beneficiary, and again it is about the lasting dynasty.

In strophe 6, God's oath is given the same amount of space as David's in strophe 2: three bicola. This balance strongly argues in favor of keeping the two verses 10 + 11ab together in strophe 5, and of seeing this unit as the counterpart to strophe 1. In both strophes, the proper names "David" and "Yahweh" are circling each other as it were, and the repetition of the keyword "swear/oath" is significant. We have landed in the middle of a generosity contest: David wants to honor Yahweh with a temple—a spatial entity, a concrete object—but God outstrips David by making his favorite king the founder of a veritable dynasty—a concept belonging to the more abstract dimension of time.

A change of voice reveals that v. 13 remains outside the oath. This has the important consequence that God's speech, which is embedded as from v. 14 and takes up no fewer than ten cola, is separated from the oath itself. And this in turn means that the status of oath—the most weighty and binding language imaginable in antiquity—remains reserved for vv. 11c–12d. The speech of vv. 14–18 has a slightly different status: it is a promise that elaborates in more detail what God's support of the dynasty implies.

If a change of voice were a watertight criterion, we would be obliged to write v. 13, which comes from the poet, as a separate one-line strophe. To prevent us from doing this, the poet has taken two measures. In the first place, the meaning of v. 13 is almost identical with that of v. 14, virtually the only difference being the change from third- to first-person singular for God. Secondly, the poet welds the B-cola into a tight unit by means of a chiasm:

| he has desired it | for his dwelling | (13b) |
| here I will dwell | for I desire it | (14b) |

Verses 13 and 14 together make up the strophe about the election of Mount Zion. What follows, in 2 + 2 verses, is the explanation of this in terms of food, salvation, and prosperity. The last strophe, i.e., the surplus vv. 17–18, is intended as a parallel to the penultimate strophe, since "clothing the priests with salvation" (16a) acquires an obvious counterpart in the "clothing of the enemies with shame," in 18a. We nevertheless hear a lot of news right at the end. Three of the four half-verses have a positive tone, in favor of "David" (read: the current king, his descendant). An inclusion has thus been created: this final strophe *pro* David—still part of the promise—is God's generous answer to the appeal *pro* David which started the second half, in v. 10. This is also indicated by the repetition of the word "anointed" (vv. 10a and 17b).

The poem as a whole proves to be one long drawn-out parallelism. At first, neither David nor Yahweh gives an inch as regards generosity toward the other. Soon, however, we notice that God's promises go deeper, and we find that the poet allows God far more speech than the king. The longer second half is the quantitative expression of the fact that God is the clear winner of this generosity contest. The structural analysis proves that v. 10 is the start of the second half; this plea serves the double function of being a parallel to v. 1, and forming an inclusion together with v. 17, marking off the second half:

Half I (vv. 1–9)	*Half II (vv. 10–18)*
strophe 1: prayer + oath (David to God)	strophe 5: prayer + oath (God to David)
strophe 2 quotes the oath literally (content: spatial)	strophe 6 quotes the oath literally (content: temporal)
strophe 3: Ark and cult (God's house)	strophe 7: election of Zion as God's house
strophe 4: protection, jubilation	strophe 8: food, jubilation
	strophe 9: prosperity and power for "David"

This analysis of Psalm 132 shows that a correct appreciation of repetition helps us to determine the demarcation of the various textual units, and that the correct division in turn is the basis for a correct interpretation of the poem. This song is an excellent example of a composition that, from its opening to its closing lines, step by step, strophe after strophe, has been meticulously proportioned with respect to length and meaning. It shows that the whole is more than the sum of its parts.

8

In search of the correct division

The power of repetition

As we have seen, a text has many layers, which are kept together by a hierarchical structure. In chapter 3, I compared these layers to a staircase. In chapters 4–7, we climbed the main steps and reached the landing of the poem as a whole, where we attained some sort of overview.

I would like to remain at this last stage just a bit longer, and explore our practice area (the poems we have discussed) one more time in detail by contemplating the importance of a correct division. The right articulation of a poem is of enormous significance: it simply makes everything fall into place. I will demonstrate this by an analysis of Psalm 103.

Turning to this poem, we quickly notice that it ends in the same way as it began, with the sentence: "Bless, my soul, Yahweh." This exhortation by the poet, addressed to his innermost self, is a soliloquy that receives a lot of emphasis. It appears twice as an A-colon in the beginning, and its repetition in v. 22c is explicitly supported by the three verses preceding it. Cola 20a-21a-22a have the same imperative in the plural, and address the heavenly hosts who also should bless God.

The word "bless" is my literal translation and deserves some explanation. In verses 3–5 the poet prompts his inner self as to how this blessing should be worded. If "his soul" listens to the command, it will start with: "blessed (Hebrew *baruch*) Yahweh who . . . ," and will then continue by naming various qualities of the deity. Sure enough, some five are mentioned in the second strophe (the vv. 3–5 mentioned above); they fill the relative clauses starting with "who . . ." with qualities of God, "who . . . forgives, who . . . heals, who . . . redeems," and so on, so that the strophe becomes a hymnic catalogue.

Blessing, however, is a combination of praising and giving thanks, which is why I do not translate *baruch* by "praise" (as NIV does) or "give thanks," as this is too limited. It is true that the song of praise and song of thanksgiving are very close within the Israelite repertoire. A number of psalms may even be found where thanks and praise seamlessly merge—see, for instance, Psalms 30, 68, 108, 118, and 124. Another example is Psalm 18: we have seen (chapter 7) that its Song of Thanksgiving is set inside a hymnic frame of 1 + 2 strophes.

It is nevertheless important to distinguish between praise and thanks; however minimal the difference, these are still two separate genres within the field of joyful-toned poetry. A hymn (of praise) lauds God's excellence, often in the form of an enumeration of his qualities. We find this in Psalm 113 (as discussed in chapter 2), and the series of Psalms 95–100 and 145–150. Even the book of Job contains a number of instances of naming a string of qualities; positively by Eliphaz, for instance (in Job 5:9–15), but subversively and with a sinister undertone by the hero in 12:13–25. And the long series of questions about the wonders of creation, which the Creator himself fires at Job in chs. 38–39, is obviously a transformation of the hymnic enumeration.

Yet, whereas a hymn remains a form of description, a song of thanksgiving by definition gives thanks *for* something: a concrete action that God has performed in favor of the speaker or the community. God has intervened in history and for this deserves thanks. Thus, a song of thanksgiving looks at history, or a concrete period in the poet's own life, and indicates what turn for the better has taken place. For instance, God has delivered the poet or the poet's friends from enemies, illness, or calumny. This kind of intervention usually illustrates the unique or incidental aspect that is characteristic of a historical event. A hymn of praise, on the other hand, is more concerned with the permanent and sometimes even timeless qualities of God.

The excellent qualities that the second strophe of Psalm 103 ascribes to God balance on the dividing line between the uniquely historical and the extra-temporal. The list that constitutes this unit (vv. 3–5) is a laudation, but we will see it is soon illustrated by "historic" acts of God in favor of the chosen people, so that the thanksgiving aspect also emerges very clearly.

Thus, the translation "blessing" covers both sides: God's actions in favor of people of flesh and blood, and his eternal qualities of being merciful, forgiving, and so on. The word "soul" is usually the last resort of a Bible translator, and only in the rarest of cases may be interpreted in a Christian sense. The original (*nefesh*) usually simply means "the whole person." In biblical Israel this is not something immaterial, as opposed to the body as an earthen vessel, since for the Israelites there was no life after death, and they had a very different concept of humans than we have. Words such as "spirit," "heart," and "soul" in Hebrew have meanings that often do not coincide with ours, and their range and function are strongly dependent on the context. As it happens, here in Psalm 103 "soul" does mean something like a spiritual life or inner self.

The unity of Psalm 103 has already been ensured by a frame which cannot be missed. But what happens inside this border? Where are the stanza boundaries, and how many strophes are there? I have checked more than thirty translations and commentaries in five different languages,[1] but the correct division of the song is nowhere to be found. This embarrassing discovery, which raises doubts as to the academic level of biblical scholarship, is all the more remarkable since the poem contains many structuring elements.

How could these signals have been missed? I perceive three factors that may explain this: an inadequate theoretical grounding, inadequate analysis, and a failure to observe all the characteristics of the linguistic work of art. First, scholars still fail to grasp the difference between strophe and stanza; most Old Testament scholars still do not distinguish between these two units, which leads to errors. Furthermore, the average biblical scholar suffers from a lack of purely literary training. Finally, although everybody is full of good intentions, in practice most scholars are content with only partial analyses. They decide that they have done a reasonable number of observations of style, and then conclude that the main lines of the poem must be such-and-such. This often misfires, since it leads to *foreclosure*: the premature shutting down of the processes of reading or interpretation. What is actually needed is a full analysis. Only after the poet's entire box of tricks has been examined, and everything observable has been noted in the poem under consideration, can a responsible conclusion be reached about how the composition has been put together.

In the case of psalm 103, the exegetes go wrong in any, several, or all of the following places: v. 8, v. 14 (which scholars separate from vv. 15–16), and v. 19 (which is thought to open vv. 19–22). Verses 8 and 19 do not open strophes, and v. 14 is not the concluding verse of a strophe. So, what is the real situation?

I will discuss the psalm in two stages: first, I will present my own translation (partly based on the JPS) and will discuss each stanza separately. My choice of words is sometimes less than perfect, but this is because the translation has been geared to the characteristics of the text and to my argument. At this stage, I will pay special attention to those aspects of style and structure that help to mark out and locate strophes and stanzas. In the second round, I will consider the poem as a whole on the basis of a slightly adapted translation, more in tune with the main connections in the poem.

Psalm 103 in stanzas

Psalm 103, stanza I

1 Bless, my soul, Yahweh,
       and all my innermost, his holy name;   strophe 1
2 bless, my soul, Yahweh,
       and do not forget all his bounties;

3 who forgives all your iniquities,
       heals all your weaknesses,   strophe 2
4 who redeems your life from the Pit,
       who crowns you with *loyalty and mercy,*
5 who fills your ways with happiness,
       so that your youth is renewed like the eagle's.

6 Yahweh performs liberating/righteous acts
       and judgments for all who are oppressed.   strophe 3
7 he makes known his ways to Moses,
       to the Israelites his deeds:
8 "*Merciful* and gracious is Yahweh,
       lenient and rich in *loyalty.*"

We note that the strophic units form an SLL series. The first strophe is a soliloquy—a rare device in ancient Israelite poetry. It is governed by imperative forms: three commands, and a prohibition at the end, which is nevertheless synonymous with the commands as it also follows the formula "minus times minus is plus." "Not forgetting" is a litotes*, which by its construction strongly recommends continued remembrance.

At the end of the second verse the original text has "his acts of retribution." Retribution is an ambiguous concept in Hebrew: it has a positive meaning in the case of the reaction to good deeds, but a negative sense when it refers to an answer to misdeeds. Here in 103:2 the word has been used in a positive sense. It anticipates v. 10 where we read: "He will not requite us according to our iniquities." We again recognize the formula "minus times minus is plus," since v. 10 deletes the negative aspect of retribution. The word has been placed deliberately and precisely, again at the end of the second poetic line (this time of stanza II).

The second strophe is clearly recognizable as a unit by virtue of its being an enumeration, consisting of a long series of adjectival clauses. These reflect what in the original text is a string of participles in honor of God. Since they fill an L-strophe, there is also a pivot: this is the middle verse, a poetic line (v. 4) that ends on two of the top five keywords of the song. These two nouns, "loyalty and mercy" form a word pair that I would like to call the thematic climax of the first stanza. Their importance is highlighted by the fact that they are applied metaphorically: God will crown "you" (as the poet addresses his own inner self) with them. The great importance of this pair, which is almost a hendiadys*, is also stressed by the fact that it is repeated in mirror-image (thus forming a chiasm) in the concluding line of the stanza: v. 8 ranges from "merciful" to "rich in loyalty." In this way, the center of the stanza is firmly connected to its conclusion.

The third strophe takes us back in time to the most constitutive phase in the history of the chosen people, the events around Mount Sinai. In various places in the Bible we are told of the covenant that God made with the people: with Noah in Genesis 6–9, with Abraham in Genesis 17 (the covenant of the circumcision), and, much later, with David and his dynasty, the poetic reflection of which we have seen in Psalm 132 (in the previous chapter). The most important covenant, however, is that made on the Sinai, during the trek through the desert, and familiar from the tables of stone containing the Ten Commandments: it clinches Israel's status as the chosen people.

The phrasing of the third strophe indicates that the song is not the personal expression of one individual, but is intended to be sung by the people: we have now entered the dimension of national history. The beneficiary (in linguistic terms: the indirect object) of God's liberating and righteous actions is indicated in strophe 3 three times by the preposition "to/for." This makes the cola of vv. 6b and 7ab into a series, and leads us to conclude that "the oppressed" in v. 6b are the Israelites: the contemporaries of the leader who in v. 7a is expressly called by his proper name "Moses." It is this generation of the Exodus to whom God "makes known his ways."

What exactly are these ways? The answer is given to us by the poet, solemnly and in detail, through the formal and weighty quotation given in v. 8. The source of the quotation makes its importance clear: these are verses from Exodus 34 with the considerable status of a self-revelation of God. Moses had returned to his people from the mountain, but had broken the stone tablets into pieces when he found the people worshipping the golden calf. After his fit of anger, however, he had decided to address a prayer to God for the survival of his people, and had climbed the mountain again. The people are granted a second chance, for God gives Moses two new stone tablets. Next, the narrator tells us what Moses hears, his face hidden in a cleft of the rock in order not to be blinded by God's appearance:

Exod. 34:5–7

5	Yahweh came down in a cloud,
	stood with him there,
	and called out the name Yahweh.
6	Yahweh passed before him, and proclaimed:

"Yahweh, Yahweh!
   Merciful and gracious God,
      lenient and rich in loyalty and fidelity;

7	who keeps faithful to thousands,
	who forgives iniquity, transgression and sin,
7c	but does not clear [the guilty]
d	and visits the iniquity of the fathers upon children
	and children's children
e	to the third and fourth generations."

What we read here in vv. 6b–7 is itself poetry, compact and rhythmic, and full of parallelisms. It resembles a creed, but most of all it is a self-portrait of God. It has a lighter and a darker side: the tricolon that concludes v. 7 has been rather a shock for many readers before us—but then there are many passages in the Hebrew Bible that are not particularly suitable for those with weak nerves.

This self-revelation is a famous passage, and it is no surprise that we find it quoted in several texts; see Psalms 86:15, 103:8, 145:8; Jonah 4:2; Joel 2:13; and Nehemiah 9:17.

It is important for us to analyze exactly what it is the poet of Psalm 103 is doing. His quotation from Exodus 34:6 is not literal, as he leaves out the word "fidelity." He has made his own combination in the word pair which places "faithful" next to "merciful." Furthermore, he does two things with v. 7cde of Exodus 34. He ignores them, by leaving them out; and he uses them, by having his poem go on to criticize these phrases. Having reached the threshold of stanza II, we prick up our ears to hear how the poet will handle the "visiting" (= punishing) side of God. We leave stanza I with the observation that God's proper name has not been mentioned in the middle strophe (vv. 3–5), whereas the poet does use the name "Yahweh" in the surrounding strophes 1 and 3, twice in each.

This arrangement is turned inside out as it were in stanza II. Yahweh is mentioned in the middle strophe, in v. 13b, but his name is totally absent in the surrounding strophes:

Psalm 103, stanza II

9	He will NOT contend forever,
	and NOT nurse his anger for eternity; strophe 4
10	he will not deal with us according to our sins,
	and not requite us according to our iniquities.

11	For as high as the heavens are above the earth,
	so great is his loyalty *toward* **those who fear him**. strophe 5
12	As far as the East is from the West,
	so far does he remove our sins from us.
13	As a father has mercy *toward* his children,
	so Yahweh has mercy *toward* **those who fear him**.

14	For he knows how we are formed,
	he is mindful that we are dust. strophe 6
15	Man—his days are like grass,
	he blooms like a flower of the field;
16	a wind passes by, and it is NO more,
	and its own place NO longer knows it.

The contours of this middle stanza are clear. The center is an L-strophe, wholly determined by a threefold application of the "as x . . . , so y" pattern. Thus, the center of the poem as a whole is devoted to the stylistic device of the simile (comparison). Around this center, there is a solid ring of negations, throughout strophe 4 and in v. 16 as the negative climax of strophe 6.

The powerful "NO(T)" does a lot of work. It marks the stanza boundaries and invites the reader to look for the connection between strophes 4 and 6. Both units focus on transitoriness, and thanks to the ring of negations the one strophe explains the other. In strophe 4, the poet does admit that God can be angry and will sometimes insist on sinners being tried and punished, but he denies that God argues all the time and never ceases to persecute. In this way, the poet is already clearly undermining the dark side (the conclusion) of the creed from Exodus 34. The poet has no use for a constantly rebuking deity. What's more, he uses strophe 6 to explain why God is not as punitive as tradition would have it:

God is aware of the brevity of man's life, and is willing to take that into account in his behavior toward mortals. The poet believes in a forgiving God, which is exactly the quality he puts first in the hymnic enumeration of strophe 2!

Strophe 5, the hub of the center, employs the chiastic word pair again, and arranges this to mirror the order in v. 8, i.e., crosswise for the second time. It is no coincidence that "loyalty" is the subject (also in a grammatical sense) of v. 11, and that its counterpart "mercy" governs v. 13, which is situated at the other side of the strophe. This quality of God's is not a latent characteristic, but is actually apparent: the keyword has been transformed into a verb here and an action.

The closely knit quality of the central strophe is further strengthened by the fact that the A-colon of each of its verses contains a merism. The pair heaven/earth introduces a "vertical" dimension, "horizontally" bisected by the pair East/West. Together, these dimensions form a system of coordinates that effectively evokes the vast reaches of creation. It reminds us of the dynamic use made of the same dimensions in Psalm 113 (see chapter 2).

Verse 13, too, contains a merism, that of father and children. Because of the cohesion of the strophe we now recognize this relationship as a metaphorical transformation or application of the heaven/earth relationship from v. 11. Yet, this argument may also be reversed. The strophe proclaims God's love for those people who show him deference and respect ("the fear of the Lord," as it was called in the King James Bible). He is that father, and the people are his children. The depth or intensity of his affection is now demonstrated by means of the widest spatial terms imaginable.

The symmetry of the middle stanza becomes even clearer when we trace the linguistic forms for "we" and "us." There are two in the central poetic line (v. 12, the pivot of the strophe, which itself is the axis of the central stanza, and hence of the whole song), and at equal distances we also find 4 + 2 forms for "us" immediately outside strophe 5, in the adjacent verses 10 and 14. Their positions become even more significant when we notice that there are no other forms of "us" in this poem. Moreover, the lines containing "us" strictly alternate with the rhyme of vv. 11 and 13, which end in "those who fear him." If we wonder who exactly "those" are, the answer is: we ourselves. Actually, the referent does not change at the end of vv. 10–14! The God-fearing group coincides with "us," and we would be justified in thinking that in that case "we" are the Israelites of strophes 3 and 7.

Strophe 3 was framed by "performing (righteousness, i.e., deeds of) liberation" and "loyalty." Strophe 7 repeats these two qualifications, makes them the subject of two nominal sentences, and places them in front position in their respective poetic lines. These are vv. 17–18; traditionally, they are read as a tricolon plus bicolon, but the sentence structure proves that this should be the other way round. Verse 17ab is a bicolon containing a remarkable enjambment, followed by a tricolon (17c + 18ab) with a threefold preposition. In the original text, this "for" is exactly the same word as the preposition translated by "to/for" in strophe 3, which is no coincidence. The tricolon again shows us the Israelites as beneficiaries; they are Yahweh's covenant partners:

Psalm 103, stanza III

17a	Yahweh's loyalty is from eternity	strophe 7
b	to eternity toward those who fear him,	
c	and his righteousness is for the children's children,	
18a	for those who keep his covenant,	
b	and for those who remember his precepts by *performing* them.	
19	Yahweh has established his throne in heaven and his kingdom *reigns* over all.	
20	Bless Yahweh, all his angels, mighty heroes, who *perform* his word, and are perfectly obedient to his word!	strophe 8
21	Bless Yahweh, all his hosts, his servants, who *perform* his will!	
22	Bless Yahweh, all his works, in all places of his *reign*! Bless, my soul, Yahweh!	

By placing the word "eternity" twice in v. 17, the poet creates a parallelism at stanza level, since it was also used in v. 9, accompanied by a synonym. We now observe a contrast in the openings of stanzas II and III, a contrast that points to the core of the message. "Eternal" does not apply to God's anger, but rather to his loyalty or mercy. This is the real essence of what the poet has to tell us about his God.

The parallelism goes further: the words "perform" (literally "do") and "heaven" from 18b and 19a also appeared in vv. 10a and 11a. To put it differently: the first three A-cola of the central stanza contain words which, in the same order, recur in (strophe 7 =) the first three verses of stanza III.

This stanza consists of two L-strophes. Their boundaries are fixed mainly by two phenomena, which demonstrate that v. 19 does indeed still belong in strophe 7; it does not open the concluding hymnic exhortation, as almost all exegetes think. First, there is the root "to reign," which occurs in v. 19b as a verb and in v. 22b as a noun, and moreover frames the concept of "all":

> his kingdom *reigns*   over *all/everything*   (v. 19b)
> in *all* places   of his *reign* (v. 22b)

This arrangement shapes the third verses of both strophes. The second phenomenon that guides the correct articulation has to do with the "population" of the strophes: the beneficiaries of God's goodness in strophe 7, and the group whose laudations put God in the limelight in strophe 8. They have been arranged in the following way:

strophe 7	*earth*	*heaven (and earth)*
	two verses: 17–18	one verse: 19
strophe 8	*heaven*	*earth (and heaven)*
	two verses: 20–21	one verse: 22

This symmetry exploits the complementariness of heaven and earth (forming as they do a merism for the universe) for two purposes: creating parallelism and creating contrast. The parallelism says that the inhabitants of both regions are obedient, given the repetition of the word "perform" and the synonymy of "covenant" and "his word." The contrast is a kind of two-way traffic: in strophe 7, God's care is directed toward the people of the covenant; in strophe 8, the angels' praise is addressed to God, so that at the last minute he again becomes the object he was in strophe 1: the target of blessing and praise.

Psalm 103 as a whole

After this discussion of the three sections of the song, we may notice other things. The words "loyalty" and "merciful(ness)" each occur four times, and the eight positions they occupy are interwoven, almost resembling wickerwork:

on the axis of strophe 2:   .. .. / .. .. .. loyalty-and-mercy

the beginning and end of verse 8,
which concludes strophe 3 and
stanza I: merciful .. .. .. / .. .. .. loyalty

strophe 5,
v. 11 + v. 13:   . .. His loyalty .. ..//   have mercy
                                                      have mercy

strophe 7, v. 17a: Yahweh's loyalty.. ..

The order in which these two appear is determined by a threefold chiasm. This is already remarkable in itself, but what strikes me as an even more effective device is the contribution that the word "loyalty" makes to the demarcation of the central stanza. It is situated on the boundaries of this stanza, or rather just outside it; in other words, stanza I ends on exactly that keyword, and stanza III opens with it. These and other points will be demonstrated by means of italics, bold type, and capitals in the following presentation of the poem as a whole:

Psalm 103

1	Bless, my soul, Yahweh,	
	and all my innermost, his holy name;	strophe 1
2	bless, my soul, Yahweh,	
	and do not forget all his works of **retribution**;	
3	who forgives all your iniquities,	
	heals all your weaknesses,	strophe 2
4	who redeems your life from the Pit,	
	who crowns you with *loyalty and mercy,*	
5	who satisfies your ways with happiness,	
	so that your youth is renewed like the eagle's.	

6	Yahweh PERFORMS **righteousness**	
	and judgments for all who are oppressed.	strophe 3
7	He makes known his ways to Moses,	
	to the Israelites his deeds:	
8	"*Merciful* and gracious is Yahweh,	
	lenient and rich in *loyalty*."	

9   He will not contend **forever**,   strophe 4
       and not nurse his anger in **eternity**;
10   he will not DEAL WITH us according to
              our sins,
       and not **requite** us according to our iniquities.

11   For as high as the HEAVENS are above the earth,
       so great is his *loyalty* toward those who fear him.
12   As far as the East is from the West,   strophe 5
       so far does he remove our sins from us.
13   As a father has *mercy* toward his children,
       so Yahweh has *mercy* toward those who fear him.

14   For he knows how we are formed,
       he is mindful that we are dust.   strophe 6
15   Man—his days are like grass,
       he blooms like a flower of the field;
16   a wind passes by, and it is no more,
       and its own place no longer knows it.

17a Yahweh's *loyalty* is from **eternity**
  b   to **eternity** for those who fear him,   strophe 7
  c   and his **righteousness** is for the children's children,
18a   for those who keep his covenant,
  b   and for those who remember his precepts
                     by PERFORMING them.
19   Yahweh has established his throne in HEAVEN
       and his kingdom reigns over all.

20   Bless Yahweh, all his angels,   strophe 8
       mighty heroes, who PERFORM his word,
       and are perfectly obedient to his word!
21   Bless Yahweh, all his hosts,
       his servants, who PERFORM his will!
22   Bless Yahweh, all his works,
       in all places of his reign!
       Bless, my soul, Yahweh!

The threefold preposition, which was so important in strophe 3 and after that in strophe 7, has been translated as consistently as possible, two times by "to," four times by "for." Stanzas I and II have the same dimensions: they both consist of 4 + 6 + 6 cola, or, to put it differently, they are both an SLL series. The permanence of God's mercy (strophe 5) is set within a ring of transitoriness (strophes 4 and 6), but is not cancelled by it: stanza III again employs the term "eternal" to make sure that mercy has the last word. The very last word is given to the hymnic ring that is drawn around all this by strophes 1 and 8.

This articulation into eight strophes and three stanzas has made everything fall into place. The correct division has here been found, and in all other cases will only be found, by paying close attention to language and style, and by tuning in to the strategic positioning of keywords and similar signals. Psalm 103 has a lot of these!

To conclude this chapter, let us look at the question of how many of the poet's decisions in this psalm have actually been based on repetition of the components of the poem. The answer yields quite a list:

- Anaphora has been used so extensively that this stylistic device has a far-reaching structural influence. Strophes 1 + 2 and 4 + 5 constitute two series characterized by a double anaphoric design. In strophe 1, the A-cola of vv. 1 and 2 are identical, so that the anaphora stretches across four words. In strophe 2, five cola start in the same way (participles in the original text = relative clauses starting with "who . . . " in translation). Strophe 4 is tightly organized by a fourfold "not" at the beginning of the cola. The verses in strophe 5 commence three times with the word "as," and the sentence structure always remains locked in comparison mode.
- These anaphoric chains already determine almost completely the parallel design of stanzas I and II.
- The hymnic enumeration in strophe 2 acquires a counterpart in the final strophe, which exhorts to praise and itself is also determined by anaphora.
- In strophe 3 we find *four* cola containing plural forms; their verses are governed by *two* verbs. The

concluding verse 8, containing the quotation from Exodus, forms the climax of the strophe, and serves as complement for vv. 6–7, by presenting *four* nominal predicates in a sort of pressure cooker, i.e., in only *two* cola.

- The distribution of the keywords is of vital importance. I have indicated most of them above, and the typographical devices I have employed in the translation will enable the reader to locate them quickly.

- An efficient form of alternation is active at strophe level. Strophes 4 and 6, which frame stanza II, both speak of the brevity of the life of humans. They interrupt the sequence about God's mercy that occupies strophes 3, 5, and 7, but at the same time give it an aspect of regularity (i.e., that of alternation).

- There are many forms of inclusio, such as the repetition of "loyalty" on (and just outside) the boundaries of the central stanza—a slim and striking ring—the collaboration of strophes 4 and 6 around the middle strophe, and one level further the collaboration of strophes 3 and 7 around/outside stanza II (as they mirror the words "righteousness" and "loyalty").

In short, it seems that there is nothing in Psalm 103 that is not based on repetition. Whatever is not repeated will always appear inside the larger framework of what is. For instance, the poet uses the phrase "who forgives" and the image of the withering grass only once, but these components always bear some relation to the context in which they occur. One possible way of describing reading and (after a lot of rereading) interpreting a poem is as a search for order and structure in a heap of language signs that at first sight seems impossible to penetrate. The order emerging from the apparent chaos is based on many and highly varied devices, themselves distributed on virtually all levels of the text. Most of these devices, however, are forms of repetition. And then there are the numerous details that are also repetition in action, of which we become aware when we do our homework and conscientiously at verse level discover and weigh one parallelism after another. In Psalm 103, parallelismus membrorum is almost always based on synonymy, and synonymy itself is a form of repetition. Still, any other form of parallelism may be analyzed as a mixture of repetition and variation.

9

Wisdom literature

The book of Job

Proverbs, Ecclesiastes, and Job

A thousand years before the people of Israel entered recorded history, a literary genre known as Wisdom and expressing itself in poetic lines had already developed in the Near East. Wisdom literature is the poetic reflection of experience and is offered in concentrated form, in proverbs and aphorisms. As early as the third millennium BCE, writers in high places were engaged in these condensing and collecting activities, which mainly took place in the courts and temples of the great powers along the Nile and in Mesopotamia.

This international genre probably started by building its atoms: individual, stand-alone aphorisms. Thus, in the book of Proverbs we may still find examples of lines which work perfectly well on their own:

Prov. 15:17   Better a meal of vegetables where there is love,
               than a fattened ox where there is hate.

This is a charming verse, a combination of extreme practicality and principle, each half-verse juxtaposing an abstract concept and a concrete term from the kitchen.

Nowadays, many of these verses do not strike us as particularly spiritual, but at the most unexpected moments we come across pearls of wisdom (!), and sometimes remarkably profound maxims:

Prov. 13:8   Riches are ransom for a man's life,
               but the poor never hears a menace.

It would seem that taking hostages for ransom is as old as the hills—that life is less stressful, the less you have. Every once in a while the meaning of a passage remains obscure, however, no matter how much thought is devoted to it. Consider this strophe about communication with a fool—a term that does not mean "silly" or "strange," but indicates a bad and dangerous form of irrationality:

Prov. 26:4   Do not answer a fool in accord with his stupidity,
                    else you will become like him.
         5   Answer a fool in accord with his stupidity,
                    else he will be wise in his own eyes.

This complete strophe apparently intends to present a masterpiece of dialectics. The first verse is still clear: it warns against lowering oneself. The second, however, is a great surprise—can a fool be spoken to after all? "To be wise in one's own eyes" is usually not a good thing in the proverb genre, as it leads to arrogance and therefore is undesirable in the eyes of the deity. This is apparently all the more so if fools think themselves wise—a double taboo, so to speak. Consequently, this should be avoided in your/our way of speaking by choosing words which put the fools in their place, probably by offering tit for tat.

Bible scholarship recognizes that chs. 1–9 from the book of Proverbs form a coherent, well-planned composition, containing one poem per chapter. As the book progresses, however, the stream of verses seems to become more fragmentized. A number of small groupings can be distinguished, partly because of occasional headings, as in the case of Proverbs 30, which is inscribed "words of Agur," or because they form an alphabetic acrostic, like the last poem. In essence, however, the approach to Proverbs 10ff. is atomistic.

This is a pity, because it is wrong. The texts following Proverbs 1–9 also obey the text model given in chapter 3 of this book. They form strophes of two to three lines, and these strophic units themselves are gathered into larger structures. But as we have already seen, the average Old Testament scholar lacks the necessary theoretical knowledge and analytical skill, and as a result has little or no awareness of such things.

I will give a brief indication of the contents: in many places a fictional character, "lady Wisdom" (in Greek one would say "lady

Sophia"), addresses the reader as "my son," and bombards him with advice and warnings. Thus, many chapters are set in the frame of a dialogue. The statements breathe the spirit of a basic and firm belief that when you follow these counsels you will be rewarded with life and health. If you do good, you will do well, and if you do evil or commit folly, you will get your just deserts. What we are told about wisdom is simply that it is obtainable; it is a practical concept, nothing like philosophy or metaphysical speculation, or the rarefied heights or voids of mysticism. It is everyday ethics, under the colors of "the fear of the Lord," which nowadays we would call "respect for God."

There are, however, three representatives of the Wisdom tradition in the Hebrew Bible: besides the book of Proverbs, which I would call the norm, there are two interesting deviants: Job and Ecclesiastes. From Job we have already heard (see chapter 6) that wisdom is nowhere to be had, so we have been warned. And Ecclesiastes assures us that life is unpredictable, offers no certainties, and that the constitution of the world will always remain unfathomable to man. The short book by this name comprises twelve chapters, and was written by an aged thinker around the third century BCE. In this case, too, biblical scholarship has not as yet been able to discover much rigorous organization, but I predict that this state of affairs will change drastically in the coming years.

The thought that the good will prosper and the wicked will suffer has a pleasing symmetry, but the Mesopotamians, like everyone else, had experienced for centuries that life is just not like that. A thousand years before Israel was established, the phenomenon of innocent suffering was already a thorny problem, and contemporary philosophers make it clear that twentieth-century philosophy has not progressed any further in explaining the origin and function of evil—at least if we reject such cheap and easy answers as "We learn by suffering" or "It is noble now to suffer, since you will be rewarded in heaven later."

Wisdom confronts us with the problem of the theodicy: How may God's goodness and justice be reconciled with the fact that the world contains so much inexplicable and especially unbearable suffering? The naive view often found in Proverbs, which in fact ignores the problem by maintaining "Do good and you will do well," leads to a dangerous reversal of the argument. This reversal is communicated to us by Job's three friends, who visit Job in his total humiliation/disgrace, and who view the stricken man with severity rather than empathy. The argument goes in three steps: the adherent of the traditional point of view finds a suffering individual, and from his condition deduces that the stricken man is being punished by the deity. He unquestioningly assumes that God is justified in acting thus, and from that deduces another fact: the sufferer must have sinned.

This is indeed what Job's friends do. They observe his pain and deprivation, and say to him, "Tell us what you have done wrong; your suffering proves you have sinned." This rigid and callous approach infuriates Job. He knows he is blameless, and maintains his innocence until his dying day.

The two heterodox representatives of wisdom (Job and Ecclesiastes) state outright that the good often suffer and the wicked do not, and voice their disapproval. They use the tools of the Wisdom genre to undermine, problematize, and further sharpen the concept of wisdom. In chapter 6 we already heard Job say that wisdom cannot be found among men, not even if you try to buy it with a bag full of gold dust. What remained in Job 28 was v. 28, a conclusion that is still practical rather than metaphysical-speculative: avoiding evil and doing good—that is what respect for the deity means. And Ecclesiastes adds that God is unknowable and unfathomable.

The book of Job is a unique, new form of the Wisdom genre, since it shapes an extremely long, complicated, and heated debate into verse, and since the author has set all this poetry inside a tight prose frame. In chs. 1–2 the writer assumes the attitude of a narrator, so that he can profit from an omniscient perspective. Thanks to this pose he "knows" that God thinks Job utterly incorruptible, and he "sees" what is being discussed in the heavenly council. God maintains that even in times of great adversity Job will not break, but his state attorney asserts that it is easy for a Job who has everything he wants to remain virtuous, and that this will change as soon as he is put to the test. This officer is simply the angel on duty, even though in Hebrew he is called *satan*. The word does not yet imply "the Devil" with a capital D, but indicates the function of "district attorney." God allows this prosecuting officer to strip Job of everything except his life. And this is exactly what happens.

By presenting the story in Job 1–2 in this way, the writer lets us in on his, and God's, superior knowledge; the intention behind granting us this surplus insight is to make unambiguously clear that Job is completely pure. The result is that we watch the total degradation of the hero with a double perspective, and that we hear his bitter complaints with understanding and compassion. Job wants a fair trial, where he can maintain his integrity and call God to account; he is perfectly right to want that. Yet, he has to wait a very long time before any recognition comes from God, a cruel fate, and he does not know what we know: that all this is "only" a test.

Starting from Job 4, the friends in turn deliver speeches that are, each time, immediately answered by Job. The entire debate is in verse, and has probably always been an extremely difficult text right from its inception—that is, from the moment it was first heard. The language is condensed, and the poet uses every square centimeter to introduce fresh statements. Almost always, one chapter equals one poem, and it is also convenient that the full poetic line in this book (as in Proverbs) coincides with the numbered biblical verse.

The majority of the poems in the book of Job develop a line of reasoning that is closely connected to the division into strophes and stanzas. For our purposes I have selected ch.10. Its composition has so far not been correctly analyzed anywhere, but a sound structural analysis will put the correct articulation beyond doubt. If we manage to distinguish the strophe level clearly from the stanza level, much will have been gained.

An articulated argument: Job 10

Job 10 is a poem consisting of seventeen bicola and five tricola, grouped into nine strophes and four stanzas. The text of the first stanza is as follows:

Stanza I: Job 10:1–6

1   My soul is disgusted with life,   strophe 1
         I will give rein to my complaint,
             speak in the bitterness of my soul.
2   I say to God, "Do not condemn me,
         let me know what you charge me with.
3   Does it benefit you to oppress,
         and to despise the work of your hands,
             while shining on the counsel of the wicked?

4   Do you have the eyes of flesh?   strophe 2
         Is your vision that of mere men?
5   Are your days the days of a mortal,
         are your years the years of a man,
6   that you seek my iniquity
         and search out my sin?

The first strophe consists of 3 + 2 + 3 cola, and its verses have several tasks: describe, command, ask questions. The hero starts with himself. He describes his own deplorable situation and in this way makes the present the basis of his exposition. Next, he introduces the second person. He addresses God directly, and straightaway makes his point by commands and questions. The subject is guilt, and the tone is desperate: although Job knows he is innocent, he nevertheless inquires about a correctly worded deed of indictment—assuming that line 2b is not a blatant challenge. In v. 3 he goes a step further and insinuates: your values are all wrong, you keep the company of the wicked (v. 3c, a defiant position). Job is not one to mince matters; he has nothing to lose, after all, and is not afraid of anybody.

Job will not let go of the second person, and continues to pester God until the end of the poem. In strophe 2 he asks two questions (vv. 4–5), doubled via parallelism, which end in a specific point. Job ponders whether we may think of God as if he were a human being. His questions, however, are rhetorical, and it is obvious that they presuppose a negative answer. They end in a clear stance: persecuting me as mercilessly as this surely does not suit a transcendent individual. It is small-minded for a god to harass a puny mortal, and in any case absurd. That's one in the eye for God.

Stanza II: Job 10:7–13

7	You know that I am not guilty,	strophe 3
	but none can deliver from your hand.	
8	Your hands shaped and made me	
	and suddenly you have destroyed me!	
9	Consider that you made me like clay,	strophe 4
	and will turn me back into dust.	
10	Did you not pour me out as milk,	
	and congeal me like cheese?	
11	You clothed me with skin and flesh,	
	strung me with bones and sinews.	
12	Life and love you made me	strophe 5
	and you visited my spirit.	
13	Yet these things you hid in your heart,	
	I know you had this in mind.	

This stanza is neatly balanced by 2 + 3 + 2 verses. The center is easily recognizable as a strophe. This unit describes in graphic detail—albeit in slightly different terms than your family doctor would use—how man grows in the womb. Job talks about himself, but his words apply to every human being. The concrete terms in vv. 9–10 are evenly distributed over the four cola and consist of two pairs of metaphors: clay/dust, milk/cheese. In v. 11, this quartet is given a perfect counterbalance by four terms which are deliberately not metaphorical (skin, flesh, bones, sinews), and are presented in half the space: another two pairs, this time squeezed into only two half-verses, which makes v. 11 the climax of the strophe.

You have made me: the simple verb "to make" has become a keyword that appears in every strophe of this stanza. In strophe 3 it is combined with the metaphor (the anthropomorphism) of God's hands. Taking a closer look at the boundary between vv. 7 and 8, we discover concatenation: the word on which v. 7 ends is the same word with which v. 8 begins. This linking figure at the heart of the strophe represents a sort of collision. God's hand in v. 7b is an iron fist, whereas in v. 8a his hands are creating, and this act of creation—the speaker suggests—must have positive reasons. Does God not shape man in order to create life and love, as the speaker himself says in v. 12a? This remains to be seen.

The opening of this stanza is a sensitive place in the text. With one or two exceptions, all the translations and commentaries I am aware of get it hopelessly wrong here.[1] Through sentence structure v. 7a is connected to the preceding verses, which in practically all cases leads to a rendering along the lines of: "Is your vision that of man, and your days the days of a mortal . . . that you seek my iniquity and search out my sin, although you know that I am not guilty, and that there is none to deliver me from your hand?"

This connection is improbable right from the start, for a number of reasons. In such a translation, strophe 2 would consist of four verses, and v. 8 would be completely isolated as a one-line strophe; v. 8 does not fit into the well-balanced strophe 4, which is already three verses long. Such a link is counterintuitive and disturbs the proportions. The Hebrew text does not contain the conjunction "although" at the beginning of v. 7, but a preposition that can mean a lot of different things. Literally, v. 7a says: "Upon your knowledge, that I am not guilty." In theory this could be a syntactic adjunct to a preceding sentence core (i.e., in v. 6b). This solution, however, is both improbable and awkward. A conspicuous aspect of the book of Job is the fact that the poet uses almost every B-colon to present a new sentence, rather than letting the statement in the A-colon gently come to a halt in an adjunct of time, place, or mode. The B-colon almost always has something new to contribute, which is perhaps the main reason why the book of Job generates such intensity and emotional impact. If not even the B-colon is allowed the luxury of adding a syntactic detail, why should the A-colon of a new line be allowed to do so?

Thus, the Hebrew of v. 7a should be viewed as a new and nominal sentence, which may be literally translated as: "It is 'upon' your knowledge that . . ." The preposition here expresses an assignment: "You have to recognize that I am not guilty!" My readers will, of course, now be perfectly justified to ask once more: Is it acceptable or defensible to differ from virtually everybody else? My answer would be that structural analysis furnishes decisive arguments to say "yes" to this question. To this end, I observe the proportions and boundaries of the stanza and its strophic units.

Even the wrong translation cannot hide the fact that vv. 7 and

13 together form a ring, as shown by means of italics and bold type in the diagram below:

v. 7 **You** *know that* **I** am innocent,
      and that none can deliver *from your hand.*

    [vv. 8–12: the body of the second stanza]

v. 13 Yet these things you hid *in your heart,*
      I know that **you** had this in mind.

The iron fist and the heart full of secret plans that characterize God form one-half of the inclusion, and they bode little good. The other half consists of the complementary relationship between "your" and "my" knowledge. "You know that I am innocent"—but it does not look as if you are drawing the correct consequences from this. What is worse, I realize perfectly well that you are following a course that will lead to my destruction. By "these things" in v. 13a Job refers to all the forms of suffering God has sent him.

Thus, the poet uses his ring construction to create a comparison between God's knowledge (which is not put to any use) and Job's powerless knowledge. Job's knowledge is ineffective in a different way, but still superior to God's. With this whole stanza Job demonstrates that God not only refuses to deal consistently or correctly with Job's innocence, but is also himself trapped inside contradiction. Job shows this by literally watching God's hands: the same hands that were so creatively shaping a human form are now bent on destroying their own creation! Verse 8 alone already manages to spell this out, but the long text passage constituted by this stanza of three strophes is as a whole also a compelling argument in favor of the position that God is beset by internal contradictions. Again, this is a point scored against God.

Strophe 4 is the detailed exploration of v. 8a, the colon about God's creating hands that itself is a continuation of "the work of Your hands" of v. 3b (in the first strophe). These vv. 9–11 form an L-strophe. Next we get the S-strophe containing vv. 12–13, and this unit, too, suffers badly in the current translations. What it really boils down to is that our translators want to remain kind to God, with the result that the tormented hero is left to fend for himself. Take, for instance, the virtuous translation in the RSV: "Thou hast granted me life and steadfast love; and thy care has preserved my spirit."

Actually, the verb in v. 12a comes from the root that makes its first appearance in v. 3b (in "work," lit. "what is made"), and continues as the verb "to make" in vv. 8b and 9a. In the first place, the context for this keyword is unfavorable, and second, both the subject and the predicate of v. 12b consist of notoriously ambiguous words. Consequently, the word "care" should at the very least be replaced by something more neutral; the predicate, "guard," is repeated very soon after the stanza boundary, even as soon as v. 14a, and because of the context of its own strophe (the sixth, vv. 14–15) acquires a clearly negative ring. For this reason, the point of strophe 5 is just as delicate as vv. 3, 6, and 8. This unit should be read as sarcasm:

v. 12   Life and love you made me   strophe 5
              and your inspection guarded my spirit.
13   Yet these things you hid in your heart,
              I know you had this in mind.

The proof for this "nasty" reading is again provided by structural analysis. The ring construction which marks and delimits the stanza comprises not only the "knowledge" of v. 7 and v. 13, but also the connection between v. 8 and v. 12. God's "making" seems positive in 8a and 12a, but is plagued by inner contradiction, and in 12b and 8b proves to refer to the negative concepts of "keeping an eye on" and "destroying."

The climax of the sarcastic strophe 5 comes in the two words that sound so lovely, "life and love" (the latter the same Hebrew word which in Psalm 103 I have translated as "loyalty"). They provide the alibi for the usual pious reading of this unit.

These two words are used predicatively in the sentence. "Life and love you made me" is a way of phrasing which to my mind points to the meaning of life: we have been created living beings as an act of loyalty (of the God of the covenant, toward his creation), and in order to ourselves lend shape to faithfulness or love (toward God and our fellow humans).[2] The combination of these two words is unique in the Bible. I suspect they are a hendiadys, as is underlined by their sound; they are closely linked thanks to alliteration (*chayyim wachesed* in the original language). Furthermore, they have been placed in a perfectly planned position. Let us just do a quick count.

Verses 12–13 (= strophe 5) as a pair form the center of the composition, which consists of twenty-two verses (also the total number of the letters in the Hebrew alphabet). The poem contains forty-nine cola—i.e., the square of the holy number 7. The odd number implies that one colon will be the middle one of the series, and this is indeed v. 12a with its "life and love." What is more, the predicate of this clause, the keyword "to make," is the exact middle of the 169 words of the original. This exact center of the poem may now be read as a secret message from the speaker to his hearer, i.e., God: be consistent, and stick to your own principles! In order to hear this appeal, however, the hearer will have to see behind the mask of sarcasm or derision.

Stanza III: Job 10:14–17

14   You guard me when I sin   strophe 6
        and do not clear me of iniquity.
15   Should I be guilty—woe is me!
        When I am right, I cannot lift my head:
            I am sated with shame and drenched in misery.

16   Whoever lifts himself like a lion you hunt me   strophe 7
        and time and again your wondrous might
            is upon me.
17   You send new witnesses against me
        and increase your vexation with me,
            troops, yea, an army against me.

This stanza speaks largely for itself. There are two S-strophes, both consisting of a bicolon plus tricolon. The *motifs* of watching closely and splitting hairs are elaborated in strophe 6. Strophe 7 leaves nothing to the imagination as regards God's hostility, since total war has been declared here. The subjects of the strophes change: strophe 6 is given to the "I" and his deep misery; strophe 7 focuses on his assailant, who just does not let up. The concluding lines of the units both serve as climaxes, since they double the negative terms. In v. 15c we find "sated with shame and drenched in misery" as the nominal part of the predicate qualifying the "I," and "You" (still God in the second person) closes strophe 7 with "troops, yea, an army."

In v. 16a I have intentionally, and in accordance with the word order in the original, left out a comma, so that the question arises who exactly is the lion, God or Job? Without the comma the colon is ambiguous, as is the original; it may be read in two ways:

(a)   Whoever lifts himself, like a lion you hunt me
(b)   Whoever lifts himself like a lion, you hunt me

Option (a) roughly says: as soon as I venture to defend myself, I am confronted by a carnivorous animal, which is how you behave. Option (b) is also correct, since the ambiguity so beloved by poets means they want to have their cake and eat it. The second option says something like: although I show the courage of a lion when I fight you, I will lose, because you keep pursuing me.

Stanza IV: Job 10:18–22

18   Why did you let me come out of the womb?   strophe 8
           If I expire, no eye would see me!
19   I would be as though I never was,
           carried from the womb to the grave!

20   Are not my days few? So desist!   strophe 9
           Leave me alone, let me feel a bit of joy,
21   before I depart, never to return,
           for the land of darkness and death's shadow,
22   a land of gloom, like dusk,
           death's shadow and disorder,
               which shines like dusk.

The drift of this stanza is also clear. I will therefore simply point out a number of striking details: strophe 8 is an echo of the extremely bitter complaint in ch. 3, which formed the prologue to the debate. It is a real death wish, working toward the climax of the poem, and phrased in terms of a daring other wish: a counterfactual dream of never having been forced to start the nightmare of this life. The same "impossible" mode has been used by Job extensively in the frenetic complaint with which the poetry of the book started.

Stanza IV is the unit of death. The massive catalogue of terms for the underworld dominates four of the seven cola. Job starts his last strophe once more with the energy/power of the command mode. He asks for nothing more, however, than a brief respite, a short break. But this short moment is soon defeated by death. All hope is swallowed up by an inventory of darkness and chaos, which threatens to go on and on. The construction of v. 20 with a double predicate in each colon is a tight chiasm, where the commands are framed by terms for brevity: a little bit of joy for just a few days.

The sentence structure in the strophe is rather paradoxical: the request "desist" is the main clause, after which the entire complex from 21a through 22c is "only" a temporal subclause. The effect, however, is the reverse. The request is phrased in only a few words, and the speaker has little confidence that it will be taken seriously. After that, we are inundated by the vast and complete darkness that usurps the strophe, as it were.

The poem now seems finished—but is it? The poet has saved his most spectacular subtlety for the very last colon. There, an oxymoron* appears: darkness that shines! By deploying this verb the poet finishes his piece in the fashion of a snake biting its tail. "Shining" is what God already did in v. 3c, a colon that straightaway in the first strophe took the criticism of God to a climax by presenting God as an ally of the wicked.

Furthermore, in the original text, the verb "to shine" in 22c is an anagram* of the word "pitch dark," which opens v. 22, so that the oxymoron is strengthened even further. The connection between the last strophe and the final colon of the opening strophe has far-reaching consequences for the significance of the poem as a whole: in this way, Job suggests that God has chosen the side of chaos, darkness, and sin by persecuting him relentlessly and without reason. These, then, are "the things you hid in your heart," as Job says. As I have stated before, there are numerous passages in the Bible for which one needs a strong stomach.

The overall composition of the poem follows an AB-A'B' pattern:

Stanza I

A   you consider me guilty
      you persecute me

Stanza II

B   my *birth:* you are my maker,
      but you plot against me

Stanza III

A'   you deny my innocence,
      you hunt me

Stanza IV

B'   my *death:* give me respite,
      before I enter total darkness

The main correspondences on which this parallelism of the poem halves is based have already been discussed. I would like, however, to draw your attention to just a few more connections. First, if we compare stanzas I and III based on their A–A' relationship, we note what strophes 1 and 6 have in common: the central notion of "my" supposed guilt versus "my" innocence. The exclamation "woe is me!" is the continuation of the complaint of the tricolon v. 1. There is a neat chiasm as well, since section A ends on injustice and sin, whereas A' (i.e., on the other side of stanza II) starts with sin and injustice. The B–B' relationship between stanzas II and IV is first of all based on a polarity: the beginning and end of human life. However, strophe 8 (the beginning of stanza IV) also provides a verbal link by twice using the word that might well be the title of strophe 4 (the L-strophe about the embryo), "womb," and by connecting this rather crassly to the grave, in one and the same colon (v. 19b). Finally, strophes 5 and 8, flanking stanza II, in the original language have the word "spirit" in common, which I have tried to echo by "expire" in v. 18b; in the context, "spirit" means something like "my life."

10

Love poetry

The Song of Songs

How religious is the Song of Songs?

Practically all of the texts in the amazingly varied collection we call the Bible are of a literary nature. This is true not only of the stories and poems, but also of the laws and commandments. Even dull catalogues such as genealogical tables (mainly in Genesis), or enumerations of dwelling places on or within the boundaries of tribal regions (cf. Joshua) are presented within a literary framework. But can all these texts also be labeled religious?

Of course, the vast majority are religious texts. The Hebrew poets, for one, are almost always concerned with God, in the second or third person, and this may often be reversed: God keeps poets occupied, in two senses of the word. Poets either express how God touches them, in a positive or negative sense, or tell us how God fascinates them with His presence, or conversely, his distressing absence; this testimony is expressed either in a minor key—in the form of complaints or protests—or in a major key—as hymns of praise or thanks. The narrators and lawgivers, too, stay within the field of religion. Even in those passages where God does not appear as a participant in the action or as a speaking character, the values expressed by the writers are moral, and in the final analysis, religious.

Thus, it is all the more remarkable that the Bible also contains a collection of poetry like the Song of Songs: a short book in which God is not mentioned at all.[1] We do not really know why the early Jewish religious community included this collection in the canon, although theories abound. Be that as it may, the Song of Songs is a marvelously fresh and uninhibited work.

Recent authors such as Francis Landy and André LaCocque have opened our eyes to the love poems' surprising subversiveness,

in view of the society in which they originated.[2] Various aspects
of the Hebrew and the appearance of a veritable Greek loan word
lead us to assume that the Song of Songs was composed around
the third century BCE. King Solomon is presented here already
almost like a fairy-tale character. Because of the pleasant alliterations with "Shulamite" (as the girl is called in ch. 7), the name of
the capital Jerusalem, and *shalom* in 8:10, his name forms part of a
web of meanings. The sound of the name is more important to the
poet than the historical figure of Solomon himself. He did attri-
bute his book of poems to the king in 1:1, but like Ecclesiastes 1:1
this is an instance of pseudepigraphy (lit. "false attribution"). In
antiquity our concept of plagiarism was unknown, and anybody
who had composed a good poem or a series of proverbs tried to
draw attention to it and enhance its prestige from the outset by
inscribing it with a famous name from the past.

Is the Song of Songs subversive? The ancient Middle East was
at least as disapproving and repressive toward eroticism and sexuality as it is now, and social control was extremely strict. The Song
of Songs also offers clear confirmation of this, for instance, in the
watchmen patrolling the town who chase the girl and beat her
until she bleeds, when she ventures to go out in the dark and look
for her beloved, 3:3 and 5:7. Free and unrestricted sexuality was
taboo.

Roughly the same may be said of the reception history of the
Song of Songs. Its poetry has for more than 1,500 years suffered
neurotic treatment at the hands of Jewish and Christian exegetes.
Out of embarrassment or (not openly admitted) outrage at the
direct and open way in which the Song of Songs speaks of sexual
attraction and the sexual act, interpreters decided to whitewash all
offensive elements wherever possible, by subjecting the book to
allegorization*. The Jews maintained that the lover is an image of
God, and that the girl represents the people of Israel. The Christians adopted their own, even more far-fetched variant: the lover
is Christ, and the girl is the Church. Both groups tried to sell this
interpretative technique as a form of spiritualization.

This method of "exegesis" (lit. "drawing out," but in this case
rather a form of "adding on") was already on its last legs two
centuries ago, but has long continued to make itself felt in the

interpretation of the Song of Songs. Many commentators and translators in the nineteenth and twentieth centuries have tried their utmost to "civilize" the lovers and make them fit for polite society by maintaining that the book was originally used in the context (or *Sitz im Leben*,* as the technical term is) of a marriage ceremony, so that the strophes exchanged by the pair could be presented as acceptable wedding songs. When the voice of one lover was replaced by that of the other, this was indicated in the margin of the translation, not by neutral terms such as "he" or "she," but by "bridegroom" and "bride"—which is still the case in the New American Standard Bible and some European translations. A shocking example of translation manipulating the reader and producing ideological pollution.

The question is now: Is it possible to civilize love? The writer of the Song of Songs would answer that love is not civilized. Neither is it uncivilized—in Nietzsche's phrase, true love is "beyond good and evil" (*jenseits von Gut und Böse*). The lovers whom the writer has allowed to fill the entire Song of Songs are never bothered by morality or religion. They are carefree, spontaneous, and pure. Their senses are wide open to enjoyment: they enjoy each other, the wide space of the landscape, and the smells and colors in which the world is now steeped. The only remaining question is a bit of a poser and concerns us rather than them: Are we as readers also allowed to enjoy ourselves?

We may certainly relax and enjoy the spring song in ch. 2 of the Song of Songs, in which the girl speaks.

The Spring Song: 2:8–17

Songs 2:8a	Hark: my beloved—there he comes!	
b	he leaps over mountains,	
c	bounds over hills.	strophe 1
9a	My beloved is like a gazelle	
b	or like a young stag.	
c	There he stands, behind our wall,	
d	he is gazing through the window,	
e	peering through the lattice.	
10a	*My beloved called and spoke to me:*	
b	"Arise, my darling,	
c	come away, my fair one!	strophe 2
11a	For look, the winter is past,	
b	the rains are over and gone.	
12a	The blossoms have appeared on the land,	
b	the time of pruning/singing has come	
c	and the voice of the turtledove is heard in our land.	
13a	The fig colors its unripe fruit,	
b	the vines in blossom give off their fragrance.	
13c	Arise, my darling,	
d	come away, my fair one!	
14a	My dove, in the crannies of the rock,	strophe 3
b	hidden in the cliff,	
c	let me see your face,	
d	let me hear your voice,	
e	for your voice is sweet	
f	and your face is comely."	
[15a	Catch us the foxes,	intermezzo: duet
b	the little foxes,	
c	that ruin the vineyards,	
d	our vineyard which is in blossom!]	
16a	My beloved is mine, and I am his,	
b	who browses among the lilies,	
17a	before the day blows	strophe 4
b	and the shadows take flight:	
c	Turn round, my love, be like a gazelle	
d	or a young stag	
e	on the cleft hills.	

These verses are faintly reminiscent of the oldest known song in English, the medieval canon "Summer is icumen in." Many details hardly require any commentary. Crucial here is the articulation into strophes. In v. 10a we notice a quotation formula, familiar from prose texts, which we may leave out of the actual poem or its meter. This line has far-reaching consequences, as it proves that the girl has verbal control of the poem as a whole, and that the young man is allowed to speak only when she lets him. Verse 10bc, a bicolon, returns without any changes as v. 13cd. This rather extensive repetition proves that the young man has not finished speaking after v. 13ab, and also indicates that we cross a threshold into a new strophe.

Thus, the young man speaks two complete strophes, but only because he has been given the floor. This means that his words, from v. 10b through v. 14f., are embedded speech, i.e., second-degree direct speech. The strophes introducing him, and thus responsible for the embedding, are spoken by the girl (strophes 1 and 4). I will leave v. 15 aside for the moment.

The girl's two strophes encircle the two spoken by the boy according to a symmetrical AB-B'A' pattern, suggesting a tight or closed construction. This proves to be correct when we look at content and images. In strophe 1, the girl compares her lover to a gazelle and its quick, jumpy movements. This simile returns in strophe 4, in v. 17cd, and here, too, the point of the comparison is movement. But from where to where? And at which time of day? In these matters of time and space, many translations are unfortunately in total disarray, and the same applies to the parallel v. 8:14, which constitutes the very last verse of the Song of Songs.

Searching for a solution, I again look at v. 17. The sentence core is an imperative in 17c (extended by another imperative, still in 17c), preceded by a temporal clause which I will here render literally: "Before the day blows / and the shadows take flight // turn round, my love, / be like a gazelle," etc. Traditional exegesis* immediately created problems for itself here by consulting the Palestine meteorological institute, where they were told that after a hot day a light breeze often blows in the evening. This information was combined with "the day blows," and resulted in the conclusion that v. 17 refers to the evening.

A sound structural analysis and some sober considerations will prevent us from falling into these traps. Reading the text from back to front, I notice that the original language speaks of shadows running away, using a verb that never means anything but "taking flight." Running away is what people do from enemies, in case of war or disaster. The question then becomes: Who is the enemy of the shadows, who forces them to fly? To which the simple answer is: the burning sun. In Palestine, the sun often rises so high that a man hardly casts a shadow. The sun wins in the morning, not at night. In the evening, the shadows gain the upper hand and within a quarter of an hour expand into total darkness. The information that the day "blows" we may now take as a metaphor: the day breathes, comes to life—which fits the morning. Then, the girl says: "turn round," which is not at all the same as saying "come," although many translations opt for this. Does she want the boy to leave?

The interpretation of v. 17 as referring to the morning is fortunately offered by the RSV, and is proved by the chiastic symmetry of the poem. Such a crosswise construction is eminently suited to expressing polarities, differences, or contrasts, in this case about the directions in which the boy is moving. Whereas strophes 1 and 4 devote the same simile to the young man's fast movements, their cohesion (symmetry-*cum*-difference) is that of coming and going. The boy comes to enjoy love and being together with his girlfriend, but he must take care to get away before the break of dawn in order not to be caught.

In the middle he invitingly sings her a song of the spring. Strophes 2 and 3 fill in the B–B' correspondence by sharing visual and auditive terms, and first of all by both starting with identical appeals from the boy to the girl. The gazelle's darting course through nature is stopped by the arrangements of culture: the lattice of her house. I interpret this as an image of society barring access to the girl. Consequently, these bars are the first item the boy addresses when he starts his textual units B–B' (= strophes 2 and 3) with his repeated appeal: he asks her to come out. Then it is her turn to move, and in this way the cultural barrier may be removed.

The young man lets himself be inspired by the fact that his girlfriend has "transformed" him into a gazelle in strophe 1, since he in turn makes her a dove. There is another parallel in the way they each use the simile: the gazelle's leaping is linked to the mountains, but there is the pleasant anticipation that "he" is coming. The girl in turn is a dove hidden in a cranny of the rock, being invited to come out. This is followed in v. 14cdef by a quartet of cola combining the senses of vision and hearing in a chiasm, and focusing on the girl's loveliness.

Seeing and hearing are also mentioned in strophe 2, and there, too, the subtleties of form are considerable. In the tricolon v. 12, the A-colon is visual and the C-colon auditory, while both versets end in an epiphora* or rhyme, "the/our land." What happens in the B-colon? In v. 12b, the poet uses a word (*zamier* in the original language) that has various meanings, and is a homonym—he wants to keep all his options open. If we translate it by "pruning," we picture the gardener at work, right after the winter, which links 12b to the visual A-colon. If on the other hand we translate it by "singing," which is just as legitimate, 12b becomes a perfect partner for the auditory C-colon. We have here a splendid example of ambiguity: a *double entendre* that indeed doubles the word meaning. The turtledove of v. 12c anticipates the dove of v. 14a. Verse 13 returns to the visual mode, and shows us the plants that are the objects of the farmer's attention. At the same time they are expressions (and metaphors) of awakening love, and together with the blossoms of v. 12a provide an inclusion for the second half of the strophe.

The seductive tones and images coming from the young man are answered by the girl. She speaks a sentence which is almost a formula: "My beloved is mine and I am his." This is in any case a key sentence with respect to her position and the part she plays, since it returns in 6:3—a crucial passage about the consummation of love, and a center of gravity in the composition of the book— and there are variations such as 7:11a and 13e. In the original text, the sounds are a beautiful alternation of the long vowels i and o— *dodi li wa-ani lo*, a sentence of unsurpassed compactness, consisting of only seven syllables. In combination with the word meanings these vowels form a chiasm, as the perfect expression of reciprocity: the two belong to each other heart and soul. The closedness of the AB-B'A' pattern symbolizes their inseparability.

This formula of reciprocity (as we may call it) is the threshold of the final strophe. Within the poem I read the girl's phrase as her "yes" to him, after he has seduced her with his song for two whole strophes. In only a few syllables she manages to speak more dia- logically than he did in seventeen cola. Next, however, she has to draw his attention to the pressure of time and the reality of soci- ety. She follows up her formula of inseparability by urgent words of leave-taking: quick, get out now, or else. . . . The very last words of the poem have the gazelle leave through "cleft hills," and if we steer clear of prudish tradition we should take this as a reference (spoken by the girl herself!) to the lover's visit to her mount of Venus, her genitals.

The rigorous AB–B'A' model of this poem, with its movements to and fro, is rudely interrupted by v. 15. Which voice is respon- sible for this pair of bicola? Nobody can offer any certainty on this point, so that readers are at liberty to view this verse in any way they please. Suddenly an "us" appears in the text, in roughly the same way as in 1:17 (after "he" has sung 1:15 and "she" answered with 1:16), which would seem to indicate that 2:15 may be viewed as a strophe sung by the boy and his girlfriend together, a duet in which they defend the garden of love against attacks from outside.

This short strophe again uses vegetative images, and again men- tions animals. These aspects argue in favor of accepting this unit in the place where it is now, for the following reasons. The foxes (elsewhere the word can even mean "jackals," for instance, in Job) are destructive burrowers, and thus are the opposites of dove and gazelle here. The vine is the privileged plant in the Song of Songs, and the vineyard is the equally privileged application of the con- cept "garden." Every now and then these words retain a little of their literal meanings, but their figurative meaning is far more important: the vineyard is the foremost image of the place where love is, then of love itself, and the enjoyment of it. It fits into a series: the trio of fig, olive, and vine, which in Judges 9 so effec- tively populates Jotham's parable-and-fable is now complete in our spring song—another signal warning us against leaving out v. 15.

Verse 15 seems highly out of place in a composition that in all its other parts exhibits such a strict symmetry. However, there is a way to integrate this strophe into the whole after all: by seeing that this disruption parallels the work of the foxes in the carefully fenced-off vineyard (compare the parable in Isaiah 5). In their duet the lovers recognize the existence of counterforces, and at the same time encourage each other to resist them. The poet integrates the strophe about disruption by himself introducing a form of disruption. This means that v. 15, in itself a poetic signal (a group of language signs that belong together), has an iconic function: by its form, and by its presence, it is an interloper, which is an image (icon, see also chapter 5) of the intruders in the vineyard.

Beginning and end of the book are linked by a number of underrated forms of inclusion, one of which is the vineyard. In 1:6cde, the girl, probably walking through the fields tending the sheep, and in any case rather sunburnt, reproaches herself as follows:

1:6c   My mother's sons quarreled with me
  d   and made me guard of the vineyards—
  e   my own vineyard I did not guard!

We see a fascinating tension between literal and figurative speech. And readers who may have missed it are further enlightened by this mini-parable from the concluding chapter:

8:11   Solomon had a vineyard
            in Baal-hamon ("place of bounty").
       He gave that vineyard to guards,
            each bringing a thousand pieces of silver for its fruit.
  12   My very own vineyard is before me,
            the thousand pieces are yours, Solomon,
                 and two hundred to the guards of its fruit.

Again we see the merging of the literal with the figurative. "My vineyard" is her own experience of love, which is priceless. Shortly before, in 8:6–7, the famous passage about love being as strong as death and not to be quenched by vast floods, she had said (in a slightly freer translation):

8:7c   If a man offered everything he possessed for love,
  d   he will be covered with insult and scorn.

Obviously, "Money can't buy you love" is an old refrain! Again, the verb "to give" has been used; on the last page it is a keyword creating a connection with vv. 11–12.

Verse 8:13 constitutes the last words from the young man; he is eager to hear her voice—a request that echoes 2:14. This is followed by the very last verse of the book, another echo of the spring song. Who is speaking? According to the standard Roman Catholic Dutch translation, this is the boy. The translators have put "he" in the margin opposite v. 11, and have inserted no further blank lines after that; this means that they believe that all the text from v. 11 through v. 14 is the boy's, starting with the parable of Solomon's vineyard (an unfortunate decision), and including the final verse. This is a particularly glaring mistake, and the translation they offer is also way off the mark:

Songs 8:14   Come quickly, my love, be like the gazelle
                   or the young stag on the hills of spices.

The fact alone that the gazelle simile had earlier been used by the girl makes this translation implausible, and it is made even more implausible because of the parallelism between this verse and 2:17. What is worse, in the original language there is no "come" or "come quickly." This rendering is a travesty of the truth, which is that the girl again simply and unequivocally uses a form of "to flee." Although choosing another root than the earlier fleeing of the shadows, i.e., a synonym, she does say "flee," using a word whose meaning is beyond doubt. The sorry height of bad translation, however, is achieved by the fact that this rendering ignores the grammatical gender in v. 14a: in the original language, both forms of the imperative are in fact masculine singular, which proves beyond doubt that it is the girl speaking here instead of the boy.

The New English Bible, which continually uses the ideologically tainted terms "bridegroom" and "bride" to designate the speakers in the Song, also uses these titles for the last two speeches. The translators do recognize that v. 13 is spoken by the boy and v. 14 by the girl. Here too, however, the verb of movement has been translated totally wrongly by "Come into the open, my beloved." Thus, in a wishy-washy manner which borders on the malicious, the Song of Songs is supplied with something vaguely resembling a happy ending; in reality, the book ends with another of the numerous leave-takings between the two, who are again deprived of each other's company because of the force of a repressive society. So, we might say that

a) the real implication of the Song of Songs is that the pair might be better off getting a marriage license, and be rid of all the hassle;

b) the translators did not hesitate to take it upon themselves to file away the rough edges of the Song of Songs, so that the reader has no opportunity to become aware of these, which in turn has the paradoxical result of strengthening bourgeois repression by making it invisible.

Guidelines for reading the Song of Songs

The entire Song of Songs is a dialogue between a male and a female voice. The rare poetic lines they do not speak are the exceptions that serve only to confirm the rule. The two voices continually alternate, often rapidly, which is the main source of the great dynamic force that characterizes the book.

The quick changes of voice are of fundamental importance to the reader. We will lose the thread if we do not remain attentive and if we do not first ask ourselves at the beginning of each verse: Who is speaking here? And is he/she actually speaking to his/her partner? This is usually the case, but occasionally the speaker is addressing his/her peer group. Anybody who reads Hebrew will be able to supply a decisive answer at the very beginning of practically every strophe. Within two or three words the grammatical gender of an imperative, vocative, etc. has become clear, so that the hearer of the original language immediately understands that the speaker is of the opposite sex. An example is 4:8a, where a voice says: "Come from Lebanon!" In English, the word "come" does not reveal anything about the sex of the addressee; in Hebrew, it always does. Here, it is a feminine form, so that by the second syllable the Hebraist can already conclude that the boy is speaking here. In 4:8a users of a translation need not wait very long, as the command is followed by the vocative "bride"—a semantic signal about the addressee that reveals the sex of the speaker.

Thus, anyone who reads the Song of Songs in English profits greatly from an indication of the sex of the speaker in the margin. For a correct understanding of the text it is crucial to be able to follow the quick changes of voice. Here, the Dutch Roman Catholic translation I criticized earlier leads by example, and has been sensible enough to use the neutral and short "he" and "she"; an apparent break with the tradition of using the saccharine terms "bride" and "bridegroom," which are far too interpretative and lead the reader astray.[3] I myself hope to be of service on this point in chapter 12, where in the "Guidelines for further reading" I give the verse numbers for all entries (i.e., changes of voice) in the Song of Songs. Anyone who loses track for a moment of who is who in the translation may find the answer there. One fact gleaned from the list is that the girl speaks thirty times, the boy eighteen times.

A second matter of fundamental importance is the question of how much unity there is in this collection of love poetry. It would be nice if we could switch off our expectations for a moment. The exegetical school that in the nineteenth and twentieth centuries succeeded the allegorizing approach and is sometimes called "naturalistic" has until recently paid insufficient attention to the various specifically literary signals of cohesion. The unfortunate result was that the Song of Songs was treated atomistically, as a long string of scattered snippets. Jews and Christians of partly or wholly fundamentalist signature would not let go of the concept of Solomon's authorship, and bent over backwards trying to prove that the Song of Songs really was extremely old, etc. Scholars went mad speculating about background, *Sitz im Leben,* and date of origin; Palestinian wedding songs from the nineteenth century were dragged in to provide parallels, and so on and so forth. This type of research, however, is about as relevant as the question when and where Rumpelstiltskin lived, what his age was, and whether he had brown or blue eyes.

During the past thirty years the tide of research has fortunately turned; scholars are more willing to let the Song of Songs speak for itself, and have discovered that listening closely is really all that is required, instead of ferreting around next to or underneath the text;[4] it is also far more productive.

Because the Song of Songs is rather mercurial in its playfulness and dynamics, it cannot be easily accommodated in an outline or diagram. From the outset the text dodges all attempts at labeling, and anyone trying to subject it to a strict division should be warned. Yet, it is worth the effort to have a shot at it. It is both possible and sensible to provide the reader with some sort of foothold, thanks to a characteristic of the Song of Songs itself: the presence and distribution of various repetitions.

The book may be seen as a composition in seven "blocks": there are seven groups of short textual units, the units being separate strophes or poems. Thus, block II consists of two poems: the spring song in four strophes, which we have just read, plus the "story" of a nocturnal quest in 3:1–4.

The outside blocks have the least rigorous structure, at least if we consider them separately. These are 1:2–2:7 and 8:5–14, and they seem to offer a fragmentary series of impressions. Thus, it is all the more striking that they have various points of contact, which I would like to see as forms of inclusion after all. Not only is there the girl's neglected but eventually nicely cultivated "vineyard," mentioned earlier (and found in 1:6 and 8:11–12), there is also a group of young men: the girl's brothers in 1:6c and their song about protecting her in 8:8–9 (eight cola), plus the boy's friends, the shepherds mentioned in 1:7 and 8:13b. Furthermore, there is the intimacy of table and home in 1:4, 12, 17, and 2:4 (about a dozen cola, spoken by the girl), corresponding to the ten cola of 8:1–3 that also come from her (and together with 8:4 constitute the conclusion of block VI).

Blocks I and II are closed by a refrain verse that contributes greatly to unifying the collection, and which deserves closer scrutiny. First, however, I will present an outline of the structure:

block	I	II	III	IV	V	VI	VII
verses	1:2–2:7	2:8–3:5	3:6–5:1	5:2–6:3	6:4–7:6	7:7–8:4	8:5–14

The circular shape of an embrace—also that of the explicit embrace in 2:6—may have inspired the poet to his demarcation of block I: an inclusion made up by the intimacy of house, wine, and embrace (the first two strophes, 1:2–4, and the last strophe, 2:4–6).

The change of voice not only is of crucial significance for the understanding of each verse, but also proves to be a prominent criterion for the main outline. The whole of block II really goes to the girl. The two strophes we have heard from the boy in 2:10–14 have been granted to him by her, but have "only" the status of embedded speech.

Block III devotes its opening to "the chorus": to the "daughters of Jerusalem," who are the girl's peers and sing of the approach of "Solomon's" palanquin, accompanied by a throng of sixty warriors. This description acquires an apt counterpart in 6:8–10, which in contrast is recited by the boy, and in which a crowd of sixty "queens" surrounds the "bride's" cortege. The girl reacts to the chorus (which spoke 3:6–10) in 3:11, and incites her friends/the girls to follow her king admiringly with their gazes.

After these female voices, the body of block III goes to the boy. In 4:1–7 he presents his first example of a so-called "descriptive song" (the Arabic term, which I like to use, is *wasf*), which is also the longest. In a series of bold metaphors, he depicts his lover's body, starting at the top with the eyes and hair. The range of the description is exactly that of a bust, and in its visual fixation on her the song resembles a photograph. It concludes with a striking parallel to the time limit I was forced to discuss earlier, together with 2:17, as it has been so ineptly translated:

Songs 4:6   Before the day breathes
                    and the shadows flee
              I want to go to the mountain of myrrh,
                    and the hill of frankincense:
      7   every part of you is fair, my darling
                    there is no blemish on you.

It is not necessary to have a dirty mind to make the connection with 2:17: the hill of frankincense is none other than the cleft hill. The verse after the colon (:) is a summary or conclusion, and employs the all-nothing contrast.

In the sequel, the idea of consummation (the sexual act) becomes more prominent. First, the young man utters an invitation (two strophes, 4:8–11) in which he represents her embraces as wine. With this, he exactly mirrors what his enamored did at the very beginning (where in 1:2 we saw the colon "your embraces are sweeter than wine"). The impressive and rough landscape of the Lebanon mountains serves as the backdrop.

In 4:12–15, the boy bursts into a stream of metaphors. These, too, are images from the landscape, but this time of more cultivated land. The central metaphor here is the garden, for the garden is you, the boy says. The girl is given one strophe (4:16) and being of the same mind says: "Let my beloved come to this garden, / and enjoy its luscious fruits"—it is easy to guess what it is that she thus permits and encourages. The ending of block III goes to the boy, in 5:1ab and cd. He does go into the garden, and eats and drinks there. Then, the final line, 5:1ef, says, using verbs in the masculine plural:

> eat, my friends, and drink / and get drunk on embraces

A nice transition, as in the A-colon we might still be under the impression that a real feast is being described, and "eating" and "drinking" literally represent eating and drinking. The metaphor in the B-colon, however, rapidly cures us of such naïveté. (Eating, drinking, and getting somebody else drunk was the lethal program to which David subjected his guest Uriah in 2 Sam. 11. When, however, Uriah's virtue did not falter in spite of all the alcohol, the king allowed him to take his own sealed death warrant to the front. That whole episode was also about consummating love, but David's adultery with Bathsheba is in strong contrast to the paradisiacal purity of the lovers in the Song of Songs!)

In the text, a series of correspondences may be found that support the idea of a concentric structure. I am certainly not going to belabor this point of a closed symmetry too much, given that the liveliness of the Song of Songs is hardly compatible with a compelling and rigorous structure. However, I do think that the line addressed to "my friends" (5:1ef) is the center of a more or less concentric design. As such, it is remarkable, because this recommendation to enjoy embraces is a concluding line by which the speaker abandons the contact for a moment; he places himself outside the intimacy of "you" and "me," and invites others to join in— it might even be an invitation to the readers! And another thing: by whom is this verse spoken exactly? Is the young man speaking to the boys? Is the couple speaking to friends both male and female? These possibilities cannot be excluded.

The question of who is speaking is also a decisive factor in block IV; this time, the entire text goes to the women. During one short strophe (5:2cdef), the girl quotes the boy—another instance of embedded speech—but all of the remaining text in 5:2 through 6:3 is spoken by the girl and her friends. In 5:2 she again tells of the arrival of her lover, and sings of her great desire for him. The ending is tragic: she receives a thrashing after a fruitless search. Next, she impresses upon the "daughters of Jerusalem" something she also said in 2:5c: "I am faint with love." This verse, 5:8, is the pivot of block IV. The second half consists mainly of another "descriptive song," this time a *wasf* sung by her about him: her only one, but a long one, of exactly twelve verses, 5:10–16. She, too, starts at the top in her part-by-part account of his body, but goes further down, to his thighs. Verse 16 is a clear form of conclusion.

On either side of the descriptive song the chorus have had two speeches. Verses 5:9 and 6:1 are two quartets of cola, i.e., S-strophes, in which the girls act as if they ask her for information about him. The parallelism is rather special here, as the A-cola are the same in both cases, and the first B-colon does not change: 9b is identical to 6:1b, a vocative addressing her as the "fairest among women." In both these questions the chorus acts as a stooge: the girl may now break out in a long description of his beautiful body, ending in 6:2–3 in short but sweet verses of . . . consummation, again through the image of the garden. This makes the end of block IV the exact parallel of the end of III.

Next, the other voice takes over again, also for a long time: block V as a whole goes to the young man. The opening is a true *da capo*, as in 6:4–7 he repeats half of his descriptive song from 4:1–7. The conclusion is also a description, so that the repeated use of the same genre here already serves to frame the block. This is the third and last descriptive song coming from the young man, in 7:1–5, and this time he works from the bottom up. The dance which he encourages the girl to perform in 6:13 draws his gaze down to her feet, so that in 7:1 he starts by describing the dance steps she makes.[5]

Block VI consists of three stanzas. The boy compares her form to that of a palm tree in 7:7–9. The girl replies with new images of garden and vine in 11–14, and completes this block with 8:1–4, a stanza that sets out to provide a roof for the desired intimacy. Enjoying each other undisturbed is not easy:

Songs 8:1   Who could make you like a brother of mine
            that also nursed at my mother's breast!
            Then I would meet you outside, I would kiss you
            and yet, no one would despise me.

The strophe once again makes clear that the partners cannot give free rein to their passion in the open air, and quickly feel watched. The scorn of v. 1d soon returns, in the colon 8:7f. mentioned earlier.

In 8:3 we find an identical bicolon to 2:6. This is the upbeat to 8:4, the exact continuation of the slightly fuller S-strophes 2:7 and 3:5, which carry the same message. This threefold refrain is one of the most powerful tools by which the poet manages to keep his collection together. A lot is going on here that merits analysis:

Songs 2:7   I adjure you, daughters of Jerusalem,
            by the gazelles or the hinds of the field:
            do not wake or rouse
            love before it pleases.

This strophe—which by its distribution marks the end of a block no fewer than three times and always comes from the girl—is remarkable for more than one reason. In the first place, the speaker places herself radically outside the intimate *tête-à-tête* that characterizes all other speech in the Song of Songs: for a moment, she relinquishes the you-and-me intimacy. On the whole, the boy and girl do not lapse into philosophical prattle, noncommittal talk about yesterday and tomorrow, or gossip about neighbors: they always concentrate on expressing the here and now that is created by love, and they speak about *their* love: attraction, desire, meeting followed by leave-taking.

However, there is one exception to this: the refrain. There, the girl generalizes about love, she is not addressing her lover but her group of friends, and she pronounces an important admonition. In these generalizations and admonishments, I recognize the tone and genre of Wisdom literature; with a minimum of adaptations, the words would not be out of place in a collection of proverbs.

Thus, in these moments of closure—in 2:7 and 3:5 and 8:4—the girl shows herself capable of drawing abstract conclusions from her actual experience. At the same time, however, the refrain enables her to deal with and use her emotions, since before and after the refrain she speaks a large number of intense strophes about the immense power of love, and from this she draws a lesson that she wants to share with her peers.

The girl's view of love is certainly not rose-colored. Her most famous verse (8:6cd) in a literal translation runs as follows: "Yea, love is as fierce as death, / hard as Hades is passion." The alliteration with the h I have used in the B-colon is a faint reflection of the hard k- and s-sounds in the original text, and "my" Hades is the underworld that the poet of the Psalms calls Sheol.

Love, then, is not a force to be toyed with, and we should not be so stupid (the girl tells her friends) as to stir it up prematurely, or manipulate it in some way, since love's authenticity will then be lost and forces released which may swallow you up. The girl speaks with authority here: all her other verses give the reader a direct and vivid picture of the forces to which she, being so much in love, is exposed.

11

The reader's attitude

Productive questions and hints

The proper reading attitude

The text is completely defenseless against any form of abuse; for the text, the reader is either a blessing or a curse. Much depends on our attitude. We may decide to work on our open-mindedness, and constantly adapt our picture of the text while reading. Curiosity is a great asset; self-criticism is even better.

Reading properly is always active puzzle-solving: comparing elements, checking on a character's history, sometimes consulting an atlas or a Bible handbook. Asking questions is more important than committing ourselves to answers. Uncertainty means that one is still open for change and rejuvenation; certainty may soon turn to atrophy. Being able to work with such simple, but basic, poetic tools as parallelism, voice shifts, verse structure, and the distribution of repeated elements is much more important in the encounter with the Bible than being devout

All this may also be formulated in negative terms: what are our biggest traps? To mention a few:

1) Our desire to know: after some reading and searching, we want to come up with a finished interpretation, and are (too) easily satisfied with a total picture based on only partial observation of the textual characteristics. In this way we commit ourselves, and forget to check our results rigorously against the text itself once more, sometime during the procedure.

2) We allow our energy and attention to be sucked up by the historical world that is connected to the origin of the text, and somewhere hides the cause of its being written. That reality, or the reality of whichever century, has a different mode of being than a story as a creative but finite string of language signs. Do not be tempted to speculate on "how it really was," there and then, so far

away and so long ago, in that utterly alien culture. The poem accommodates these far horizons in its own way, but never exclusively consists of referencing them. Through the medium of our attention and our act of reading, it constructs its own world in words, which has only a tenuous and indirect contact with what is irretrievably past and gone.

3) An insidious form of delusion arises from the spectacles we ourselves are wearing: our unspoken hopes; expectations; our preconceived notions about Moses, Jesus, and ancient Israel; and especially our prejudices, beliefs, and unshakeable convictions. Fixed ideas about aspects of faith and the world will influence, lead, and regularly impede us, even unconsciously. The Bible is so complex that it differs by definition from any religious belief, no matter how exalted our own creed or value scale may be. Only by keeping an open mind and by asking questions can we discover *how* different the Bible is. The Bible is not a picture book for our own ideas, which we open only if we want our opinions confirmed or our vanity tickled. Nor is it a box of proof texts.

This book is an exercise in grasping the overall shape of a text, and in reading from within. An old rule says: the whole is more than the sum of its parts. I have tried to make this insight truly operational, so that at many levels it becomes practical and manageable for readers. From the viewpoints of creation and knowledge, proper reading, and literary experience, the whole has priority over the parts: it comes first in the writer's mind, and it is the beacon on which we set course while traveling, in our reading, past numerous details.

Questions to be asked of biblical poetry

1. Who is speaking, an "I" or a "we"? Can we picture this lyrical subject? Does it change in the course of the poem?

2. Whom is the lyrical subject addressing? Is the addressee visible in the text, or can we put a face to him/her? Does the addressee change? Do we encounter apostrophe*?

3. How long are the sentences? Check every time whether the syntactic unit coincides with the colon, the verse, or even a strophe. In other words: Does enjambment occur?

4. Which verb tenses are used? Are the various tenses (present, past, future) distributed over the strophes?

5a. Which modes are used besides the indicative? Wishes, commands, exclamations?

b. Are there actions, or descriptions of qualities?

6. How do space and time function in the lyrical world?

7. Can a diagram be drawn of the relations between the lyrical characters—for instance, a triangle such as me-God-enemy?

8. How long are cola and verses, generally?

9a. How much parallelism (both semantic and morphological) is there between half-verses? Ask yourself regularly if the "A, what's more, B" rule applies.

b. How much parallelism exists between the verses? And between the strophes?

10. Try to find the demarcation of strophes and stanzas. What devices does the poet use to create these units? Are there any boundary markers?

11. Is the cohesion of the strophe internal or external? Try to indicate the nature of the internal cohesion.

12a. Does the poet use simile?

b. Metaphors?

c. Metonymy? Synecdoche*? Symbols?

13. How are the verses related in regard to meaning?

14. And the strophes? Are they steps in a line of argument?

15. How does the theme develop? Is a specific line of thought followed?

16. What are the keywords?

17. Be sensitive to contrasts, oppositions, and transitions.

18. Try to make the most of various forms of repetition by listening for it and testing the function of variation–in–repetition.

12

Guidelines for further reading

150 and more poems, and their divisions

Unless stated otherwise, in the following the single slash represents the blank line separating two strophes. A double slash is used to separate stanzas; triple slashes mark sections.

Genesis 49
1b–2 // 3–4 // 5–6 / 7 // 8 / 9 / 10 / 11–12 // 13 / 14–15 / 16–17 // 19 / 20 / 21 // 22 / 23–24 / 25 / 26 // 27
Judah and Joseph are the only ones to be allotted a complete stanza of their own: vv. 8–12 and 22–26, respectively.

Exodus 15
Three refrain-type verses—v. 6, v. 11, and v. 16cd—create four stanzas:
I = vv. 1–5, II = vv. 7–10, III = vv. 12–16b, IV = vv. 17–18.

Numbers 23–24
Three poems by the seer Balaam:
I = four strophes consisting of two bicola: 23:7 / 8 / 9 / 10
II = four S-strophes and one L-strophe: 23:18–19a / 19b–20 / 21ab / 22–23a / 23b–24
III = 24:3–4 / 5–6 / 7 / 8 / 9, i.e., an SLSSL series

Deuteronomy 32
Four sections: A = vv. 1–9, B = vv. 10–18 + 19–29, C = vv. 30–41 + 42–55, D = vv. 56–62 + 63–69.
There are eleven stanzas and twenty-seven strophes: vv. 1–3 / 4–6 / 7–9 // 10–11 / 12–14 // 15–16 / 17–18 // 19–21 / 22–23 // 24–26 / 27–29 // 30–32 / 33–34 // 35–36 / 37–39 / 40–41 // 42–44 / 45–46 / 47–49 // 50–52 / 53–55 // 56–57 / 58–60 / 61–62 // 63–64 / 65–67 / 68–69

Judges 5
Three sections, seven stanzas, and twenty strophes: vv. 2–3 / 4–5 // 6 /
7 / 8 /// 9–11c / 11d–13 // 14–15c / 15d–16 / 17–18 // 19 / 20–21b
/ 21c–22 / 23 /// 24–25 / 26 / 27 // 28 / 29–30 / 31

1 Samuel 2:1–10
vv. 1–2 / 3 // 4–5 / 6–7 / 8 // 9–10a / 10b–e (detailed analysis in
NAPS IV)

2 Samuel 1:17–27
Discussed in ch. 1 of this book; for a detailed analysis see NAPS II, ch.
XV.

2 Samuel 22
The main contours are discussed in ch. 5 of this book. For a detailed
analysis, see NAPS III; for the division, see the figures for the parallel
text Ps. 18.

Isaiah 40–55
I.e., Deutero-Isaiah: two cycles, according to W. A. M. Beuken's com-
mentary (in Dutch, 1979–83), i.e. chs., 40–48 and 49–55. In these cycles,
Beuken distinguishes seven parts:
I = 40:1–42:13, containing the following literary units: 40:1–11 / 12–31
/ 41:1–7 / 8–16 / 17–20 / 21–29 / 42:1–9 / 10–13
II = 42:14–44:23, units: 42:14–17 / 18–25 / 43:1–7 / 8–13 / 14–21 /
43:22–44:5 / 6–22 / 23
III = 44:24–48:22, units: 44:24–45:8 / 9–13 / 14–17 / 18–25 / 46:1–13
/ 47:1–15 / 48:1–19 / 20–22
IV = 49:1–6 / 7–12 / 13
V = 49:14–26 / 50:1–3 / 4–9 / 10–11
VI = 51:1–8 /9–16 /17–23 / 52:1–6 /7–10 /11–12
VII = 52:13–53:12 / 54:1–17 / 55:1–13

Lamentations
This division as proposed in J. Renkema's commentary (in Dutch, 1993),
but without his terminology. N.B. In chs. 1, 2, and 5 the traditional verse
numbers coincide with the strophes, as a result of the alphabetical structure of the acrostics. In these chapters, the single slash separates stanzas.

ch. 1
vv. 1–3 / 4–6 // 7–9 / 10–11 // 12–13 / 14–16 // 17–19 / 20–22

ch. 2

vv. 1–3 / 4–5 // 6–7 / 8–10 // 11–13 / 14–15 // 16–17 / 18–19 / 20–22

ch. 3

Eleven strophes: vv. 1–3 / 4–6 // 7–9 / 10–12 // 13–15 / 16–18 / 19–21 // 22–24 / 25–27 / 28–30 / 31–33

ch. 4

1–2 / 3–5 / 6 / 7–9 / 10–11 // 12–13 / 14–16 / 17 / 18–20 / 21–22

ch. 5

Eleven strophes: vv. 1–2 / 3–4 // 5–6 / 7–8 / 9–10 // 11–12 / 13–14 // 15–16 / 17–18 // 19–20 / 21–22

150 Psalms (148 poems)

(Stanzas are usually, but not always marked.)

Psalm no.

1 1–2 / 3 / 4–6

2 1–3 / 4–6 // 7–9 / 10–12

3 2–3 / 4–5 // 6–7 / 8 / 9

4 2 / 3–4 / 5–6 / 7–8 / 9

5 2–4 / 5–7 // 8–9 / 10 // 11 / 12–13

6 2–4 / 5–6 // 7–8 / 9–11

7 2–3 / 4–6 // 7–9a / 9b–10 // 11–12 / 13–14 / 15–17 // 18

8 2ab / 2c–3 / 4–5 / 6–7 / 8–9 / 10

9–10 9:2–3 / 4–5 // 6–7 / 8–9 // 10–11 / 12–13 // 14–15 / 16–17 // 18–19 / 20–21 // 10:1–2 / 3–4 // 5–6 / 7–8 // 9–11 // 12–13 / 14a–d // 15–16 / 17–18

N.B. Psalms 9 and 10 together form one song.

11 1–3 / 4 / 5–7

12 2–3 / 4–5 // 6–7 / 8–9

13 2–3 / 4–5 / 6

14 1–2 / 3–4 / 5–6 / 7

15 1–2 / 3–4b / 4c–5c

16 1–2 / 3–4 // 5–6 / 7–9 / 10–11

17 1a–d / 2–3 // 4–5 / 6–7 // 8–9 / 10–12 // 13–14b / 14c–15

18 2–4 / 5–6 / 7a–d // 8–9 / 10–11 / 12–13 / 14–15 / 16a–d // 17–18 / 19–20 // 21+25 / 22–24 // 26–27 / 28–29 / 30–31 // 32–33 / 34–35 // 36–37 / 38–39 / 40–41 // 42–43 / 44–46 // 47–49 / 50–51

19 2–3 / 4–5 / 6–7 // 8 / 9 / 10 / 11 // 12–13 / 14–15

20 2–3 / 4–5 / 6 // 7 / 8–9 / 10
21 2–3 / 4–5 // 6–7 / 8 // 9–10b / 10c–11 // 12–13 / 14
22 2–3 / 4–6 // 7–9 / 10–12 /// 13–14 / 15–16 // 17–19 / 20–22
    ///   23–24 / 25a–d / 26–27 // 28–29 / 30a–d / 31a–d
23 1–3 / 4a–d // 5a–d / 6a–d
24 1–2 / 3–4 / 5–6 // 7–8 / 9–10
25 1–3 / 4–5 // 6–7 / 8–9 // 10–11 / 12–13 / 14–15 // 16–17 /
    18–19 // 20–21 / 22
26 1a–d / 2–3 // 4–5 / 6–8 // 9–10 / 11–12
27 1a–d / 2a–d / 3a–d // 4a–f / 5a–d / 6a–e // 7–9a / 9b–10 //
    11–12 / 13–14
28 1a–d / 2a–d // 3a–d / 4a–d / 5a–d // 6–7 / 8–9
29 1–2 / 3–4 / 5–7 / 8–9 / 10–11

30 2–4 / 5–6d // 7–8a / 8b–9 / 10–11 // 12–13
31 2–3 / 4–5 // 6–7 / 8–9 // 10–11 / 12a–d / 13–14 // 15–17 /
    18–19 / 20–21 // 22–23 / 24–25
32 1–2 / 3–4 / 5a–d // 6–7 / 8–9 / 10–11
33 1–3 / 4–5 / 6–7 // 8–9 / 10–12 / 13–15 // 16–17 / 18–19 /
    20–22
34 2–4 / 5–6 // 7–9 / 10–11 // 12–13 / 14–15 // 16–17 / 18–19 //
    20–21 / 22–23
35 1–3 / 4a–d / 5–6 // 7–8 / 9–10 /// 11–12 / 13–14 / 15–16 //
    17–18 / 19–21 /// 22–23 / 24–25 // 26a–d / 27–28
36 2–3 / 4–5 // 6–7 / 8–9 // 10–11 / 12–13
37 1–2 / 3–4 / 5–6 // 7a–c / 8–9 / 10–11 // 12–13 / 14–15 /
    16–17 // 18–19 / 20 / 21–22 / 23–24 // 25–26 / 27–28b /
    28c–29 // 30–31 / 32–33 / 34a–d // 35–36 / 37–38 / 39–40
38 2–3 / 4–5 // 6–7 / 8–9 // 10–11 / 12–13 / 14–15 // 16–17 /
    18–19 // 20–21 / 22–23
39 2a–d / 3–4 // 5–6b / 6c–7 / 8–10 // 11–12 / 13–14

40 2–3 / 4a–d / 5a–d // 6a–e / 7–9 // 10–11b / 11c–12 //
    13a–e / 14 / 15–16 // 17a–d / 18a–d
41 2–4 / 5–7 // 8–10 / 11–13 // 14
42–3 N.B. Ps. 42 and 43 together form one song:
    2–3 / 4a–d // 5a–f / 6a–d // 7a–d / 8a–d / 9–10 //
    11a–d / 12a–d / 43:1–2 // 3–4 / 5a–d
44 2a–d / 3–4 // 5–6 / 7–9 /// 10–11 / 12–13 // 14–15 / 16–17
    /// 18–20 / 21–22 // 23–25 / 26–27
45 2–3 / 4–6 // 7–8 / 9–10 /// 11–13 / 14–16 / 17–18
46 2–4 / 5–7 / 8 // 9–11 / 12

47   2–3 / 4–5 // 6–8 / 9–10
48   2–3b / 3c–4 // 5–6 / 7–8 // 9a–d / 10–11b / 11c–12 //
      13–14b / 14c–15c
49   2–3 / 4–5 // 6–7 / 8–10 // 11–13 // 14–15b / 15c–16 //
      17–18 / 19–21

50   1–3 / 4–6 // 7a–c / 8–9 / 10–11 // 12–13 / 14–15 //
      16a–c / 17–18 / 19–20 // 21a–c / 22 23
51   3–5 / 6a–d // 7–8 / 9–11 // 12–13 // 14–15 / 16–17 //
      18–19 / 20–21
52   3–4 / 5–6 / 7–9 // 10a–d / 11a–d
53   2a–d / 3a–d // 4–5 / 6a–e / 7a–c
54   3–5 / 6–7 / 8–9
55   2–4b / 4c–6 / 7–9 // 10–12 / 13a–d / 14–16 // 17–18 / 19 /
      20a–d // 21–22 / 23a–c / 24a–f
56   2–3 / 4–5 // 6–8 / 9–10 // 11–12 / 13–14
57   2a–d / 3–4 / 5a–d / 6 // 7a–d / 8–9 / 10–11 / 12
58   2–3 / 4–6 // 7–8 / 9–10 / 11–12
59   2–3 / 4–5a / 5b–6d // 7a–c / 8–9 / 10–11a /// 11b–12 / 13–14
      // 15a–c / 16–17b / 17c–18

60   3–5 / 6–7 // 8–9 / 10–11 / 12–14
61   2–3 / 4–5 // 6–7 / 8–9
62   2–3 / 4a–d / 5a–e // 6–7 / 8–9 // 10a–d / 11a–d / 12–13
63   2–3 / 4–5 // 6–7 / 8–9 // 10–11 / 12
64   2–3 / 4–5 // 6–7 / 8–9 // 10–11
65   2–4 / 5a–d // 6a–d / 7–9 // 10a–d / 11–12 / 13–14
66   2–4 / 5–7 // 8–9 / 10–12 // 13–15 / 16–18 / 19–20
67   2–4 / 5–6 / 7–8
68   2–4 / 5–7 // 8–9 / 10–11 /// 12–14a / 14b–15 // 16–17 /
      18–19 // 20–21 / 22–24 /// 25–26 / 27–28 // 29–30 /
      31–32 // 33–34 / 35–36
69   2–3 / 4–5 / 6–7 // 8–10 / 11–13 / 14a–d //
      15–16 / 17–19 / 20–21 // 22–23 / 24–25 / 26–27 / 28–29 //
      30–32 / 33–34 / 35–37

70   2 / 3–4 // 5a–d / 6a–d
71   1–2 / 3–4 // 5–6 / 7–8 // 9–11 / 12–13 ///
      14–16 / 17–18 // 19–20b / 20c–21 // 22a–d / 23–24
72   1–2 / 3–4 // 5–6 / 7–8 // 9–11 / 12–14 // 15–16 / 17a–d / 18–19
73   1–3 / 4–5 / 6–7 // 8–9 / 10–12 // 13–14 / 15–17 //
      18–20 / 21–22 // 23–24 / 25–26 / 27–28

74   1–3 / 4–5 // 6–7 / 8–9 / 10–11 // 12–13 / 14–15 / 16–17 //
       18–19 / 20–21 / 22–23
75   2 / 3–4 / 5–6 // 7–8 / 9a–d / 10–11
76   2–4 / 5–7 // 8–10 / 11–13
77   2–4 / 5–7 // 8–10 / 11–13 // 14–16 / 17–19 / 20–21
78   five sections: vv. 1–8, 9–31, 32–43, 44–60, and 61–72;
       fourteen stanzas and thirty-two strophes:
       1–3 / 4a–d // 5–6 / 7–8d /// 9–11 / 12–13 / 14–16 //
       17–18 / 19–20 / 21–22 // 23–25 / 26–28 / 29–31 ///
       32–33 / 34–35 // 36–37 / 38–39 // 40–41 / 42–43 ///
       44–45 / 46–47 // 48–49 / 50–51 // 52–53 / 54–55 // 56–58 /
       59–60 /// 61–62 / 63–64 / 65–66 // 67–69 / 70–72
79   1–3 / 4–5 // 6–7 / 8–9 // 10a–d / 11–12 / 13a–d

80   2–3a / 3b–4 // 5–6 / 7–8 // 9–10 / 11–12 / 13–14 //
       15–17 / 18–20
81   2–4 / 5–6b // 6c–8 / 9–11 // 12–13 / 14–15 / 16–17
82   1–2 / 3–4 / 5a–c / 6–7 / 8
83   2–3 / 4–6 / 7–9 // 10–11 / 12–13 / 14–15 // 16–17 / 18–19
84   2–3 / 4a–f // 5–6 / 7–8 // 9–10 / 11a–d / 12–13
85   2–4 / 5–6 / 7–8 // 9–10 / 11–12 / 13–14
86   1–2 / 3–5 / 6–7 // 8–10 / 11–13 // 14–15 / 16–17
87   1–3 / 4–5 / 6–7
88   2–3 / 4–5 / 6–7 // 8–10 / 11–13 // 14–16 / 17–19
89   three sections: vv. 1–19, 20–38, 39–52; eleven stanzas and twenty-
       two strophes:
       2–3 / 4–5 // 6–8 / 9–11 // 12–13 / 14–15 // 16–17 / 18–19 ///
       20–21 / 22–24 // 25–26 / 27–28 // 29–30 / 31–33 // 34–36 /
       37–38 /// 39–40 / 41–42 // 43–44 / 45–46 // 47–49 / 50–52

90   1–2 / 3–4 / 5–6 // 7–8 / 9–10 / 11–12 // 13–14 / 15–16 /17a–c
91   1–2 / 3–4 / 5–6 // 7–8 / 9–10 / 11–13 / 14–16
92   2–4 / 5–6 // 7–8 / 9–10 / 11–12 // 13–14 / 15–16
93   1–2 / 3–5
94   1–2 / 3–4 / 5–7 // 8–9 / 10–11 // 12–13 / 14–15 //
       16–17 / 18–19 // 20–21 / 22–23
95   1–2 / 3–5 / 6–7b // 7c–9 / 10–11
96   1–3 / 4–6 // 7–8 / 9–10 // 11–12 / 13a–d
97   1–3 / 4–6 // 7–9 / 10–12
98   1a–d / 2–3 // 4–6 / 7–8 / 9a–d
99   1–3 / 4–5 // 6–7 / 8–9

100 1–3 / 4–5
101 1–2b / 2c–3b / 3c–4 / 5a–d / 6a–d / 7a–d / 8a–d
102 2–3 / 4–6 // 7–9 / 10–12 // 13–15 / 16–18 // 19–20 / 21–23 //
24–26 / 27a–d / 28–29
103 1–2 / 3–5 / 6–8 // 9–10 / 11–13 / 14–16 // 17–19 / 20–22
104 1–2 / 3–4 // 5–6 / 7–9 // 10–11 / 12–13 // 14–15 / 16–18 //
19–20 / 21–23 // 24–26 / 27–28 / 29–30 // 31–32 / 33–34 /
35a–d
105 1–3 / 4–6 / 7–9 / 10–11 / 12–13 / 14–15 / 16–17 / 18–19 /
20–22 / 23–25 / 26–27 / 28–29 / 30–31 / 32–33 / 34–35 /
36–38 / 39–41 / 42–43 / 44–45
106 1–3 / 4–5 // 6–7 / 8–9 / 10–11 // 12–13 / 14–15 / 16–18 //
19–20 / 21–22 / 23a–e // 24–25 / 26–27 // 28–29 / 30–31 /
32–33 // 34–35 / 36–37 / 38–39 // 40–42 / 43–44 / 45–46 //
47a–d / 48a–c
107 1–3 // 4–5 / 6–7 / 8–9 // 10–12 / 13–14 / 15–16 // 17–18 /
19–20 / 21–22 // 23–24 / 25–27 / 28–30 / 31–32 // 33–34 /
35–36 / 37–39 // 40–41 / 42–43
108 2–3 / 4–5 / 6–7 // 8–9 / 10–11 / 12–14
109 1–3 / 4–5 // 6–7 / 8–10 // 11–13 / 14–16 / 17a–d / 18–19 /
20 // 21–22 / 23–25 // 26–27 / 28–29 / 30–31

110 1a–d / 2–3 // 4–5a / 5b–7
111 1–3 / 4–6 // 7–8 / 9–10
112 1–2 / 3–4 / 5–6 // 7–8 / 9–10
113 1–2 / 3–4 // 5–6 / 7–9
114 1–2 / 3–4 // 5–6 / 7–8
115 1–3 / 4 + 8 as an envelope around 5–7 // 9–11 / 12–13 // 14–16
/ 17–18
116 1–2 / 3–4 // 5–6 / 7–8 // 9–11 / 12–14 // 15–16 / 17–19
117 1–2
118 1–4 / 5–7 // 8–9 / 10–12 / 13–14 // 15–16 / 17–18 / 19–20 //
21–22 / 23–24 / 25 // 26–27 / 28–29
119 Nineteen octets have a strictly binary structure; only the *aleph,*
zayin, and *lamed* stanzas each contain three strophes: LSL, LLS, and
LSL, respectively.

120 1–2 / 3–4 / 5–7
121 1–2 / 3–4 // 5–6 / 7–8
122 1–2 / 3–4b / 4c–5 // 6–7 / 8–9
123 1 / 2a–f / 3–4

124   1–2 / 3–5 // 6–7 / 8
125   1–2 / 3a–d / 4–5
126   1–2b / 2c–3 // 4–5 / 6a–d
127   1a–d / 2a–d // 3–4 / 5a–d
128   1–2 / 3–4 / 5–6
129   1–3 / 4–5 / 6–8

130   1–2 / 3–4 // 5–6 / 7–8
131   1a–d / 2a–d / 3
132   1–2 / 3–5 // 6–7 / 8–9 /// 10–11b / 11c–12 // 13–14 /
        15–16 / 17–18
133   1 / 2–3b / 3cd
134   1a–c / 2–3
135   1–2 / 3–4 // 5–7 / 8–9 / 10–12 // 13–14 / 15–18 / 19–21
136   1–3 / 4–6 / 7–9 // 10–12 / 13–15 // 16–18 / 19–20 / 21–22 //
        23–24 / 25–26
137   1–2 / 3–4 / 5–6 // 7a–d / 8–9
138   1–3 / 4–6 / 7–8
139   1–3 / 4–6 // 7–8 / 9–10 / 11–12 // 13–14 / 15–16 / 17–18 //
        19–20 / 21–22 // 23–24

140   2–4 / 5–6 // 7–9 // 10–12 / 13–14
141   1–2 / 3–4 / 5–6 / 7–8 / 9–10
142   2–3 / 4–5 // 6–7 / 8
143   1–2 / 3–4 / 5–6 // 7a–d / 8–9 // 10a–d / 11–12
144   1–2 / 3–4 // 5–6 // 7–8 // 9–10b / 10c–11 // 12a–d / 13–14a /
        14b–15
145   1–2 / 3–4 // 5–7 / 8–9 // 10–13b // 13cd–14 / 15–16 //
        17–18 / 19–20 // 21
        (N.B. the lost *nun* line 13cd has been inserted with the support of
        the Septuagint and one of the Dead Sea Scrolls containing the
        Psalms)
146   1–2 / 3–4 // 5–7b / 7c–9 / 10
147   1–3 / 4–6 // 7–8 / 9–11 // 12–14 / 15–17 / 18–20
148   1–2 / 3–4 / 5–6 // 7–8 / 9–10 / 11–12 // 13–14
149   1–2 / 3–4 // 5–6 // 7–9
150   1–2 / 3–6

The letters in this list reveal how many cola I distinguish in a biblical verse; "5a–d," for instance, means that I discern four cola in
verse 5. Occasionally my cola total for a verse will differ from that
in RSV, JPS, and NIV.

Students of Hebrew may find the detailed underpinnings for these colon, verse, and strophe divisions in *Major Poems of the Hebrew Bible,* Volume II (published October 2000) and Volume III (in preparation).

The book of Job

I present the Job material in three parts:

1. My own division of Job 3-14, i.e., Job's complaint in ch. 3 (the Prologue), plus the entire first round of the debate; the scholarly basis for this division may be found in Volumes I and II of *Major Poems*.
2. Next, two divisions for Job 15–31: my own provisional articulation in italics, and the division given in the best book on the articulation of this poetry: Pieter van der Lugt's *Rhetorical Criticism and the Poetry of the Book of Job*, Oudtestamentische Studien xxxii, Leiden, 1995. This double notation shows that matters are far from simple, and that opinions may easily differ. I give it here as a challenge to the true lovers of puzzles: they can set to work on the question of what they think is the best division, and why.
3. Finally, I offer only one division of the chapters in which Elihu and God speak: Van der Lugt's.

Job chapter
3   3–5 / 6–9 // 10–12 / 13–16 / 17–19 // 20–23 / 24–26
4   2–4 / 5–6 // 7–9 / 10–11 // 12–13 / 14–16 //
     17–18 / 19–21
5   1–2 / 3–5 / 6–7 // 8–9 / 10–11 / 12–14 / 15 16 //
     17 18 / 19 20 / 21–23 / 24–26 / 27
6   2–4 / 5–7 / 8–10 / 11–13 // 14–16 / 17–18 / 19–21 //
     22–24 / 25–27 / 28–30
7   1–2 / 3–4 / 5–6 // 7–8 / 9–10 / 11–12 / 13–14 / 15–16 //
     17–18 / 19–20 / 21a–d
8   2–4 / 5–7 / 8–10 / 11–12 / 13–15 / 16–17 / 18–19 / 20–22
9   2–4 / 5–7 // 8–10 / 11–12 // 13–15 / 16–18 //
     19–21 / 22–24 // 25–26 / 27–29 // 30–32 / 33–35
10   1–3 / 4–6 // 7–8 / 9–11 / 12–13 // 14–15 / 16–17 //
     18–19 / 20–22
11   2–4 / 5–6 // 7–9 / 10–12 / 13–14 / 15–16 / 17–18 / 19–20
12   2–3 / 4–6 // 7–8 / 9–10 / 11–13 // 14–16 / 17–19 /
     20–22 / 23–25

13   1–3 / 4–6 // 7–9 / 10–12 / 13–14 // 15–16 / 17–19 /
      20–22 // 23–25 / 26–28
14   1–3 / 4–6 // 7–9 / 10–12 // 13–14 / 15–17 //
      18–20 / 21–22

At the beginning of a poem, Van der Lugt sometimes labels a strophe separately as A; twice, an isolated end strophe B occurs. Here
and there, he divides long stanzas into substanzas. I read his Roman
numerals as stanza numbers and the Arabic numerals he adds as
indicating a substanza.

15:2–16   2–3 / 4–6 // 7–8 / 9–11 // 12–13 / 14–16
15:17–35   A = 17–19 // I.1 = 20–21 / 22–23 / I.2 = 24–25 /
           26–27 //
II.1 = 28–29 / 30–31 / II.2 = 32–33 / 34–35

N.B. Van der Lugt distinguishes two poems in Job 15; on the
other hand, he sees chs. 36 + 37 as one literary unit.

15   *2–3 / 4–6 // 7–8 / 9–10 // 11–13 / 14–16 // 17–19 / 20–21*
      // 22–24 / 25–27 // 28–29 / 30–31 // 32–33 / 34–35

16   A = 2–4b + 4c–6 // I.1 = 7–8 / 9–11 / 12–14 //
      I.2 = 15–16 / 17–18 // I.3 = 19–20 / 21–22 //
16   *2–3 / 4–5 / 6–8 / 9–11 / 12–14 / 15–17 / 18–19 / 20–22*

17   II.1 = 1–2 / 3–5 / II.2 = 6–7 / 8–10 //
      II.3 = 11–12 / 13–14 / 15–16
17   *1–2 / 3–4 // 5–7 / 8–10 // 11–12 / 13–14 / 15–16*

18   A = 2–4 // 5–7 / 8–10 // 11–13 / 14–16 // 17–19 / 20–21
18   *2–4 / 5–6 / 7–8 / 9–10 / 11–13 / 14–15 / 16–17 / 18–19 /*
      20–21

19   A = 2–3 + 4–5 // 6–8 / 9–10 / 11–12 // 13–15 / 16–17 /
      18–19 // 20–22 / 23–24 // 25–27 / 28–29
19   *2–3 / 4–6 // 7–8 / 9–10 / 11–12 // 13–14 / 15–17 /*
      18–20 // 21–22 / 23–24 // 25–27 / 28–29

20   A = 2–3 // 4–6 / 7–9 / 10–11 // 12–14 / 15–17 / 18–19 //
      20–21 / 22–23 // 24–26 / 27–29
20   *2–3 / 4–6 // 7–9 / 10–11 // 12–14 / 15–16 //*
      17–18 / 19–21 // 22–23 / 24–25 // 26–27 / 28–29

21   A = 2–4 // 5–7 / 8–10 / 11–13 / 14–15 // 16–18 / 19–21 /
      22–24 / 25–26 // 27–28 / 29–30 / 31–33 / B = 34

21   *2–4 / 5–7 // 8–9 / 10–11 / 12–13 / 14–15 // 16–18 /*
      19–21 // 22–24 / 25–26 // 27–28 / 29–31 / 32–33 / 34

22   2–3 / 4–5 / 6–7 / 8–9 / 10–11 // 12 / 13–14 / 15–16 /
      17–18 / 19–20 // 21–23 / 24–25 / 26–28 / 29–30

22   *2–4 / 5–6 / 7–9 / 10–11 / 12–14 / 15–17 / 18–20 /*
      21–22 / 23–25 / 26–28 / 29–30

23   A = 2 / 3–4 / 5–7 // 8–9 / 10–12 // 13–14 / 15–17

23   *2–3 / 4–5 / 6–7 // 8–9 / 10–12 // 13–14 / 15–17*

24   I.1 = 1 / 2–4 / 5–6. // I.2 = 7–9 / 10–12. // II.1 = 13–14 /
      15–16 / 17–18. // II.2 = 19–20 / 21–22 / 23–24 / 25

24   *1 / 2–3/9! + 4 // 5–6 / 7–8 / 10–12 // 13–14 / 15–16a /*
      16b–17 // 18–19 // 20–21 / 22–24 // 25

25–26   according to Van der Lugt, Job 24 is a speech by Bildad, and
      25 + 26 together form one literary unit, a speech by Job!
      25:2–3 / 4–6 / 26:2–4 // 5–7 / 8–10 / 11–13 / B = 14

25   *2–3 / 4–6*

26   *2–4 / 5–6 / 7–8 / 9–10 / 11–13 / 14*

27   I.1 = 2–4 / 5–7 // I.2 = 8–10 / 11–13 //
      II = 14–15 /16–17 / 18–19 / 20–21 / 22–23

27   *2–4 / 5–6 / 7–8 / 9–10 / 11–12 / 13–15 / 16–17 /*
      18–19 / 20–21 / 22–23

28   I = 1–2 / 3–4 // II.1 = 5–6 / 7–8 // II.2 = 9–10 / 11–12 //
      III.1 = 13–14 / 15–16 // III.2 = 17–18 / 19–20 //
      IV.1 = 21–22 / 23–24 // IV.2 = 25–26 / 27–28

28   My radically different division has been presented and motivated
      in chapter 6.

29   I.1 = 2–3 / 4–6 // I.2 = 7–8 / 9–10 // II.1 = 11–12 / 13–14 //
      II.2 = 15–16 / 17–18 // III.1 = 19–20 // III.2 = 21–22 / 23–25

29   *2–3 / 4–6 // 7–8 / 9–11 // 12–13 / 14–15 / 16–17 //*
      18–20 / 21–23 / 24–25

30   I = 1–3a / 3b–5 / 6–8 // II.1 = 9–10 / 11–12b // II.2 =
      12c–13c / 14–15 // III.1 = 16–17 / 18–19 // III.2 = 20–21 /

22–23 // IV.1 = 24–25 / 26–27 // IV.2 = 28–29 / 30–31
30   *1–3a / 3b–5 / 6–8 // 9–10 / 11–13a / 13b–15 // 16–17 /*
         18–19 // 20–21 / 22–23 / 24–26 // 27–29 / 30–31

31   I.1 = 1–2 / 3–4 / 5–6 // I.2 = / 7–8 / 9–10 / 11–12 //
         II.1 = 13–15 / 16–18 // II.2 = 19–21 / 22–23 //
         II.3 = 24–26 / 27–28 //
         III.1 = 29–30 / 31–32 / 33–34 // III.2 = 35–37 / 38–40
31   *1–2 / 3–4 / 5–6 / 7–8 / 9–10 / 11–12 / 13–15 / 16–18 /*
         19–20 / 21–23 / 24–25 / 26–28 / 29–30 / 31–32 / 33–34 /
         35–37 / 38–40

The strophe division for the remaining chapters, according to Van der Lugt:

32	6–7 / 8–10 / 11–13 / 14–16 / 17–19 / 20–22
33	1–3 / 4–5 / 6–7 / 8–9 / 10–11 / 12–13 / 14–15 / 16–18 / 19–20 / 21–22 / 23–24 / 25–26 / 27–28 / 29–30 / 31–33
34	2–3 / 4–6 / 7–9 / 10–12 / 13–15 / 16–18 / 19–20 / 21–22 / 23–24 / 25–26 / 27–28 / 29–30 / 31–33 / 34–35 / 36–37
35	2–3 / 4 / 5–6 / 7–8 / 9–10 / 11–12 / 13–14 / 15–16
36	2–4 / 5–7 / 8–10 / 11–12 / 13–15 / 16–18 / 19–21 / 22–23 / 24–25 / 26–27 / 28–29 / 30–31 / 32–33
37	1 / 2–3 / 4–5 / 6–7 / 8–10 / 11–12b / 12c–13 / 14 / 15–16 / 17–18 / 19–20 / 21–22 / 23–24
38:2–38	2–3 / 4–5 / 6–7 / 8–9 / 10–11 / 12–13 / 14–15 / 16–18 / 19–21 / 22–24 / 25–27 / 28–30 / 31–32 / 33–35 / 36–38
38:39–39:30	38:39–41 / 39:1–2 / 3–4 / 5–6 / 7–8 / 9–10 / 11–12 / 13–15 / 16–18 / 19–20 / 21–23 / 24–25 / 26–28 / 29–30
40:7–41:26	7–9 / 10–12 / 13–14 / 15–18 / 19–22 / 23–24 / 25–28 / 29–32 / 41:1–3 / 4–6 / 7–9 / 10–13 / 14–17 / 18–21 / 22–24 / 25–26
42:2–6	2–3d / 4–6

The book of Proverbs

The following strophe division is certainly correct for chs. 2 and 8, but is only a proposal in the case of the other chapters. The reader should bear in mind that a translation will sometimes introduce other links than those contained in the Hebrew text. For instance, the material of Proverbs 1 (JPS) is articulated differently by means of a striking "because/since," capitalized twice (vv. 24 and 29). The division I propose is based on analysis of the original text.

Proverbs chapter
1   2–4 / 5–7 / 8–9 // 10–12 / 13–14 // 15–16 / 17–19 //
    20–21 / 22–23 / 24–25 // 26–27 / 28–30 / 31–33
2   half I: (a) 1–2 / 3–4 // (b) 5–6 / 7–8 / (c) 9–11
    half II: (a) 12–13 / 14–15 // (b) 16–17 / 18–19 / (c) 20–22
3   1–2 / 3–4 / 5–6 / 7–8 // 9–10 / 11–12 // 13–15 /16–18 /
    19–20 // 21–22 / 23–24 / 25–26 // 27–29 / 30–32 / 33–35
4   1–2 / 3–4 / 5–6 / 7–9 // 10–11 / 12–13 // 14–15 / 16–17 /
    18–19 // 20–22 / 23–25 / 26–27
5   1–2 / 3–4 / 5–6 / 7–8 / 9–11 / 12–14 // 15–17 / 18–19 /
    20–21 / 22–23
6   1–2 / 3a–d / 4–5 // 6–8 / 9–11 // 12–13 / 14–15 / 16–19 //
    20–22 / 23–24 // 25–26 / 27–29 // 30–31 / 32–33 / 34–35
7   1–3 / 4–5 // 6–7 / 8–9 // 10–11 / 12–13 / 14–15 / 16–17 //
    18–20 / 21–23 // 24–25 / 26–27
8   1–3 / 4–5 / 6–7 / 8–9 / 10–11 // 12–14 / 15–16 / 17–19 /
    20–21 // 22–23 / 24–26 / 27–29 // 30–31 / 32–33 / 34–36
9   1–3 / 4–6 // 7–9 / 10–12 // 13–15 / 16–18

The Song of Songs

I give all the changes of voice; in the case of a longer speech, I also have indicated the start of a new strophe. Furthermore, as indicated in ch. 10, n. 5, I present two versions of the strophe division in the Song of Songs: one for the original (Masoretic) text and the JPS, and one for the other translations.

The girl starts or continues to speak in:
Masoretic text/JPS:

1:2	1:5	1:7	1:12	1:16	2:1
2:3	2:4	2:7	2:8	2:16	3:1
3:5	3:11	4:16	5:2ab	5:3	5:4
5:8	5:10	6:2	6:12	7:10b	7:11
8:1	8:4	8:5cde	8:6	8:10	8:14

Other translations:

1:2	1:5	1:7	1:12	1:16	2:1
2:3	2:4	2:7	2:8	2:16	3:1
3:5	3:11	4:16	5:2ab	5:3	5:4
5:8	5:10	6:2	6:12	7:9b	7:10
8:1	8:4	8:5cde	8:6	8:10	8:14

The boy starts or continues to speak in:
Masoretic text/JPS:

1:8	1:9	1:15	2:2	2:10b	2:13c
4:1	4:8	4:12	5:1	5:2c	6:4
6:8	6:11	7:1c	7:7	8:13	

Other translations:

1:8	1:9	1:15	2:2	2:10b	2:13c
4:1	4:8	4:12	5:1	5:2c	6:4
6:8	6:11	6:13cd	7:1	7:6	8:13

The girls (the heroine's "peers"), who form the chorus as it were, speak in 3:6–10, 5:9, and 6:1, 6:13ab (MT/JPS 7:1ab).

There is also a group speaking in 6:10 and 8:5 (complementary verses); these might be first the boys, then the girls.

In 8:8–9 the girl's brothers are speaking.

The boy and girl may be singing together in 1:17, 2:15, and 5:1ef.

Glossary

allegorization
> interpretation of a text as an allegory, i.e., reading/explaining a text from an extrinsic point of view, not borrowed from the text itself. The text is seen through a strange or alien metaphor.

alliteration
> the use of the same consonants

anagram
> a word or phrase whose letters can be rearranged to form another word or phrase, such as "astronomers—moon-starers" or "the best things in life are free—nail-biting refreshes the feet"

anaphora
> identical openings of cola or higher-level textual units

antecedent
> element in a preceding phrase or clause, to which a relative pronoun refers

apostrophe
> The poet addresses a person or object directly; in the Psalms often "O Yahweh!"

apotropaic
> intended to ward off (by magic or verbal arts)

assonance
> identity of vowels

bicolon
> bipartite verse; *adj.*: bicolic

binary
> consisting of two aspects; arranged in two components

caesura
> interruption of the poetic line, often around the middle, which occurs in much poetry, usually indicated by a slash by exegetes

chiasm
> arrangement of four elements according to an AB-B'A' pattern; a form of mirroring, named after the Greek letter *chi,* which looks like an X

colon
> verset; often a half-verse

concatenation
> linking: i.e., by the repetition, at the beginning of a textual unit, of an element that also occurred at the end of the previous unit

counterfactual
> the mode indicating what has not really happened/is not really happening; in English often with the auxiliary "would (have) . . ."

double duty
> the construction in which one word governs two cola/objects, etc.

elegy
> lament, esp. for the dead

ellipsis
> omission

enjambment
> construction in which a sentence extends beyond the colon or verse boundary

epiphora
> identical endings of cola or higher-level textual units; sometimes coinciding with end rhyme

etymology
> the explanation of a word via its *etymon* (root or origin)

eulogy
> speech of praise

exegesis
> explanation, interpretation

hendiadys
> lit. "one through two": trope in which one concept is expressed by two words

hermeneutics
> the science of interpretation

homonym
> a word that is pronounced or spelled in the same way as another, but has a different root and meaning; for instance "feet/feat"

iconic
> term from semiotics★, and the adjective of "icon," from the Greek for "likeness, image"

inclusio
> "inclusion," frame

indicative
> mode indicating a positive statement (as opposed to a wish or a command)

intransitive
> a verb that cannot have an object, as, for instance, "to go" or "to swell"

litotes
> construction stating something positive by denying its opposite: "not bad"

merism
> a trope by which a whole is indicated by mentioning two components, or two extremes: "the rich and the poor"

metaphor
> lit.: "transference"; meaning is conferred through images rather than literally

metonymy
> figure of speech based on a shift in meaning: something is stated, but an adjacent or contiguous concept or entity is meant, as when "the Crown" is used to refer to the monarch

monocolon
> a full poetic line consisting of no more than one colon/verset

morpheme, zero-
> A *morpheme* is the smallest meaningful syntactic unit; for instance, the verb ending *-ed*, which indicates the past tense; a zero-morpheme is a morpheme that has been omitted.

morphology
> study of linguistic forms and structures

oracle
> word from God

oxymoron
> expressive combination of contradicting terms; for instance, "black milk" or "icy fire"

polemics
> a dispute or argument; a verbal combat

predicate
> part of the sentence in which something is stated about the subject; together with the subject, the sentence core

prosody
> orchestrating quantity and rhythm at various textual levels

rhetorics
> the art of (verbal) persuasion

scansion
> the rhythmic reading and/or division of a poetic line

semanticize
> confer meaning to

semantics
> the study of (esp. linguistic) meaning

semiotics

>   the study of signs and symbols (active in various branches of science, and relating to a range of human activities and fields of research)

signified / signifier

>   the two sides of the linguistic sign (word), according to Ferdinand de Saussure, the founding father of modern linguistics: roughly equivalent to "meaning" and "form," respectively

simile

>   comparison

Sitz im Leben

>   the context in which a text was produced

synecdoche

>   a figure of speech in which the whole is substituted for a part, or a part for the whole

syntax

>   sentence structure

theophany

>   the appearance of a deity

transitive

>   a verb that can/must take an object; for instance, "to read" or "to see"

tricolon

>   tripartite poetic line

vocative

>   form used for an address (in some languages, this is a separate case, but not in English or Hebrew: "O King!")

volitive

>   verb mode indicating a wish

Bibliographical notes

A. Readers who would like to know more about poetry will find the following books rewarding, as they are (mainly) about poetics in the English language:

—M. H. Abrams, *A Glossary of Literary Terms,* 7th ed. Harcourt College Publishers, 1999.

—John Ciardi, *How Does a Poem Mean?* Boston: Houghlin Mifflin, Co., 1959.

—Section on poetry in Sue Collins, *Approaching Literature: An Introduction to Literary Criticism,* Chicago: NTC Publishing Group, 1993.

—Jonathan Culler, *Literary Theory: A Very Short Introduction,* Very Short Introductions, OUP, 2000.

—Edward Hirsch, *How to Read a Poem, and Fall in Love with Poetry,* New York and London: Harvest Books, 1999.

—Philip Hobsbaum, *Metre, Rhythm and Verse Form,* New York and London: Routledge, 1996.

—Herbert Kohl, *A Grain of Poetry: How to Read Contemporary poems And Make Them a Part of Your Life,* New York: HarperCollins, 2000.

—Stephen Matterson and Darryl Jones, *Studying Poetry,* Arnold, 2000.

B. To readers who read Hebrew and would like to acquire a broader orientation in biblical poetry, I can recommend the following well-known titles:

—Wilfred G. E. Watson, *Classical Hebrew Poetry, A Guide to Its Techniques,* Sheffield Academic Press, first impression 1984, revised editions in 1986 and 1995; JSOTS 26 = no. 26 in the series *Supplements* of the *Journal for the Study of the Old Testament.* Together with the next title, this book offers a virtually complete inventory of the poet's box of tricks, and an extensive bibliography for every section.

—Wilfred G. E. Watson, *Traditional Techniques in Classical Hebrew Verse,* JSOTS 170, Sheffield, 1994.

—Robert Alter, *The Art of Biblical Poetry,* New York, 1985 (Basic Books), a beautifully written general introduction.

—Adele Berlin, *The Dynamics of Biblical Parallelism*, Bloomington, Ind., 1985; clear, instructive, with many examples.

—Luis Alonso Schökel, A *Manual of Hebrew Poetics*, Rome, 1988 (Pontificio Istituto Biblico).

C. Some of the analyses in this book continue or echo research results I have published earlier for the scholarly community. The following titles (all in English) may be viewed as further motivations and illustrations of my structural approach to poetry.

—In *Oudtestamentische Studiën* (OTS) 21 (1981) I have discussed the overture to Deutero-Isaiah (Isa. 40:1–11).

—*OTS 26* (1990) contains a structural analysis of what is probably the most difficult poem in the Psalter, Ps. 68.

—Judges 5, the Song of Deborah, I have discussed in detail in the *Festschrift* for Jacob Milgrom, titled *Pomegranates and Golden Bells*, and edited by D. Wright, D. N. Freedman, and A. Hurvitz; Winona Lake, Ind., 1995 (Eisenbrauns).

—I have written about the oracle to King Cyrus (Isa. 44:24–45:7) in the *Festschrift* for W. A. M. Beuken, Bibliotheca Ephemeridum Theologicarum Lovaniensium 132 (1997).

—The Song of Hannah in 1 Sam. 2, David's Lament (2 Sam. 1) and David's long Song of Thanksgiving in 2 Sam. 22 (= a variant of Ps. 18) have been discussed in Volumes II–IV of my tetralogy *Narrative Art and Poetry in the Books of Samuel*, Assen 1981–93 (Van Gorcum).

—Chapter 10 of my *Reading Biblical Narrative* (Westminster John Knox Press/DEO Publishing, 1998) deals with poetry within the framework of biblical narrative, and the poetry-prose relationship there.

—Three fragments of the present book have appeared earlier, in a slightly different form, in the Dutch literary magazine *Raster:* no. 80, 1997, an issue titled *In den beginne* and devoted to the Bible as literature.

—Three famous and very diverse poems, Exod. 15 (Moses' Song at the Red Sea), Deut. 32 (the long didactic poem), and Job 3 (the complaint that constitutes the prologue of the poetry in the book of Job), I have analyzed in detail in Volume I of my *Major Poems in the Hebrew Bible*, Assen, 1998.

—Volume II of *Major Poems* (Van Gorcum, Assen, 2000) contains succinct but complete descriptions of prosody and structure of 94 poems: 85 psalms (83 poems) plus Job 4–14. In this book, I present the revolutionary conclusion that the Hebrew poets did most assuredly count their syllables, and frequently made the figures for cola, verses, strophes, and stanzas a feature in (the structure of) their compositions. Volume III is in preparation and will deal with the remaining 65 psalms.

Notes

Chapter 1

1. I know only one text that is original to the New Testament and may be read as poetry: Paul's famous text about love in the First Letter to the Corinthians, ch. 13.

2. Of those 1,574 pages, 24 are in biblical Aramaic, the rest in classical Hebrew; the Aramaic passages are Jer. 10:11, Dan. 2:4–7:28 (with some bits in verse), and Ezra 4:8–6:18, 7:12–26. The standard edition, known among scholars as the BHS, is the *Biblia Hebraica Stuttgartensia*, fourth edition, 1977.

3. The 150 psalms are really 148 poems, since Pss. 9 and 10 together form one literary unit, as do Pss. 42 and 43.

4. The poetry in Job covers chs. 3–41, which almost always coincide with literary units (= poems) and are marked by a change of speaker some 15 times. Around these, there is a frame of narrative prose where the author acts as narrator and through his prose introduces us to Job, his excellence, and his terrible ordeal (Job 1–2), plus the good outcome in the final half (vv. 7–17) of the last chapter, 42.

5. The short book of Jonah is in prose: a prophet's legend (or rather anti-legend), interrupted or enriched in 2:2–9 by a psalm. The remaining eleven short books bear the names of Hosea, Joel, Amos, Obadiah, Micah, Nahum, Habakkuk, Zephaniah, Haggai, Zechariah, and Malachi.

6. Some six short poems: the vengeful song of Lamech in Gen. 4:23–24, the oracle of birth to Rebecca in Gen. 25:23, Isaac's blessing of the firstborn in Gen. 27:27b–29, God's self-revelation in Exod. 34:6–7 (quoted several times in Psalms and the Prophets; a kind of creed, very sacral), the oracle by which Saul is rejected in 1 Sam. 15:22–23, David's lament for Abner in 2 Sam. 3:33b–34; next, four medium-sized, coordinated poems by the seer Balaam in Num. 23:7–10 + 18–24, and 24:3–9 + 15–19.

7. For the structure of 1 Sam. 27–2 Sam. 1, and for the overall coherence of both these books, see the analysis contained in chs. XIV–XVI of my *Narrative Art and Poetry in the Books of Samuel, A Full Interpretation based on Stylistic and Structural Analyses*, vol. II, and the last pages of vol. IV. There I demonstrate that the lament forms the axis around which the structure of 1–2 Samuel revolves, and that it should be read in close conjunction with the Song of Hannah and the Song of Thanksgiving in 2 Sam. 22.

Chapter 2

1. The term "verset" for colon (often literally a half-verse) I have borrowed from Robert Alter, *The Art of Biblical Poetry,* New York, 1985, p. 9.
2. I am here referring to counting pre-Masoretic syllables. The adjective "Masoretic" (from *masorah*, tradition) refers to the rabbis of the sixth–tenth century CE. These syllables are found by reconstructing the structure of the words in ancient Hebrew—the Hebrew actually used by the poets, who for the most part were active in the period 800–300 BCE. The recipe for this, the defense of this recipe, and its application to ninety-four poems are given in the book mentioned in n. 3 below.
3. This recent investigation was my own, and its results are presented in volume II of *Major Poems of the Hebrew Bible, at the Interface of Prosody and Structural Analysis,* Van Gorcum, Assen, 2000.
4. Thus my own slight adaptation of two lines attributed to Horace Walpole. The Dutch poem goes: *Hier ligt Poot / Hij is dood,* and is attributed to Gerrit van de Linde (1808–1858), better known as the Schoolmaster. It is an epitaph on the seventeenth-century Dutch poet Poot.
5. *De sacra poesi Hebraeorum,* 1753.
6. The parallelism of the adjectival clauses, and the alliterations of the first three words in the Hebrew text, enforce the improved division of v. 1ab I am offering here; for additional arguments see my *Major Poems of the Hebrew Bible,* vol. II, ch. II, § 1.
7. Thus says James Kugel on p. 58 of his book *The Idea of Biblical Poetry: Parallelism and Its History,* New Haven, Conn., 1981. The complete sentence runs: "Biblical parallelism is of one sort, 'A, and what's more, B,' or a hundred sorts; but it is not three." I will return to the A and B formula in due course. In *The Art of Biblical Poetry* Robert Alter says on p. 13: "The predominant problem of biblical poetry is to move from a standard term in the first verset to a more literary or highfalutin' term in the second verset."
8. Here and in ch. 3, I am indebted to Adele Berlin's lucid work *The Dynamics of Biblical Parallelism,* Bloomington, Ind., 1985. I will adopt some of her many illuminating quotations from biblical poetry.
9. For my book on the Psalms the proportion of bicola and tricola to the whole corpus has been investigated; this turns out to be more than 99 percent—cf. *Major Poems,* vol. II, and the appendix containing the figures for all the poems. There are verses in the Psalms consisting of only one colon, but they mainly serve as the conclusion to a strophe, stanza, or poem. The book of Job does not contain a single monocolon (= poetic line consisting of one colon), according to Pieter van der Lugt on p. 478 of his book *Rhetorical Criticism and the Poetry of the Book of Job,* Leiden, 1995. The book of Proverbs, too, probably does not contain any monocola.
10. To have *three* predicates in one colon, however, is extremely rare. This is also the maximum, and this situation has been recognized by Michael O'Connor in his extensive syntactic study *Hebrew Verse Structure,* Winona Lake, Ind., 1980 (reprinted 1997), p. 138. Examples: Deut. 32:15b; Judg. 5:12b; and

Pss.10:10a (three verbs that all have the lowly as their subject! RSV, NEB, and NIV are correct; JB and JPS are not), 46:11a, and 98:4b.

Chapter 3

1. The two or three exceptions only serve to make the regular situation all the more interesting. As stated before, there are strong literary arguments in favor of taking Ps. 9 and Ps. 10 as one poem, and the same holds for Pss. 42 and 43. In Job, the traditional chapter division almost always coincides with the boundaries of the separate poems, but around ch. 25 we run into problems. It is not even clear who is speaking here, Bildad or Job himself. Van der Lugt (op. cit., pp. 274–96) argues that Job 24 is Bildad's third speech, and that 25:2–6, together with 26:2–14, are a speech of Job's, his third reply to Bildad.

    Contrast this with the prophetic literature: in many places in these books the correct demarcation of most literary units is difficult to find. Biblical scholarship has made a great effort in the various commentaries, but there are still numerous chapters in Isaiah and Jeremiah (and in the Minor Prophets from Amos to Malachi) about which there is no consensus. It will take decades of purely literary, and especially prosodically grounded, study before any agreement is reached.

2. See for both cases (one or five stresses) my *Major Poems*, vol. II, ch. 2, n. 55. Also compare the discussion, in the same chapter, of the syntactic model of the colon advocated by O'Connor and his follower Cloete (in his study on Jer. 2–25).

3. Some examples: Pss. 14:7a, 15:5c, 29:7 and 9c, 49:9e, 50:21c, 125:5c, and 128:5a.

4. The exact figures, taken from *Major Poems*, vol. II: of the 2,795 verses I allocate to the Psalms, 348 are tricola and 2,426 bicola, that is, 86.3 percent. In his study on the book of Job, p. 475, P. van der Lugt records 82 tricola in Job (as opposed to 912 bicola), that is, 8 percent. The book of Proverbs (c. 921 verses in all) contains about 40 tricola.

5. P. van der Lugt makes more "cuts" in Job than I do, and sees seventeen one-line strophes: 3:3; 5:1, 8, 17, 27; 6:14, 24; 7:19; 21:34; 23:1; 24:1; 25; 26:14; 35:4; 37:1, 14; and 40:2. Some of these may be discarded (cf. my discussion of Job 4–14 in *Major Poems*, vol. II, and of Job 3 in vol. I); some hover on the edges of literary units (= poems), such as, for instance, the opening verse of chs. 23, 24, and 37, or the ending of Job 24.

    In my opinion (Van der Lugt thinks differently), the book of Job does not contain any four-line strophes, with one interesting exception, viz. the bitter and vehement complaint that constitutes the prologue and does not yet form part of the debate: ch. 3. The special characteristic of this first poem is the fact that here the regular dimensions 2 and 3 are increased by one. The strophic structure is a strict alternation of 3–4–3–4–3–4–3 poetic lines (see *Major Poems*, vol. I, ch. 5)—a division already noted by Delitzsch 136 years ago, but strangely enough by no one else after him.

6. The strophes of four verses: Pss. 31:20–21, 118:1–4, 135:15–18, 145:10–13, and 150:3–6.

7.   If we decide after all to describe Ps. 18:21–25 as a combination of a two-line and a three-line strophe, this has all sorts of consequences; the total number of strophes in this psalm will then change from 23 to 24, in a poem in which the numbers 22 and 23 are also prominent, and the cola totals for the halves, sections, and stanzas of this song also matter; a detailed analysis will appear in *Major Poems*, vol. III (in preparation).

8.   The remedy here is to publish the poetry in a typography that does justice to the prosody, including strophe boundaries, on the basis of a sound literary-critical analysis. As a contribution toward this goal, I am publishing, at about the same time as this book, the complete Psalter in Hebrew with the demarcation of cola, verses, and strophes as substantiated in vols. II and III of *Major Poems*, thus showing these works of art in their true colors.

9.   See my analysis of Judg. 5 in the *Festschrift* for Jacob Milgrom, *Pomegranates and Golden Bells*, edited by D. P. Wright, D. N. Freedman, and A. Hurvitz, Winona Lake, Ind.: Eisenbrauns, 1995; I have also given the correct division in *Reading Biblical Narrative*, p.185.

10.   See *Major Poems*, vol. II for all the details, the underlying theory, and the demonstration on the basis of full syllable counts for 85 psalms and Job 4–14.

11.   Psalm 119 itself, moreover, has the norm figure 8 as the average colon length: I allocate 355 cola and count 2,861 syllables; their division yields 8.05. If we assume that originally there were 2,860 syllables, which is very well possible, this colossal didactic poem would then also yield a round figure for the syllable total per stanza, with 2,860 : 22 = 130 syllables as the average number per octet.

    Since an octet here mostly consists of S-strophes, Ps. 119 also contains nineteen instances of a stanza consisting of four strophes.

12.   See further on Ps. 97 ch. 2 § 6 of *Major Poems*, vol. II.

Chapter 4

1.   Adele Berlin in *The Dynamics of Biblical Parallelism*, p. 79: "It is not word pairs that create parallelism. It is parallelism that activates word pairs."

2.   I have already argued for this correction in *Narrative Art in Genesis*, Ph.D. thesis, Assen, 1975, p. 35; it is an excellent confirmation of the theory that structural analysis also yields improved understanding of the text. My thanks to Johs. Pedersen (*Israel, Its Life and Culture*, Kopenhagen, 1926, vols. I/II, p. 397 and his note on p. 533f.), who seventy-five years ago already noticed that the preposition is a so-called *bet pretii*.

    A count of the pre-Masoretic syllables in the three poetic lines 9:6–7 yields: 6 + 8 = 14, 6 + 6 = 12, and 8 + 8 = 16, i.e., three times six plus three times eight = 42. Exact average: 7. In Lamech's song of revenge (Gen. 4:23–24), the exact average of the six cola is 48 : 6 = 8.

3.   At least, this is how it appears in v. 5b. The student of Hebrew will notice from the *BHS* apparatus that there is a better reading, suggested by Septuagint and Peshitta. The mem has been the victim of haplography; read the

participle *m^etsawweh* in the B-colon (plus elliptical subject "he") and render the colon predicatively. The problem is that the appeal (containing the imperative) comes far too early. The reading with the participle is confirmed by the exact syllable totals for all strophes and for the poem as a whole—see for full details *Major Poems,* vol. III.

4. The compelling structure of Isa. 40:3 is ignored by De Moor and Korpel in *The Structure of Classical Hebrew Poetry: Isaiah 40–55,* Leiden, 1998; a fairly unique feat.

5. The formula was launched by James Kugel in *The Idea of Biblical Poetry,* New Haven, 1981 (subtitled "Parallelism and Its History"); see pp. 51–58.

6. I have taken the "binocular" metaphor from Adele Berlin's book on biblical parallelism (see n. 1); on p. 99 she says: "Parallelism focuses the message on itself but its vision is binocular. Like human vision it superimposes two slightly different views of the same object and from their convergence it produces a sense of depth."

Chapter 7

1. For a more extensive analysis of Ps. 8, and an account of the syllable figures I have presented here, I refer the reader to ch. II, § 1 of *Major Poems of the Hebrew Bible,* vol. II.

Chapter 8

1. I have checked the following translations of Ps. 103: *Bible de Jérusalem* (also the English version), *RSV, TaNaKh* by the Jewish Publication Society of America, *NEB,* several Dutch translations (*Leidsche Vertaling,* NBG, KBS 2 and 3, *Groot Nieuws Bijbel*), *Nueva Biblia Española,* Buber & Rosenzweig's *Verdeutschung, La Bible* by Edouard Dhorme, and the German so-called *Einheits-Übersetzung.*

   I have consulted a number of Dutch commentaries (J. Ridderbos [COT], Noordtzij [*Korte Verklaring,* Kampen], de Liagre Böhl and Gemser, Th. Booij [*Prediking van het Oude Testament*], Pieter van der Lugt [dissertation *Strofische structuren in de Psalmen,* Kampen 1980], J. P. van der Ploeg [*Boeken van het Oude Testament*], and also: Kissane, Allen [Word Biblical Commentary, Waco, Tx.], Dahood [Anchor Bible], Buttenwieser, Girard, Beaucamp; Delitzsch, Gunkel, Kittel, Kraus, Weiser, Deissler, Seybold.

Chapter 9

1. The two commentators who have seen that v. 7a does not qualify the preceding verse, and that a better solution has to be found for "your knowledge," are S. L. Terrien (Neuchâtel, 1963) and N. H. Tur-Sinai (Jerusalem, 1967). But for Job 10:7a the King James Bible is correct.

2. Although the Hebrew text literally says: "You have done/proved life and loyalty with/toward me," in my exposition for non-Hebraists I have to stick with the keyword "to make."

Chapter 10

1. For those who read Hebrew: I realize that there is one word, *shalhebet-yah,* at the end of Songs 8:6 that does seem to refer to God; however, it is by no means certain how we should interpret this form and its final syllable, and it would be unwise to have this one word determine our interpretation of the book.

2. Francis Landy, *Paradoxes of Paradise: Identity and difference in the Song of Songs,* Sheffield, 1983 (Almond Press), and André LaCocque, *Romance, She Wrote: A Hermeneutical Essay on Song of Songs,* Harrisburg, Pa.,1998 (Trinity Press International). The latter author contends that the book was written by a woman; there are no arguments against this possibility.

3. The recently revised edition of the *Bible de Jérusalem* (Paris 1998) values neutrality: a good balance has been struck there by designating the lovers as *le bien-aimé* and *la bien-aimée.*

4. I am thinking of the work of Leo Krinetzki, who at first was still bent on pacifying the Holy See with his so-called anthological exegesis, but who seven years later (in "Retractationes," a significant title, in *Biblica* 52, 1971) admitted that compromises with the allegorizing school are erroneous; in his first book, titled *Das Hohe Lied* (Patmos Verlag, Düsseldorf, 1964) he proves himself sensitive to literary aspects; later, in his second book (*Kommentar zum Hohelied,* Lang, Frankfurt/Bern, 1981) he is both literary and Jungian. Then there is the structural analysis by Cheryl Exum in *Zeitschrift für die alttestamentliche Wissenschaft* 85, 1973, who takes the many forms of repetition seriously. Finally, there is the intense book by Landy, which I mentioned in n. 2 above.

5. I would like to draw the reader's attention to the fact that the verse numbers in the original text (and in the JPS translation) differ by one point from those in the translations: what in most translations is 6:13 is in the original text justly (and much more correctly) labeled 7:1. Thus, the numbers of the subsequent verses are also increased by 1. This explains why in ch. 12 I have been forced to provide two versions of the strophe division in the Song of Songs: one for the original (Masoretic) text and the JPS, and one for the other translations.

Index of biblical passages

This index incorporates biblical passages from chapters 1 through 10 only. It is not useful to offer the masses of figures from the lists of chapter 12 here. The letter *n* after a page number indicates a note.

A. Cited (i.e. translated and written in full) passages